PRIVATE MEMBER

PRIVATE MEMBER

Leo Abse

MACDONALD · LONDON

Copyright © Leo Abse 1973

First published in Great Britain in 1973 by
Macdonald and Company (Publishers) Limited,
St Giles House, 49 Poland Street, London W.1.

Made and printed in Great Britain by
Redwood Press Ltd
Trowbridge, Wiltshire

ISBN 0 356 04602 8

CONTENTS

ILLUSTRATIONS

Acknowledgements

The judgements made in this book are my personal responsibility: but I am deeply grateful to those friends of mine with whom, while I was contemplating or writing *Private Member*, I have had so many dialogues. My especial thanks are due to paediatrician Joe Jacobs, Professor of Paediatrics at the McMaster Chedoke Medical Centre, Hamilton; to psychiatrists John Denham, Medical Director of St Clement's Hospital, and Richard Tilleard-Cole, Director of the Oxford Institute of Psychiatry; to sociologist Ronald Fletcher; to psychoanalysts Wilfred Abse, Professor of Psychiatry, University of Virginia, Arthur Hyatt Williams and Augusta Bonnard; and to solicitor Richard Oerton. I am also indebted to Barbara Kirton, my amanuensis for twenty years in my political and professional life, for all the help she has again afforded me.

Lewis Hawser QC, Ronald Waterhouse QC and Dr Dannie Abse generously read my original draft and I owe my thanks to them for their helpful suggestions.

To Marjorie
Tobias and Bathsheba
in love

and to the Electors of the Eastern
Valley of Monmouthshire
in gratitude for their forbearance.

But if a man don't occasionally sit
   in a senate
how can he pierce the dark mind of
   a senator?

EZRA POUND
Pisan Cantos LXXX

Prologue

I

In 1958, for some obscure and unexplained reason, the Labour Member of Parliament for Pontypool was elevated to the House of Lords and a by-election declared in the constituency. In this borderland South Wales valley, on the fringe of the Celtic world, the news was received with sulky indifference, for the Member's parliamentary performance had already petered out and, politically, he had died before his death.

But for me the announcement brought travail: I was seized with conflict. I had the private arrogance of a certitude that, if I chose, the seat could be mine; yet I was reluctant to seek it. I did not need, as many M.P.s do, the compulsive verification of identity in hollow external success. After the locust years of the R.A.F. and the war, painstakingly I had erected my little citadel. Within my carefully tended garden and walls I had achieved an inner stillness. I had travelled too far to despise the pedestrian rhythm of my provincial life. My family, my professional work and my role as burgher were belatedly but firmly established; and the inner fortress of personal happiness, if not impregnable, was sufficiently secure. Westminster, I knew, meant total devastation. I did not lack the confidence to jostle with my peers in the Commons, but I feared that, amongst the ruins, amidst the clamour of the squalid, the plagiarists and the tawdry, I would never again hear the esoteric, familial melodies that, looking at the past and anticipating the future, bring alive the living.

I had married late, in 1955, when I was thirty-eight. Now I had two children. I had already learnt what later experience confirmed, that there is nothing more rewarding than parenthood. So many women are mothers from their very earliest years, but men cannot imagine their eternity before they find themselves linked to it. There is a Talmudic saying that the world survives in the breath of little children, and I knew that it was a true one. My son, a premature baby, had had serious early illnesses and my wife and I had battled with success to save him. The close links which were formed then between him and me have always remained; and my new baby girl was, of course, beautiful and irresistible.

I was aware that becoming the Member for Pontypool could place my domestic happiness at risk. After the birth of the children my wife, a considerable artist, no longer produced her exotic fabrique collages but poured all her talent into the home. Nowadays the glossy magazines ask to photograph the homes she has created for me, and the fashionable but uncertain Chelsea designers masochistically submit to her gentle chidings at our London dinner table. For myself, I was aware long since of her unerring taste. We had recently bought a large Edwardian villa with some ground in the suburbs of Cardiff and my wife had begun the never-ending process of rebuilding. For indeed there is truth in the saying that when you stop building your house it is time to die. But she needed always, in return for her eyes which she gave to me, support. Her startling vision and sensuous Celtic imagination needed some anchorage. She was precariously poised. I had married her because she had an extra dimension: I could have married a much simpler woman and lived more prosaically, certainly less turbulently and passionately. But if you dare to scale the heights, footholds must be secure all the way; for one slip can be fatal. The turbulence of a dishevelled and peripatetic M.P.'s life could, I knew, so easily precipitate an avalanche. And never-ending separations from my children, in the earliest and most formative years, might be no less disastrous. In the event, only by the skin of my teeth did I avoid a rupture in the bond between my daughter and myself, and that by much and persistent wooing.

My fears were to be proven not unfounded, for I was to find in the House of Commons the bachelors and childless are often the pace-setters in the investment of political time, so playing an unwitting part in the disruption of the family life of their colleagues. Even more than most of their fellows they generate a feverish competitiveness into life at Westminster. With the act of reproduction the son not only asserts his biological function, he also achieves the ultimate goal of his ordained competition with his father: now he has become the father. When he gives a child to his wife he himself has become a link in the chain of generations between his father and his child and has then reached a further stage in his psychosexual maturity. To the childless this is denied, and unassuaged competitiveness and rivalry have to be carried on until death with a ferocity that first disturbs and then spurs on their parent colleagues who too often meet the challenge by an abandonment of the aims of fatherliness. Too frequently, the parent Member of Parliament yields to the temptation of his ambitions and, channelling his physical and emotional energies away from primary experiences with his family, he alienates his children and his emotionally impoverished family life becomes a wasteland.

Doubtless the childless M.P.s have a considerable functional value.

The elderly and middle-aged childless sons, incessantly in rebellion and forever battling against paternalistic authority, dominate the left wing of the Parliamentary Party: no-one indeed could gainsay the lively contributions made to national debates by Michael Foot, Eric Heffer, Stan Orme, Norman Atkinson and Jack Mendlesohn. And often, too, when the failure of the childless adult politician to become his own parent leads him to an avid search for parental figures, it can take harmless forms, like the mildly fetishistic framed Queen Victoria's stocking set off by photographs taken with Papa Pope in courageous St. John Stevas's home; and even the tasteless expressions of such yearnings, like the absurd and sustained apotheosis of Wilson by his one time Secretary of State for Wales, bachelor George Thomas, can be shrugged off. Or again, when those like the late Victor Yates or Fergus Montgomery or Raymond Gower, who have no children to rear, choose instead to nurse their constituencies by such non-stop canvassing that their colleagues have taunted them with their failure to take out pedlar's licences, such conduct need arouse little more than mild exasperation.

But it cannot be conceded that politicians who lack the experience of parenthood or who, for ambition's sake, betray it, are not disadvantaged: fatherliness entails discipline, modifications of personal conduct, concern, care and tenderness. In the life cycle of every man there is a period from infancy to adolescence when the vector of metabolic and psychological processes is self-directed and later, towards the end of life, as ageing comes and the positive extraverted tendencies ebb away, we are again left with the self-centred tendencies, for old age compels us to be restrictive and energy conserving. But in between, during our reproductive period, the vector is expressed in the expansive giving attitude of parenthood. It is during this period that parenthood can establish the confident sense of identity that integrates the biological and social functions of the personality. The public, therefore, have a right to be exceptionally wary of the politician who affects to be the father of the nation without the experiences of first being the father of his own child.

It is in times of crisis that the celibate bachelor becomes particularly vulnerable. Adult man, single or married, faced with difficulties that appear almost overwhelming can still secretly feel a need to cry out for help from his mama: but his self esteem demands that he does not yield to such regressive tendencies and he must find an escape route to avoid recognizing his feelings of helplessness and dependence. At such a time a man increases his narcissistic defences: he can dangerously over-react to situations and individuals which remind him of his conflicts. To relieve himself of his anxieties the bachelor, unable to sustain and enrich his inner life by deep personal relationships, blatantly attempts to shore up his self esteem in a frenzy of external public activities which he then spuriously claims to be for the benefit of others. More genuinely felt self esteem is rooted in a confident sexuality, in the body giving and receiving love. Those who feel themselves sexually inadequate often convert their disappointment into an aggressive and feverish competition in the world of power.

To the politician husband there are, however, other ways of overcoming his difficulties that leave the public undamaged. Through his virility, in his conscious desire for procreation, he can overcome his regressive tendencies. His gratification in heterosexual love reassures him of his masculinity and elevates him above his fears; his desire for reproduction becomes a process of reparation, a means of overcoming anxiety. It is open to him to quench his anxieties and to resolve his conflicts privately, not to project them on to the public scene.

With Heath as our Prime Minister, the role of the bachelor in politics cannot be dismissed as irrelevant. The opinion polls persistently reveal how popularity eludes Heath and how much suspicion is felt towards him in the country; but there are additional and special reasons why this unease always hovers over his parliamentary supporters. The Tory Party is essentially a father-orientated party. It is basically authoritarian in mood, believing in an elite, at ease in a structured fag system, and of course, in the House, ready to accept a whip's rule that would be intolerable to a party more democratic and more sceptical of leadership principles. The Labour Party is essentially mother-orientated. It is the welfare party, maternally concerned, the provider, the bountiful: indeed, if a leader does evoke the image of the tyrannical father, all hell is let loose, for the rebellious temperaments which brought so many of the Parliamentary Labour Party members into politics are then at once provoked. The Party is more at ease when it has leaders who are, or give the appearance of being, neutral, of being chairmen rather than leaders. This was Attlee's strength, and Gaitskell's weakness, in relations with the Party: Wilson's colourlessness may explain in part the absence of rebellion against him during his premiership. But the Tories delight in strong leadership, and it is demonstrably difficult for them to project the image of a powerful father figure upon a celibate. This factor, among others, accounts for the unease which now exists between the Conservative Party and its leader, and, sensing it, Heath reacts with a dangerously over-determined aggressiveness, carrying his masculine identity on his sleeve.

Certainly I doubt whether in normal times the nation can benefit from having an inadequate father as a political leader. The nation is an extended family and those who are incapable of the sacrifice imposed by parenthood fail more readily to give the security and consolation that remains the yearning of even an adult nation. Only perhaps in wartime does political leadership require the ruthless qualities reminiscent of the castrating father of the primal horde. In such seasons bad fathers make good premiers. But they remain bad fathers. Certainly the children of Britain's war-time premiers in this century suffered: few of Churchill's and Lloyd George's children survived their disastrous early deprivation. Even so lively a woman as Lady Megan Lloyd George, whom I was to know well, was emotionally stunted. No conversation could be sustained for long without reference to 'the old man', without quotations and recollections of her father. The visitor to Criccieth could be embarrassed as she conducted him around the shoddily furnished house, picking up trivial mementoes and reciting well-worn associative tales. This determined worship of her father never masked for me the clear and bitter sense of betrayal with which she wrestled all her life. And one felt that Lloyd George's main legacy to his children was the certainty of a lifetime of incestuous quarrels: in vain they were doomed to fight amongst themselves for a greater share of the love and the security which had been denied to them all.

Too frequently the fate endured by the children of our war-time premiers is one shared today by the families of less prominent politicians. The demands made upon a Member of Parliament are legion and growing, and M.P.s are rarely coy or diffident people. Often their narcissism demands that they are always on stage, forever listening to or fighting for the applause of the public, and, yielding to their own weakness, they can render their family lives fitful and impoverished. This situation has sometimes been exacerbated by poverty: the derisory salaries until recently paid to M.P.s have precluded for so many the possibility of two homes, one in the constituency and the other in London. Everything conspires to ensure that the M.P. and his children grow further and further apart.

It was not, therefore, surprising that I was later to hear so many of my colleagues sadly admit that their children had grown up without their knowing them. Some of the worst casualties have attained a cruel notoriety; and in the House able and distinguished men of all parties have told the nation authoritatively how to run its affairs while their own lost children end in prison, in suicide or in drug addiction. Less dramatically, but more frequently, the children of M.P.s simply fail the expectations of their actor-like fathers. These fathers, having given them little in the early years, leaving them to public schools or to isolated mothers, still expect their children's achievements to reflect further glory upon themselves, and they admit their inevitable disappointment only with a sulky reluctance. The growth of a child demands that both love and time shall be given, and given when they are needed, and in the House these commodities are in both short and unpredictable supply. It follows that M.P.s sometimes seem to have more interest in the next edition of the newspapers than in the next generation. In the tea rooms of the House of Commons the early evening papers are avidly read before lunch, but though members talk so much of the latest events many of them talk extraordinarily little of their children. It is a striking contrast to what I find at election times, when household after household has to be canvassed and a draining bonhomie to be maintained: then I always avoid talking politics and ask the voters about their children and talk of my own. Ordinary folk will then so often lose shyness or hostility and selflessness emerges as they tell of their hopes for their little ones, of their anxieties and their triumphs. Thus in the deeper sense we share our hopes for the future of humanity.

I was well aware, as I wrestled with the challenge of deciding whether to enter Parliament, that my marriage certificate and the birth certificates of my children, although helpful, certainly spelt out for me no guaranteed immunity against the inflammatory conceit of Parliamentary life: pathogenic elements in my character could flare up dangerously in such an ambience. I feared that to yield to my narcissism and to contest Pontypool would be self-destructive. My children, in whom I revelled, were my links with the cosmos: and I feared that the erosion which comes from the prosaic drudgery of political life could snap those links. But I felt, too, that such a political commitment would sever other pathetically tenuous links, perhaps droll to others but precious to me. I was painfully aware that total abandonment to public causes could lead to an ugly aridity in the interior life: I did not want to have washed away for ever the source from which fitfully springs an illumination of a blessed vision which sometimes envelops me.

Very occasionally and alas, for me, increasingly rarely, some curious combination of circumstances precipitates a magic awareness. These are the moments when each stone in the moonlight is alive and separate, each tree is human and alone; and the threnody of the stars, as they speed through the expanding universe, can be piercingly heard. When the mood snaps, it is as if the link with the whole world, organic and inorganic, has gone; and sadly, I am painfully aware that our present ego-feeling is but a shrunken residue of an all-embracing feeling which in the beginning coalesced self and universe. These oceanic emotions have been compared by Freud to pathological mental disturbances in which the boundaries between the ego and the external world become totally uncertain, but Romain Rolland reproved him, insisting that these intimations of eternity brought with them none of the vulgar and absurd consolations of personal immortality proffered by most religious systems. As a young man, making love in the open air has sometimes acted as the catalyst: in the strange, post-coital mood, within the little death, suddenly the whole evolutionary process is intuitively divined, and as I lie flat on the earth the stillness is broken only by the throb of the diurnal swing of the world. All the teleology within life becomes suddenly, marvellously and quietly revealed.

There are paintings by Giorgiorne, like the mis-named *Tempest*, that miraculously capture this super-reality. This painting presents a calm and serene scene, just after a storm has passed. The sensuous, but sexually quiescent mood, is economically stated by the contrast between a clothed man and a naked woman feeding her child. Between them flows the eternal river of life and although in the distance there are leaping bridges, in the foreground there is a broken column, a spent penis symbol. Out of the flux of time Giorgiorne snatches the still moment, and for a few seconds all our alienation dissolves within the golden tones that bathe the canvas. And Picasso, too, uses the strange moment when, all passion spent, vision is re-born: his paintings juxtaposing sleeping man and woman, with cut fruit, open books and limp, beautiful, phallic musical instruments hanging downwards, fill the void of consummation with a pristine and heightened awareness. But the gifts of even the great painters are but shadows of those gained by experience, and I am jealous of these elusive and too infrequent moments.

For some, it is true, the inner life contains only fear; and some of these flee to politics to relieve themselves of the terror of their hidden tensions by externalizing their problems – all too often causing havoc to the unsuspecting community. I myself acted out unrestrainedly my own turbulent adolescence and now feel a poignant empathy with those young people of today who still believe that a millenium can be created by a restructuring of our external world. But they are wrong. Life is not easily lived; and the most extravagant of our young revolutionaries, as the most devout religious zealots of history, scorning stoicism, are passionately seeking consolation for its hardships. There is, however, no escape from the threefold threat which must envelop us throughout our transient flicker of existence: no journey to the moon should raise hopes that man can totally usurp nature; no antibiotic or heart transplant can do more than postpone the inevitable decay and dissolution of our bodies; and no one can be totally cocooned from the cruelties of his fellow men and women, both of those he loves and of those he hates.

In my youth we sought, as do the worthwhile youth of every generation, for apocalyptic solutions in our frantic rebellion against fate, and Marxism was to be the science to lead us to the new Zion. I had followed, as perhaps must the young thinkers of today, the well worn path from illusion to disillusion and delusion. But in the post war world no such routes in search of the millenium tempted me. My painful youthful political experiences had left me totally suspicious of the grand design and quite untempted by the pursuit of the unattainable. I sought my political fulfilment in the immediate, modest and real objectives that lay within the field of local government. To contemplate entering Parliament, exchanging the microcosm for the macrocosm, was at this moment particularly painful for, after long wooing, the city of my birth, my Jerusalem, had at last yielded to me.

The conquest had taken many years. On my return from the war I had found Cardiff still dominated, as ever, by a sluggish Tory council led by a few patricians and administered, for the most part, by unimaginative and timorous bureaucrats. I brought back with me the impatient mood of the ex-serviceman and found infuriating the excessive acquiescence of the local Labour movement, almost wholly working class, which was accepting too readily the inevitability of its minority role upon the city council. They had no right to such modesty for some of these elderly Labour councillors and local Party officials had acquired an encyclopaedic knowledge of local government which they were ready to use in the service of their caring attitudes; they lacked formal education but possessed wisdom. I gave them the respect they well deserved, and, free of envy, they gave me every facility to use my propagandist talents for the local movement, and to arouse it, and indeed the city, from its political torpor. They indulged my wish to contest half a dozen safe Tory seats in succession so that I was able to activate the local party workers and familiarize myself with the problems of the city; and then generously they influenced the movement to make me Chairman of the City Labour Party and a city councillor with a firm base in a large working class ward. The selflessness of these older men, believing the torch must be handed on to a new generation, came from a religious devotion to the cause of socialism which was part of the South Wales scene. Together we were able to erode the Tory majority, and then, because of our success with the tenants of the large council housing estates in attaching an authoritarian label to the Conservative city leaders, we finally swept them out of office for the first and only time in the history of the city – and that at a time when the national tide was not in favour of the Labour Party.

The local Tory patricians had failed to realize that rent and housing policy, largely because of its psychological significance, is one of the most sensitive issues in the whole field of politics: the home tends unconsciously to symbolize the mother and her attributes, the womb and the breast, and those who lay down and enforce policies about housing and rents are always in danger of arousing the same feelings of hostility as the interfering and authoritarian father bent upon disrupting the delicate and infinitely precious relationship which exists between the occupant and the thing which protects, encloses and comforts it. The purblind and rigid Tories refused my demands for the modification of the unjust,means test rent structure which they were imposing. I took the issue into the housing estates, speaking on the street corners, and impressed upon the angry tenants an image of the tyrannical city fathers. At the head of thousands of tenants I marched to the City Hall: I was fortunate to have the aid of the older stabilizing Labour colleagues, for I had unleashed deep emotions, and it was only their presence that protected the demonstrators from falling into the hands of the dangerous and illiterate paranoid leadership which arises spontaneously in every large mass agitation. The Tories, however, remained unyielding and predictably and with relish at election time, the electors committed the necessary parricide in the polling booths. In my own ward I received an unprecedented majority.

With Labour's success came the spoils of victory and the challenge of government. I was readily given the chairmanship of the Watch Committee which had control of the police and the ultimate power to appoint, promote and dismiss the members of the force. My colleagues no doubt thought that my interest in the control and prevention of crime had prompted my desire to head this committee and at the time that was how I rationalized my decision to myself. Now, in retrospect, I am compelled to recognize that my motives were not so pure. So closely are the police identified with authority that there exists, in the minds of many people, a half acknowledged feeling, however illusory, that to have control of the police is to have an authority verging upon omnipotence; and I derived a certain satisfaction from playing so deeply symbolic a role. It is true that the authority with which the police are thus endowed is essentially benevolent in nature: the anthropologist Geoffrey Gorer, in a work on the English character, published in 1955, was surprised to discover the depth and almost unqualified regard in which the police are held by all sections of the community. He suggests indeed that the policeman may represent a model of the ideal male character, self-controlled, possessing more strength than he ever has to call into use except in the gravest emergency, fair and impartial, serving the abstract of Peace and Justice – in short perhaps, an idealized father figure. This benevolent image, as I was to point out in the final capital punishment debate in 1969, when I clashed with Eldon Griffiths (the adviser in the House of Commons to the Police Federation, which had organized an irrational hanging lobby), is unfortunately changing; and indeed by 1973 I was co-sponsoring with a colleague a Bill designed to stiffen the complaints procedure against errant policemen. But by assuming the chairmanship of the Watch Committee I was subliminally at that time conveying the nature of the strong and benevolent leadership which I wished to give to the city and, far less creditably and only half consciously, I was, by innuendo, showing that the ultimate authority of the Labour Council rested with me.

Having so set the stage, the prospect of quitting a leading part almost before the play had begun was one which filled me with foreboding as well as regret. The maintenance of Labour's majority and the success of an untried Labour council, I felt, depended on the alliance between these older colleagues and myself: we needed each other. If I left for Westminster I would go with their expressed good intentions but deep down these people, with whom I had worked for nearly a decade, would inarticulately feel betrayed; and their sense of betrayal would be strengthened if they fumbled the challenge of power and quickly lost control of the council. In the event all my forebodings were fulfilled, save only that – such was their generosity – my guilt was to last longer than their silent reproaches.

Nor could I contemplate quitting my professional work as a solicitor with any equanimity. The estrangement which exists between man and work is no novelty, though it is nowadays more fashionable to emphasize it. The curse of work was placed on man at the time of the expulsion and, not surprisingly, most people look back with yearning to idle Eden. People generally work only under the stress of necessity. The frustration and pain of living can for some be alleviated by the pleasures gained from creative work; and some, like myself, can ward off the threat of powerful aggressive and narcissistic drives by channelling them into a professional career and all the human relationships which that involves. But for most people work can bring little pleasure. The miner, it is true, has the real consolation of the comradeship of the pit, the intimacy of the darkness. But even this, as I witness in my constituency, becomes lost as the prestige within the community of being a miner diminishes, and a flight from the mines into my valley's modern car component and man-made fibre industries ensues. There the men are condemned to the anomie of the modern factory which for some becomes endurable only with the relief of absenteeism, of periodic flights into illness or, perhaps more salutory individually although socially disastrous, of aggressive strikes. The economists have little understanding of the significance of work for the economy of the libido and we are a long way from having created a society which diminishes as far as possible the tensions between the urge for dalliance and pleasure and the need for work as a therapy to control our brutish impulses. Meanwhile the people of Britain, aware of the present imbalance, assert the right to be lazy, are deaf to the pleas for greater productivity and attract from obsessional managements the same hostility as puritans display towards the joys of sex.

For my part, the challenge of the law engaged me as I had never been engaged before. Second sons have a notorious passion for justice and a constant suspicion of authority and sometimes it is best to accept, albeit wryly, the role determined by one's place within the family constellation. In my practice I did this with verve. Soon after I put up my plate I was fortunate enough to be joined by a pure young man of considerable skill, Isaac Cohen, who determinedly chose me as a partner. He possessed a detached, academic interest in money and, taking complete control of the finances of the practice, and indeed of my own, he freed me for law and politics.

I have never been interested in money. It is true that I have, out of whim, whilst in the House of Commons been prepared to devote just sufficient time to money making to ensure that I earn each year at least as much as the Prime Minister; but that no doubt is a little private game which I play in order to ensure complete immunity from the temptations and corruptions of pelf and place at Westminster. That I am able to do this without a disproportionate expenditure of energy is wholly due to Cohen's detailed execution of any imaginative scheme which I may perhaps conceive during a parliamentary recess. But the pursuit of wealth as a way to happiness is never freely chosen. The millionaires I have known, and for whom I have acted professionally, have almost all been mad; and their sad, compulsive conduct would be recognized as insane in a healthier society. The desire for money, as has well been pointed out, is not an infantile wish, though it may come to represent one, and since our fitful happiness comes from the fulfilment of our earliest yearnings there is no surer route to disenchantment than the dedication of our lives to the acquisition of wealth.

My own careless attitude to money has no doubt been largely determined by my familial background. My grandparents became wealthy
but their sons were feckless and easily duped and robbed, and their
cinema empire crashed totally when I was a small boy. But my generous,
ineffective and good father never accepted defeat: tomorrow would bring
the dawn, and one wildcat scheme succeeded another, so that I was brought
up in a home crippled with indebtedness but with absolutely no awareness of poverty. No one thought of pennies but, as is the wont of those
who live in the fantasy shadow-world of films, only in telephone numbers.
The realities caught up with me in my 'teens, but those formative years
had already insulated me. Even when I was dependent for years as an aircraftsman on half-a-crown a day I felt richer than my officers. It has
always seemed quite appropriate to me that, given the application of some
of my intelligence, I should have ample money for my needs and I have,
of course, lived up to my expectations. Those solicitors who, seduced by
the ease with which their untutored clients make money, yield to avarice
and, becoming impatient with the discipline of the law, turn wholly to
commerce and property development are doomed to caverned lives.

The early years of my own practice had been fascinating. Cardiff has
an unenviable crime record: it ranks high in the crime league of the cities
of Britain, and the opportunities for advocacy in the courts were considerable. The understatements and restraints of the formalized higher
courts find no place in the magistrates' courts of a Welsh city, where
panache is appreciated and daring and novelty are not considered bad
form. Histrionics, provided they are backed by knowledge of the law, are
savoured by court and local press, and cross-examination does not stop
short at the boundaries of genteel conversation. The infinite boredom
and repetitiveness of crime can be elevated to the level of high drama in
a little Welsh court and it is possible to reveal the tragedy of deprivation
which lies behind the vain quest for identity of petty thief and murderer.
In such courts Welshmen, and of course Irishmen and Jews, can flourish,
but they are no place for English solicitors and still less for Welshmen
simulating the style of highly mannered, mincing English barristers. In
their homes and dress the Welsh may lack style, but with rhetoric they can
still move the stars to dance and make the Anglo-Saxon appear a stammering yokel. It is spiteful of the English to have made oratory unfashionable.

Criminals have their own subculture, and local papers, though their
·influence is being eroded now by television, can still shape a town into a
community. In any case, the Welsh, blessed with ceaseless curiosity about
people, have no difficulty in reducing a city of a quarter of a million to the

dimensions of a village. A professional reputation, therefore, be it good, bad or indifferent, can speedily be built up and, however undeservedly, my waiting rooms were thronged not only with the men of commerce, but also with the accused pariahs of the city. I would note how often the arrest of a habitual criminal improved his stance and his physical appearance. His furtive, hangdog look seemed for a while to slough off him. He was no longer as lost as before: he had indeed been found by the courteous police and questioned by the attentive probation officer and he had acquired a solicitor who displayed interest in him. He was somebody. And when the great day of the trial came he stood in the very centre of the stage in the elevated dock. Here the stipendiary magistrate, the prosecuting solicitor, the clerk, the evidential rules and indeed the whole process, as well as his own advocate, protected and respected him. In many courts he was addressed as 'Mr' and when he gave his wild, fanciful account, denying his guilt, his absurdly improbable story was treated with a total seriousness. Until sentence was pronounced, for a little hiatus, he was a person. Then, thrust back into prison, he lapsed once more into his bewildering anonymity – his name taken from him, a number substituted, garbed impersonally, a nobody, utterly confirmed in his lack of identity.

Yet few of these men really wanted to be acquitted. On the contrary, when I succeeded in persuading the court that a case was not proved beyond reasonable doubt, I sensed the resentment of my client as he muttered a surly and ungracious thank-you. I have many grateful letters from men whom I have defended but whom the court convicted and sentenced to long terms of imprisonment, thanking me for having fought on their behalf, but I have none from those who were acquitted. And in truth there are many criminals, neurotically burdened with a sense of guilt for the childhood crimes they have committed only in fantasy, who stagger inexorably, like doomed characters in a Greek myth, towards the punishments which they demand as their right. Lacking the imagination of a Lawrence of Arabia to justify the flagellations for which they ache and which alone can bring temporary relief, they commit the most petty and stupid of crimes to ensure that the blows of society will fall upon them. To guarantee that their claim for punishment shall not be overlooked, they all but leave their visiting cards behind when they commit their offences. Some immediately rush off to the police to enjoy the agony of confession, a few even selecting and insisting upon seeing a particular officer in whose presence the self-abasement must be conducted. The majority, on being challenged, readily offer an incriminating statement which they sign and later repudiate, often suggesting that they have been threatened or beaten into submission by the police. The hapless, embarrassed policeman has in fact rarely yielded in this way to their masochism and in the witness box tries to step out of the fantasy role which his determined victim, with exquisite delight, projects upon him. The charade is maintained to the very end of the trial and the plea of Not Guilty insisted upon even after conviction; for this is the only way in which the last remnants of self-respect can be maintained. But the defending solicitor who cheats the accused out of his punishment is not loved. It is true that the accused requires someone to present the denial of his guilt with fervour, so that the shameful need for punishment can remain private, but the most terrible denouement for such a man is to be acquitted. Fortunately for him the whole process of a trial in Britain is so constructed that the sadism of the court and the masochism of the accused, though most amply assuaged, is most decently concealed. It is not for nothing that British justice has gained the admiration of the world.

Skills gained by an advocate in criminal trials could, as I speedily discovered, be transferred without difficulty to the magistrates' matrimonial courts, for theoretically the accusatorial system prevails there. But lay magistrates have perversely ignored the historical duty which the law places upon them to probe pruriently into the personal lives of their fellows and then adjudicate upon their guilt. They slyly insist upon using the occasion to explore the possibility of reconciliation between the parties and often, by partial hearings and repeated adjournments, they delay the final rupture so long that it never takes place. The husband and wife, having aired their grievances, real and imagined, released by the catharsis, and being of conservative disposition, decide eventually to avoid the discomfiture of change and lapse back into the habit of marriage. Solicitors, if sufficiently mature themselves, soon adjust to the rhythm of these courts and, by suitable conspiracies with probation officers, help to provide unimaginative husbands and wives with exotic reasons for forgiving one another.

None of this is taught in law schools. There students, potential judges among them, learn all about criminal law and procedure but little or nothing about the causes and treatment of crime – all about divorce law and practice but little or nothing about the art of healing marriages. So far as magistrates are concerned, the truth is that they are a captive audience, there to listen, and that once people have been listened to they are surprisingly open minded in receiving any suggestions put to them. Unfortunately the load of anxiety carried by so many people means that they cannot listen because they cannot tolerate their own silence. A greater number of formalized listening posts in the community would indeed contribute to a much needed stability.

None needed such supportive help more than the large Arab and Somali communities which formed a ghetto in the dockland. Although the dwindling importance of the Cardiff docks has now forced most of them to leave they had, in the early years of my practice, two mosques and the only Arabic newspaper in Europe. Only when they clashed with the law did many of these Adenese, Yemenites and Somalis make contact with their white fellow citizens, and they began to seek my services as an advocate. But it soon became clear that members of this community needed a counsellor and friend more often than they needed a solicitor. Sailors would sit for hours in my waiting room in order to greet me and deposit a sum of money for collection by a wandering cousin who would appear months or even years afterwards: banks were too impersonal for them. Often they would eschew the courts and ask me to adjudicate on their tortuous commercial disputes, honourably accepting my unenforceable rulings. Colourful, superbly dressed sultans from Somaliland, making their way via Cardiff to Whitehall, would descend upon me so that I might formalize in lengthy memoranda the grievances which their people wished to present to the Colonial Office.

And of course, dolefully attended by a retinue of friends and suborned witnesses, they would come to me for protection against the rigours of the criminal law. The first murder case which I defended concerned a Somali. Bewildered, lost and far from his native land, he regressed, quit the docks and lived native in some nearby moorlands. Seeing enemies everywhere, he descended one day from his tree and killed a hapless passing farmer. More usually they were accused of rape, gross indecency or seduction of young girls – crimes, according to our inconvenient laws, and punishable by terms of imprisonment, but sometimes amounting in their own countries scarcely to breaches of etiquette.

On festive days I would be invited to their mosques and, donning my yamalka, the skull prayer cap of the Synagogue, I would join them in their services, later to be offered stale Lyons' cakes – for I had been injudicious enough to express polite appreciation when these were first offered to me and so I was plied with them on every subsequent occasion.

I doubtless felt a particular empathy towards these people. My father and all his family, unlike the Ashkenazi Jews who constitute the vast majority of Jews in Britain, were totally Arabic in appearance. My strange name is not shared with any other family of Jews in Western Europe or the United States of America and is probably Phoenician in origin. Arab Moslems in the seaports of Saudi Arabia and Arab Christians and Moslems in Syria and Lebanon have the name, and all speak of its Phoenician source. I suspect that my ancestors were in Tyre long before the Jewish tribes arrived in Canaan. I remember an occasion soon after my arrival in the House of Commons when I was walking across Westminster Hall with Nye Bevan; as we stepped upon those sacred stones, fearing I would be intimidated, he told me with his stammer, as I suppose he had told others and as no doubt he told himself when he first came to Westminster, to cultivate irreverence. I told him haughtily that however the English ruling classes might appear to a Celt, to a Phoenician they were mere parvenus.

The links I had formed with the Arabs were but one facet of my professional life. It was my connection with a different section of the South Wales community which was to determine my departure for the House of Commons. The claims I was daily fighting for men injured in industrial accidents were bringing me fatefully close to many of the Trade Union leaders and their members. To lose health or a limb can be to suffer a living death, and it is doubly bitter if the failure to obtain financial compensation, inadequate though this must always be, leaves one economically dependent on State or relatives.

Wales is notorious for its industrial accidents. Superficially this may seem to be due to the hazardous nature of its older industries, but comparison with similarly industrialized areas throws doubt upon this view. One of the great difficulties which the Coal Board has found in dealing with absenteeism in the Welsh pits is the refusal of the Welsh miner to become a totally corrupted consumer. Having bought his own terraced house, or continuing to rent it for a very small sum, and having amply furnished its small rooms and perhaps bought a modest car, his needs cease. He has his beer and his brisket and that suffices. He has the impudent rationality to consider it droll to work merely in order to keep up with the Joneses: indeed the Joneses within a tight mining community are his cousins, and they will join him in the miners' club wanting no more than he. Such a rejection of the opportunities of contemporary society can, as I have observed, infuriate English Coal Board executives baying for less absenteeism and more productivity. Of course the traditional miner's attitudes and, no less important, those of his wife and daughter, cannot be maintained indefinitely. The millions spent on advertising are not totally squandered. Television, mobility and the erosion of the extended family system all exert their pressure on the miner who, as four fuels overtake one fuel, increasingly becomes a factory worker. But often he drags his feet, for the Welsh, who had the wisdom to resist the call to go to the Crusades for God and plunder, and who have never joined the English in their enthusiasm for empire-building, maintain a resentment of the enforced tempo of modern industry. They can tolerate an extraordinary degree of disorganization without anxiety, as anyone will testify who has witnessed a Welsh miners', or Welsh Labour movement, demonstration: no one keeps in step – and this is only partly due to the traditional exemption of miners from military service. What the Welsh find hard to endure is organization and regulation. They are perhaps endowed with too much imagination fully to accept the fact that two and two must always make four. Indeed, insistence on such rules can make them ill. The number of doctor attendances in South Wales is extraordinarily high, and the attempt to dismiss this as the legacy of deprivation in the 'thirties can hardly be maintained much longer. But for the more self-aware, illness is too cowardly a way of retreating from work. Despite the indulgence of the Welsh wife, who is in any case inclined to treat her husband as just another boy in the house, malingering is not acceptable to everyone. An industrial accident, however, is demonstrable proof of incapacity which no one can impugn. What is needed to reduce these accidents is not safety precautions, but happy factories. The Welsh tend anyway to doubt the efficacy of safety precautions because they believe in luck – as the profusion of betting shops in the towns of South Wales, the highest number in the United Kingdom relative to the population, will amply testify. But happy factories are not easily created, and temperament therefore makes a serious contribution to the large number of industrial accidents within the Principality.

The courts, in assessing blame and damages for industrial injuries, eschew such speculations and are concerned only to decide whether the facts establish, on a balance of probabilities, that someone other than the injured workman can be held primarily to blame for the accident. In my experience it was often more difficult to succeed on the injured man's behalf when the accident really was the responsibility of his employers or fellow workmen than it was when he was unconsciously but determinedly the agent of his own misfortune. The fluent and paranoic capacity of the self-injured man to project guilt and responsibility on those around him is sometimes proof against all logic. I had one client whose so-called accident-proneness became a source of terror to his employers and their insurers when I established to the satisfaction of the court, on three occasions over a small span of years, that he was the victim and not the cause of the industrial accidents which befell him. My relish of his rationalizations, which remained undented under all cross-examination, almost equalled the awe in which I held a woman client for whom I obtained three divorces on the ground of cruelty by successive husbands: unerringly she selected passive men, married them, deftly provoked them to violence, and left them bewildered and shocked by the acts of aggression which she had managed to elicit and which she was able, through me, to catalogue against them. An advocate must present his client's case as well as he can and I suspect that many advocates, were they to worry at all about the results of their cases, would be perturbed as often by their successes as by their failures.

In the field of industrial accident work, however, both my successes and my failures had brought me friendships in many of the Trade Union branches in the valleys of South Wales. Those friendships did not fail me when, ambivalently and without enthusiasm, I yielded to my political destiny: my friend Ron Mathias, then boss of the Transport and General Workers' Union in Wales, dropped the hint to his seven branches in the Pontypool Constituency and, speedily and loyally, they nominated me as their contender for the candidature.

No event is trivial in Wales: magic, ceremonial and drama must envelop every occasion and, if reality is too dull, then imagination must triumph over fact. All parliamentarians know that the gossip of government is to be found at the table traditionally and exclusively reserved for Welsh members in the tea room of the House of Commons. Here Celtic wisdom mocks at the absurdities of Anglo-Saxon phlegm and reticence. Here no one crouches behind the affectation that policy is more important than personality and, if there are dog days when grey politicians are so lacking in lustre that scandal is short, then it is in this little corner of Wales in Westminster, without malice but with delicate seasoning, that it will be invented.

Obviously, therefore, a selection conference for a safe Welsh seat cannot be a trivial occasion; and no self-respecting Welsh valley would allow Transport House to devalue the festival by turning it into an odious, headcounting, bureaucratic process. The first rule is that there must to the very end be total uncertainty as to the result. The run up to selection day must be long, preferably punctuated with hotly-contested adjournments, and with as much unprovable cheating and sustained canvassing as can be devised. If Transport House can be provoked to intervene by some such minor infringement of the regulations as claiming votes for delegates from a mine that has gone out of production, or a tin plate works that has closed down, then that is quite delicious. To be sure of favours from their future M.P., all delegates will give unconditional but strictly private assurances of support to every likely contestant. Throwaway remarks about the drinking habits, indebtedness, or marital disorders of the candidates are permissible. But vulgarity such as the passing of money is not allowed; nor of course, given the intimacy and curiosity of the Welsh, would anyone be foolish enough to attempt impersonation. These are days when old scores can be settled, blood links renewed or severed and friendships tested. Those who complain that in these safe seats a mere two hundred people are deciding who is to be the M.P. for the whole constituency do not understand how deep are the grass roots of democracy in our Welsh valleys. Contestants seeking votes must make their approaches sensitively and obliquely through influential cousins of the delegates, weighty magistrates and county councillors oft times holding some delegates in thraldom. Crude and direct assaults upon the delegates are a sign of desperation and reveal weakness. When the great day comes, the involvement of all the opinion formers of the area is total; and so nicely balanced are the forces at work that, miraculously, the ability of the contestant himself really counts. The whole performance is one of great complexity. The nationally known lobby correspondent, who was on the short list and entered the conference hall in my company with high confidence, left with but a handful of votes, bottom of the poll and utterly bewildered. He was accustomed only to the intrigues of Cabinet Ministers, which lack the sophistication and the feints and infighting of Welsh political life.

In Wales you must enter the contest as a David, never as a Goliath. It is a simple rule, and its non–observance has led to the rejection of not a few worthy candidates. Even if rebelliousness and irreverence did not preclude it, a win by the favourite would be an anti–climax and therefore unthinkable. Only a churlish iconoclast would so defuse the drama. So the contender must at all costs simulate the role of outsider until the very last vote is counted. Only thus can the last drop of excitement be wrung out of the selection conference and only then, reluctantly and lingeringly, can the tensions relax and the chores of the actual election, with its pre-determined result, begin. Pontypool, border country as it is, was sufficiently Welsh not to renounce any of the zest of such a conference. People still mulled over the last occasion on which a selection conference had taken place, twelve years before. The need for it arose then through the death of Sir Arthur Jenkins, the sitting Member and the father of Roy Jenkins, and Roy Jenkins himself, then a young man, was among the nominees, as were Eirene White, later M.P. for Flint and Minister of State for Welsh Affairs, and Ernie Fernyhough, later M.P. for Jarrow and Parliamentary Private Secretary to Harold Wilson. Unwisely and petulantly, the conference had rejected the future Chancellor of the Exchequer. This decision was no tribute to their judgment, though I was later to benefit indirectly from it, for if Roy Jenkins had been accepted he would undoubtedly be still the Member of Parliament for Pontypool.

His father, Sir Arthur Jenkins, was regarded warmly by the valley since he was a solicitous and attentive Member, but the constituency had clearly developed a distaste for his wife. She was convicted of snobbery, a peccadillo elsewhere, but fortunately a grave offence in the eastern valley of Monmouthshire. The clustering together of local doctor, local mine manager, solicitor, comfortably-off shopkeepers and forge manager has been a feature of valley life which, lacking any true aristocracy, enables the petit bourgeoisie to play act as lords and ladies and deliberately to dissociate themselves from the overwhelming solid proletarian majority which threateningly surrounds them. Their mincing antics are quickly observed and healthily disliked. Lady Jenkins came from such a group. I met her once, after she had become a widow: she seemed a silly woman. But silly mothers assume the most extraordinary importance in the lives of even the most brilliant sons. She evidently ruined Roy's chances of taking over his father's seat. He was young, an ex-captain, comparatively recently down from Oxford, doubtless foppish and with an accent unknown to the parents and pupils of the local Abersychan Grammar School which he had quit but a few years earlier. The valley's loyalty to the father was based upon his record, and this included a short term of imprisonment which had followed his involvement in a clash between miners and police. It was known that this prison sentence had for years been concealed from the son, not out of protectiveness but from sham respectability, and this hurt the political pride of the party activists. The temptation to return the slights, real or imagined, which they had received from his mother, and to debunk the young man, was too much for the mischievous and egalitarian Welsh. More concerned to bring about Roy Jenkins's defeat than with the selection itself, the buzzing conspiracies led to the choice of an undistinguished local man whose contribution to the constituency and the Commons, and later to the Lords, proved slight.

Roy Jenkins felt his defeat keenly, as I saw when twelve years afterwards I myself arrived in the Commons. On every occasion during the first year when I spoke to him or brushed against him in the Lobbies, he would involuntarily close his eyes for a few seconds, blotting me out as an unpleasant reminder of his earlier humiliation. But I ignored this unusual brusqueness and irrational rudeness, of which I suspect he was unaware, and persisted courteously when occasion arose, for I was conscious both of his considerable quality and of the cause of his unease. The rejection he had received had made him almost phobic where Wales was concerned, and the other Welsh Members, many of them ex-miners who had known his father, resented his insularity and were unforgiving, often implying in robust language that his mother's snobbery was irrevocably encapsulated within him and brushing aside my attempts to defend him.

When Jenkins, asked in a television interview whether he considered himself Welsh, described himself, with more honesty than political sagacity, as a border man, the Welsh Labour Members, echoing their constituents, were furious. The very term 'border man' in Monmouthshire and Brecon is used only by a fringe of determinedly anglicized hunting and fishing county Tories. Jenkins's comment was interpreted as a repudiation of his origins and as final proof of his identification with the notorious pretentiousness of his mother. But, unlike many others, Roy Jenkins was to improve with success and, when in the Cabinet, he was ready, with forgiveness on his side, at long last to return in triumph to his rejecting Monmouthshire for official engagements. Yet even then I was aware, there by his side, of a lingering gaucherie and lack of rapport which he displayed among his own people but never showed on his feet in the Commons. The gulf was to be bridged further when he became deputy leader of the Labour Party and in the autumn of 1970 he yielded to my persuasions and met again the Pontypool Labour Party, facing many of those who a generation before had so foolishly rejected him. He was wise enough when speaking to them to recall the event and, with wit, to relieve them of their embarrassment. The reconciliation appeared to him to be complete and this reflected the measure of his new found security; but sadly as I was to find when I was lined up with him on the issue of entry into Europe, the ambivalence in Pontypool remained. The fact that I was in agreement with Jenkins was held to be strong evidence by anti-common marketeers in those older parts of the constituency, with folk memories, of my perfidy.

There is no doubt that Jenkins's fascination with and yearning for the values of an essentially alien English culture leads him to a romanticism that blurs his political judgments. No true Welshman, for example, wastes time on honour: that is an indulgence in which only the ruling class of a ruthless dominating nation can afford to luxuriate. The Welsh, however, have been compelled to learn to survive by guile and guerilla war, and if Roy Jenkins's mother had brought her son up as a Welsh valley boy he certainly would not, on the provocation of infantile political thuggery by Wedgwood Benn, believing his honour to be at stake, have unnecessarily resigned in 1972 his deputy leadership of the Parliamentary Labour Party. Nor would he have so overvalued Harold Wilson's coolness; repeatedly, seeking to be scrupulously fair to a man whom he has every reason to dislike, this deeply emotional Celt has paid public tribute to what he regards as Wilson's remarkable coolness in the face of government crises. Jenkins admires what he evidently regards as Wilson's possession of English sangfroid, a quality unknown in Wales. But I doubt his diagnosis: a less fanciful interpretation, on the basis of my observations, is that Wilson's seeming calmness is a regressive schizoid phenomenon. Unnatural states of calm and detachment in the face of serious difficulties are essentially a schizoid reaction. No rational person could lay claim to an ego so unified and stable in its higher levels that in no circumstances whatsoever would any evidence of basic splitting come to the surface: few of us have not experienced a transient sense of 'looking at oneself' in some embarrassing or paralysing situation. But Wilson's reactions, in my judgment, reveal a more profound schizoid splitting, and the calm which Roy Jenkins romantically eulogises is in fact a dangerous political vice. It is unfortunate that the influence of Roy's mother who looked consciously eastwards, like so many of Monmouthshire petit-bourgeois, to the English side of the county and to the various values it epitomizes, away from the more Welsh proletarian valleys, has lingered overlong upon the judgment of this brilliant man who otherwise has a style, conviction and lack of deviousness which give him a rare excellence in leadership.

In my own selection conference, unlike his, the miners' nominee had the handicap of being the favourite, but the decline which had begun in the coal industry was already reflected in the quality of its leaders. When I was a lad, I would creep surreptitiously past the careless stewards into the miners' conferences which were traditionally held in Cardiff's seedy temperance hall. There I would listen to the bright little alert men as they elevated some local issue on the coalfield to the status of a glorious philosophical dialogue – and all of them were anarchists. The young anarchists of today seem curiously oblivious of the anarchosyndicalist traditions which exist within their own land, and they resort to foreign ancestor figures to fill the gap created by the symbolic destruction of their own fathers. But the essential sense of locality, the comparatively small pit where all worked (when work was available), the isolation of the valley village or township – all these were similar to the environmental conditions which created the anarchosyndicalist movement of Spain.

In the history of the South Wales miners' movement, some leaders were overtly anarchosyndicalist and had international links with syndicalists in other lands, and their attitude was implicit in the movement as a whole. It was the redolent rhetoric of the miner-novelist Lewis Jones – the man who would attend the Comintern conferences in Moscow and who, alone of all the world-wide delegates, would ostentatiously refuse to stand up when Stalin arrived – and the passion of the sensitive Arthur Horner, President during my boyhood of the South Wales miners, that drove me into activity in the Labour movement. But these men, although declared communists, were inevitably in constant conflict with the Communist Party machine: although Moscow detained Horner for many months in an attempt to 'correct' his attitudes, they could never cast him into the Stalinist mould. The miners' Lodge was the centre not only of industrial life but of all political and social life as well. Local health schemes began there and ultimately blossomed into the National Health Service, as Nye Bevan applied to the nation the lessons he had learned in Tredegar and Blaenavon. From the Lodge came the miners' institutes, their clubs and their libraries. Through the Lodge they acquired their own cinemas, their billiard halls in the valleys, and even a corporately owned brewery. They governed themselves, and indeed their leaders had anticipated the Marxist millennium since for them the State had already withered away. There was an extraordinary contempt for external authoritarian disciplines. When South Wales miners hear music, they sing: they do not march.

Even the famed Chartists, who went down through my valley to meet the soldiery on the coast, walked through that wet, ill-fated night and on to the deportation of their leader John Frost, bedraggled and unmarshalled; but they were far removed, as were their descendants in my own adolescence, from today's unkempt hippie demonstrators. In my teenage years the nation was shameless and shrugged off the responsibility for the grim unemployment and the pitiless means test techniques which callously broke up the whole family life of the region. Yet even in those terrible seasons we were unable to demonstrate on a Sunday – not because our protests would have clashed with the services of the chapels, but because the proud men would not demonstrate on that day without their Sunday-best suits and they had none to wear. Our South Wales Labour movement was the most respectable and unselfconscious anarcho-syndicalist movement ever. Now it remains to be seen whether its unique quality will peter out in the prim spawning suburbs of the towns on the South Wales coastal conurbation.

But already, during the fifties, the old traditions were fading. The more intelligent and hence more mobile men were moving out of the pits and into the new factories. The miners' leaders were floundering and the last of the giants of the coalfield, Bill Paynter, was to leave Wales to become the Secretary of the National Union of Mineworkers. Those left behind lacked the political and intellectual equipment to cope with the complex problems of a declining industry and a declining union membership. To our syndicalist miners, Westminster had always been unimportant, for the local Lodge was the real centre of power. The House of Commons had so often in the past been used as a dumping ground for those in the union who were supernumerary, awkward, or even slightly senile. And now the miners lacked the capacity, even if they had acquired the will, to produce men young and able enough to command support in a selection conference where the miners' delegates were no longer an overwhelming majority.

Then, too, many of the middle-aged ex-miners were becoming shop stewards on the floors of the emerging diversified factories. It is unlikely that the wisdom distilled out of the bitterness of the slumps and the struggles with obdurate coal owners can survive in the vacuums of these huge and anonymous modern factories: such wisdom is germinated and thrives only in the small hot-house pits beneath our mountains. But at the time of my candidature for the Labour nomination, such a legendary ex-miner, his front room packed with well-thumbed books from Marx to Keynes, was the Transport and General Workers' Union Branch Secretary in Pontypool's huge nylon works. There, on the factory floor, he subtly controlled some four thousand men. We knew and respected each other. In my interest he took charge, and with zest and cunning began the pre-selection conference manoeuvres.

With these set in motion I quit Wales and went away, alone, to Spain. In retrospect this seems an extraordinary gesture, and by the standards of any experienced politician it was clearly a lunatic step to take in the middle of a tough selection conference campaign when all the other candidates would undoubtedly be canvassing the delegates. But it was a measure of my uncertainty. I did not know whether I wished to endure the life style of an M.P. I went, in fact, into retreat. We each must find our own oases for meditation, and perhaps, in choosing Spain as my Mount Horeb, at that odd moment in the midst of a selection campaign, I was moved by forces of which I was only half aware.

I had been to Spain once twenty years before. Then I had gone as a young man on a less personal mission, not to find myself but to test the credibility of the requests being made through the Franco government by parents for the return of their Basque children, whom we had been sheltering in Wales while the civil war raged. Then, with the connivance of the Unions, I had been signed on a cargo boat and had slipped into the Basque province which was still under tough military control, to find that many of the coerced parents were in San Sebastian gaol. But on this later visit I spun a cocoon around myself to keep away such painful memories of the civil war and tried, within the quietude of the cathedrals, in the astonishing and neglected Museum of Catalonian Art in Barcelona, and in the Prado, to find the very pulse of the machine.

Yet once during this visit my carapace was painfully pierced. Unexpectedly, I passed a signpost pointing to Brunete. In 1937, at the battle which took place at Brunete, my closest teenage friend, Sid Hamm, had been killed. The tender Welsh communist leaders had screened the volunteers for the International Brigade so that few of them were youngsters; but Sid, impetuous and so romantic that he died without ever knowing a woman, slipped through the mesh. The deaths of those near to us always brings guilt. Usually, mourning bountifully dissipates it but, more than thirty years later, I am still encompassed by my responsibility for his extinction.

Decisions are sometimes taken in the deed, and sometimes they are reached unknowingly in contemplation. It was perhaps in the Velásquez rooms of the Prado that my conflict of feelings about the vacant seat at Pontypool was resolved. Thousands of painters and sculptors have used the subterfuge of the theme of the Madonna and the infant Jesus to portray the infinite nuances of the relationship which exists between mother and child; but few have revealed, either directly or behind the mask of some historical or mythological tale, the symbiosis between father and son. Velásquez apparently had no son, but his link with his father must have been exquisitely compassionate. Even in his most famous painting, *The Surrender of Breda*, which portrays the fall, after a valorous defence, of the Dutch city to the besieging Spaniards, Velásquez tells of his father. If, for a moment, we disengage ourselves from fascination with the Baroque interplay of movement, light, air and distance, we may find significance in the fact that the source of the Velásquez composition was an old print recounting a story of the archetype of fathers, Abraham. In the Prado painting the large key is apparently handed by the younger, capitulating Justine of Nassau to the elderly conquering Spanish army grandee, but its destination is as ambiguous as is the depicted situation. To the viewer with insight, the guilty painter does not conceal the transposition which he artfully makes: in reality it is the father who is handing the keys of the city to his son, and although the younger man pays homage to the father-like Marquis, the Marquis is no conqueror, for he exudes love. For we who are godless, our eternity is our children. And if, out of private selfishness, we deny our duty to plan the city, what key, and what evil kingdom, shall be our children's inheritance? Still possessed with the wonder of my pristine parenthood I recalled, on that afternoon in the Prado, the credo of the noble anarchist Professor Camillo Berneri, who was assassinated in Barcelona in 1937: 'Grant that the remoteness of the city of the sun shall not lead me to abandon the cities of the world.' And I returned to Wales, ready to do battle.

The calumnies and apotheoses inspired by the contending protagonists were by now echoing throughout the valley. Since my more weighty rivals were not professional men, attention had been well drawn to their suitability as engineer or miner, to represent this essentially working class seat. But I was too idiosyncratic a candidate to be ensnared by such innuendoes, however subtly expressed, for I had held a union card for years as a worker on a factory floor before I became a lawyer. And my opponents were too wily to call me an intellectual, for that accusation would have done them no good. In England the term is pejorative, but in Wales, where scholastic achievement was for so long the only means of escape to economic security, the intellectual is over-valued. Nor would they draw attention to my Jewish origin, for that would have been an offensive violation of the rules within the tolerant Welsh Labour movement. Had I been English the situation would, of course, have been quite different: their tolerance had its limits.

And in the meanwhile, my own lads had not been slow to boast of my war record. In pacifist Wales, even in just wars, the real heroes must be anti-heroes, and in this respect alone I was uniquely qualified. I found that the story of my arrest, which occurred while I was serving in the R.A.F. in Egypt, had been circulated, with many apochryphal additions, to all receptive delegates to the selection conference.

In Cairo, when I was an aircraftsman in 1944, a number of us had created, with the approval of the forces' education authorities and as part of the recreational facilities for the troops in the Delta and for those on leave from the desert, a mock Parliament. Here the citizens in uniform were able to debate the shaping of the post-war world for which we all yearned. When elections were held the Parliament acquired a very large socialist majority and this, together with its continued success, provoked the bewildered Colonel Blimps of Middle East Headquarters to fury. One fateful night, when some six hundred of us were gathered there, they moved in with the military police bent, in effect, upon suppressing the alien institution, just at a time when I, as Chancellor of the Exchequer, was about to nationalize the Bank of England. The Blimps' intervention was not relished, and the young servicemen of all political parties protested against it. That night I nationalized the Bank; but in the morning I was arrested. The military authorities refused my challenge of a court martial, and I was taken under escort to Suez and kept in custody to await the arrival of a boat which was to take me to a hot and arid island in the Persian Gulf, where I was to be quarantined. They also ordered a rigorous censorship of all forces' letters for Britain, but fortunately my Sergeant Prime Minister, later to be M.P. for Hull, and his Cabinet, with the aid of pilot friends in Air Transport Command, quickly smuggled news of my arrest to Westminster.

There Manny Shinwell, Nye Bevan and, most persistently, D. N. Pritt raised the matter. Pritt, a great lawyer who in his day selflessly defended everyone from Ho Chi Minh to Jomo Kenyatta, was an incorrigible fellow traveller whose splendid libertarian activities would not have allowed him to survive for a week in the Soviet Union. While, characteristically, he was forcing a debate in the Commons, the stupid Cairo Colonels' panic became undirected and, to my astonishment, I was escorted to Port Tewfiq and placed upon a boat bound not for the Persian Gulf but for Liverpool. Later an embarrassed Air Minister had to explain to a sceptical House of Commons that I had been moved because my 'enthusiasms' were disturbing the forces of the Middle East.

But at the end of the day it was perhaps my rivals' misogynist tendencies, rather than my past record, which determined the result. Politicians seldom like women, though they may often lust for them. Strangely, M.P.s frequently forget that half the electorate are women. With my spirited wife, I am not prone to such fatal absentmindedness, but so many M.P.s have submissive, almost apologetic wives, that their amnesia is understandable. No doubt, as prima donnas, they dislike attention being drawn to the supporting cast. There are happy exceptions to this rule. Pearl Binder, an original and disconcerting woman, saves her husband, Sir Elwyn Jones, from an excessive talent and adaptability which could otherwise have made him an urbane smoothie; Susan Barnes has a transatlantic freshness and vigour which prevents Tony Crosland from becoming an effete; and Jill Craigie, winsome and creative, has her own province in the Foot home. Some M.P.s, too, have their wives working with them as secretaries, instead of working for them as deductible expenses for their income tax return, and within such genuine partnerships there are worthy boy scout–girl guide relationships. But original choice, early marriage and the exposure of the M.P. to a myriad unshared experiences, often lead him, in his middle age, to the possession of a tedious wife.

Following the M.P.s' pattern, the aspiring trade union candidates spoke at the selection conference as to a hermetically sealed masculine branch meeting: interest in equal pay for women in the trade unions has always been a protective mechanism and has not sprung from any genuine belief in the equality of women. As I waited my turn in a little ante-room, I could hear the contenders booming at the delegates in the main hall as they would boom at the pithead or the factory gate; and predictably each laid claim to a longer period of service in the Labour movement than the last, and each ignored the dozen women delegates who were able to sway the result.

When my turn came and I had to declare my own length of service in the party, I took the advice given me by my elderly mother a few hours earlier: 'Tell them, son, that you went with me to Labour Party meetings six months before you were born.' I did; and the tension in the hall broke as the men melted into needed laughter and the child stirred in the bellies of the women. Pontypool was mine. And the yiddisher momma had sent her boy to Westminster exactly a hundred years after the first Jew, Lionel de Rothschild, was finally, and reluctantly, admitted to the House of Commons.

II

All achievements bring guilt, and those most yearned for in childhood, on attainment, bring the heaviest neurotic burdens. The new M.P. enters the House trailing clouds of glory and with the plaudits of his local supporters still in his ears, but within a few weeks depression follows, and it is more than the usual trough that follows excessive elation.

He arrives into the Chamber with blood on his hands; and it is not only the other contenders and candidates for the constituency that he has slain. The distinction of the unfamiliar letters now to be attached to his name, as soon as he submits to an oath of loyalty to the Monarch, is more than a mark of Cain who slew only his brother: this mark, which will single him out, giving him an identity of Authority, of Membership of the Supreme Court of Parliament, which he will enjoy and hate and the loss of which will be his death, is the symbol of the fulfilment of his most secret, terrible early infantile dreams. And although he, and all the older Members, will, in a grand and formal conspiracy, affect to wipe out his awful deed by an immediate public affirmation of allegiance to the Crown, the ostentatious display of loyalty will not quench the primal disloyalty. Parliament, born out of near regicide, and strengthened by actual regicide, is too evocative to erase the buried parricidal wishes. The son has become a ruler of the land, and princes only become kings on the death of their fathers.

My own gentle, ailing father, with an exquisite sense of timing, on the way to my eve-of-poll meeting, succeeded in being knocked down by a car, and I spent election day rushing between constituency and hospital. The gesture, fortunately, proved to be over-theatrical, and he survived; but the point was well made. Although no-one speaks of such daemonic displays at Westminster, the House of Commons is old enough to understand them just as well as the Greeks. Not for nothing did the Members fear a Bradlaugh who refused as a condition of entry to submit in the name of a god-father to the monarch: the form of words, the sacred incantation, was naturally all-important for the change of one word would unleash a crushing avalanche. To join the rulers, one killing is permitted: but chronic parricide would jeopardize the whole institution.

And to make certain that the newcomer, intoxicated with his own success, does not again over-reach himself, the conventions are laid down firmly. The fresh M.P. must be relegated, and must accept his relegation. The constituency-conquering hero must become a supplicant child praying in his maiden speech the indulgence of the House for daring even to make a contribution. The insensitive or arrogant who dare to challenge these rules are soon humiliated: the millionaire, Captain Robert Maxwell, possessed of boundless animal energy and born too poor to afford deference, is soon humiliated by mockery; a John Davies, with the hubris of the unfeeling successful accountant showing his contempt for parliamentary process, is speedily and mercilessly savaged. No one can avoid the initiation ceremony: no one can crash the House. The outsize man must accept his new infancy, and again must learn, if he is to survive, to grow up slowly in Westminster, and the process can be an agonizing one. Sir Owen Temple-Morris who eventually escaped from Parliament to become our most assured senior County Court Judge, was afflicted with an hysterical temporary blindness while delivering his maiden speech. Although such copy book imitations of Oedipus, paying his price for parricide, may be rare, few escape from their personal guilt which the House of Commons, making them children yet again, corroborates.

When I delivered my first speech the *Daily Telegraph* recorded: 'Mr Abse made a fine maiden speech. He spoke with a force and clarity approaching that of an experienced parliamentarian. The House welcomed his contribution, and agreed that "Abse made the heart grow fonder." ' The outward calm was, however, a sham. The first year of my parliamentary involvement was one of the most painful periods of my life. The nights after I left the Commons for my lonely hotel room were full of nightmares and terror: seemingly for hours I would, in a twilight world between dream and wakefulness, be gripped by vertigo. The whole room would spin round me, now slowly, now like some ghastly merry-go-round totally out of control, and again and again my attempts to impose order and stillness on the whirling furniture would fail. I was unbalanced and had lost my bearings.

It did not help me that I came in on a by-election at the fag end of a Parliament. At General Elections the newcomers arrive as a group, and prop each other up, like a new class entering the grammar school from a junior school: but I entered alone, at the end of term, with the great examination, the General Election, soon to take place, and anxiety enveloped the Palace. Most examinations, if failed, can soon be taken again but the election result is final. Failure to the average M.P. means the destruction of his identity and his world. So often a hollow man, he becomes increasingly and utterly dependent upon his role: nothing exists behind the mask of his persona. His rejection by the electorate is not coolly appraised as disapproval of his political party: it is interpreted as personal rejection. The election is not simply experienced as such: it is not conceptualized as an event in itself, as something unrelated to his real inner life, as essentially extrinsic to his self evaluation. Failure means oblivion: today a somebody, tomorrow nothing. To lose means the dissolution of his world: all the various constellations of his relationships, all the projects and plans which he has assigned to himself will melt away. The implications of failing to surmount the hurdle are so awful, so intrusive, that for months before the election they cannot be put aside. I was surrounded by M.P.s fearful that the achievement of the milestone was uncertain; their roads were trembling with uncertainty and their possible collapse confronted them with the pointlessness of their lives, made them alone within their separate worlds. To wrest some calm and stability from them was impossible: and the anxiety oozing from them disturbed me still further, leaving me wretchedly disorientated.

In pre-election months, even after my fourteen years in the House and my five parliamentary elections, I still remain sensible to so many of my colleagues' sense of aloneness, though now I am no longer vulnerable to infection from their anxiety. The run-ups to elections are ugly days, not only because of the absurd and gross oversimplifications publicly displayed in the debates in the Chamber and Committee Rooms, but because of the desperate conviviality which has to be endured. The M.P.s, in their club, flee from their loneliness, immersing themselves in sociality in the busy impersonal everyday life, but they fail to ward off their anxiety. Compulsively the conversations return to the election prospects and the M.P. cannot tear himself away: his world, his life, his identity all call him back as problematical, as being at stake and threatening to corrode into meaninglessness. He feels his world is coming apart.

But these repetitive preoccupied conversations are stamped with what has been described by the American psychotherapist Harry Stack Sullivan, who strove so heroically to fuse psychiatry and social science, as the selective inattention technique. The excruciating sense of inadequacy, caused by the anxiety-provoking situation, calls into existence a security operation, through which the M.P. avoids coming to grips with the fundamental meaning to him of the coming election – the fear that he is not an adequate human being. He regresses into the stage where as a juvenile his parents and his peers all expected him to attend to what is deemed to be socially relevant and appropriate, and where violations of these requirements meet with ridicule and disparagement; as a result as a juvenile he was educated, primarily by anxiety, to control his focal awareness, to notice and concentrate on that which is socially acceptable. But such a selective inner tension technique of avoiding anxiety, in adults, must lead to dangerous denials of reality.

So it was to come about that my private conviction, oft-times expressed to my colleagues, that the continued leadership of Wilson would result in disaster for our party in 1970 was always unacceptable as anxiety-provoking. The electorate, goaded into punitive attitudes by the public display of unjustified vanity by Wilson in his vulgar presidential campaign, without fear of recrimination, unobserved, in the absolute privacy of the ballot box, predictably and determinedly punished him for his overweening pride. But even, when beaten, the Parliamentary Party reassembled as an opposition, still their closely fitting delusionary habitudes could not be sloughed off: completely deceived into believing victory was inevitable, their technique of selective inattention had caused them to evade all painful contradictions, and suavely to avoid all the anxiety-provoking meanings and consequences of the bunglings of the 1966–70 government. It was not that they were unaware of the events: but they had to be dismissed, for to have accepted their full implications was to have accepted their death as men, for being alive and being an M.P. was sadly for many of them, an equivalent. At the first private meeting of the Party in the present Parliament they packed the large Committee Room and huddled together like a pack of hypnotized rabbits, silent, utterly immobilized and submissive when called upon to reaffirm Wilson's leadership: such conduct, so rare in so notoriously opinionated a group, showed how traumatic an experience they had just endured. Their scramble for their personal survival had left them prostrate, exhausted, panting with personal relief but without spirit. My weariness, however, came from other sources. I was tired of a manipulative leadership lacking style and goals, and alone I challenged Wilson and placed the responsibility for the debacle upon him personally. I was listened to with respect, without anyone demurring, without anyone approving: the tongue-tied mob, unable to adjust to the fact that the listening opposition leader no longer could bind them by patronage or magic, sat frozen. And when, at last, the well intentioned Left, shamed by my intervention, rose, they characteristically fumbled the occasion.

However, my capacity to swim confidently against the tide certainly did not exist in my first years in Parliament. Then it was I who was drowning, and to escape and gain confidence, I moved into the shallows. I confined myself almost exclusively to the problems of my constituency, involving myself with a passionate parochialism in the affairs of Monmouthshire and South Wales. It was with irony that I discovered how grim was the state of hospitals and housing in the County which had enjoyed, through Nye Bevan, a Member who had commanded the Ministries of Health and Housing. There were strange ambivalences on Nye's part to his birthplace: and just as all of us show an impatience towards the foibles of an elderly mother that we would willingly indulge in other old ladies, so Nye in many ways showed more concern for the nation than his own area. Perhaps Tredegar and Ebbw Vale were too constricting, as had been his assertive mother: and Nye preferred to soar among the stars rather than to forage around the coal tips.

But it meant that tumble-down hospitals, and the lack of bathrooms and flush toilets in the old terraced houses of the valleys, were accepted with a slothful complacency: and the effect of these conditions was reflected in the South Wales infantile mortality rates, some of the worst in the kingdom. I aroused concern over these needless deaths of the newly born children, shaming authority into action: the Coal Board, the largest landlord in my constituency, was cajoled into a programme of renovations and, under my prodding, more funds were diverted to speed up hospital-building programmes. Today the infantile mortality rates of the region, although too high in our valleys, are little different from the national average: but any contribution I have made to this result, made me as much a beneficiary as the mothers. Such successful campaigning in and out of the House enabled me to regain my confidence and inner poise. It enabled me to have the courage to acknowledge to myself that my life-long involvement and interest in extravagant partisan party politics had ceased to exist the very year I had been elected to the House of Commons.

I had reached the point where I found the unselfconscious approach of the fully committed politician intolerable. The projection of all fault on to the other side, and the absolute exemption from blame of your own party, leads to absurdities which are clearly pathological. The baying that, with such frequency, punctuates the debates as the final division on an issue approaches, cannot be explained merely as expressions of strongly held differing views. I sit on the benches surrounded and fronted by men screaming puerile insults, distorting each others' motives, falsifying facts, and frequently creating an uproar totally disproportionate to the gap between the Parties. The advent of Heath's rigidly ideological politics has of course prompted a surfeit of such storms: each side of the House claims the other side are persecutors coercing, by stratagem and conspiracy, the supporters of the opposing party. Party politics cannot be understood if the elements of institutionalized paranoia embedded within them are ignored: and to a large extent in the House of Commons the source of this paranoid conduct is to be found in the repressed homosexuality of many of its members.

It is certainly not an historical accident that Freud's monumental contribution to the aetiology of paranoia rested initially upon the study of a German politician-lawyer, Dr Schreber, who stood as a candidate for the Reichstag in 1884. Poor Schreber's illness, his paranoia and his megalomania, arose from his failure to sublimate his homosexual component, and his faulty attempt to repudiate his homosexuality led to his extraordinary delusions. Fortunately for the community our contemporary British politicians do not usually founder so fatally: but a paranoid imprint is nevertheless stamped too heavily on their partisan contributions.

We can perhaps not expect it to be otherwise. The man who lives comfortably in the Party, in the smoke rooms, and the essentially male world of the Commons, can disperse much of the homosexual component of his emotional life in a circumscribed esprit de corps, in a measured comradeship and sometimes, more worthily, in a love of mankind. We too often overlook the erotic element, with the sexual aim inhibited, that bathes social relationships: but it cannot be disputed, that, like actors, politicians are usually narcissistic, and this is the nub of the problem, for each stage in the development of a man's psychosexuality affords the possibility of a fixation, and those still excessively enslaved to their narcissistic phase are exposed to particular dangers.

Freud has explained that there comes a time in the development of the child when he unifies his sexual impulses, which have hitherto been engaged in auto-erotic activities, in order to obtain a love object: and he begins by taking himself, his own body, as his love object, and only subsequently proceeds from this to the choice of some person other than himself, first choosing a similar person – that is a homosexual object choice – and thence to heterosexuality.

The residue of homosexual feeling still possessed by the heterosexual can usually be sublimated, and the banding together with other men to achieve a political object affords considerable opportunity for sublimation. But people who are not freed from the earlier stage to the homosexual one, the stage of self-love, are exposed to the danger that some unusually intense wave of libido, unable to find a narcissistic outlet, may surge up to sexualize their social impulses. Then, their now recharged homosexual impulses can no longer be sublimated in this social and political activity. Their homosexual impulses are running too strongly to be contained, and to protect themselves from the dangerous sexualization of their social instinctual cathexes, a remedy, however desperate, has to be found. Freud explained the remedy is paranoia. The man, not daring to face the true proposition of 'I love him', declares 'I do not love him – I hate him' and then justifies this assertation by saying 'I do not love him – I hate him because he persecutes me'. This paranoic technique, albeit usually in its milder forms, I see operating everyday in Westminster.

The Party system depends upon it to a large extent for its continuance: and those whose narcissism is greatest have greater need for the Party game. The accusations the Party players can levy against their opponents, the delusions of persecution or exploitation they rationalize – all protect them from the weak spot in their development lying somewhere between the stages of auto-erotic narcissism and homosexuality. Our solitary Prime Minister needed and enjoyed the disciplined and disciplinary role of chief Whip. In a rare glimpse of his fantasy life Heath has revealed how incapable he is of moving away from his self-attraction to enjoy any real relationships with others. 'I have always had a hidden wish, a frustrated desire, to run a hotel,' he once said. It is a sad dream corroborating his evident incapacity to enjoy developed object relations.

The hotel keeper greets his guests with the ever present meaningless smile, like Heath's fixed smile, which is charming, pleasant and correct but distant; and, of course, all who come soon go, ships that pass in the night. Not for Heath the dream of a home, wife and children: only the impersonal hotel over which he presides and where undemanding transitory acquaintances but not relationships are formed. Heath's fate is to hug himself, as he often does on the front bench: and then at piano or organ it is his pleasure to play all alone. Such a personality type needs the protection of a party system; his deliberative and provocative ending of consensus politics is the fulfilment of a personal need, but whether it is the need of the nation is another matter.

It is in the Members' dining room that the prevailing paranoic mood is epitomized, and it is a mood which would surprise practising lawyers. Lawyers battle against each other in court and then break off during an adjournment and amiably lunch together. Such detachment, and capacity to see both sides, may well account for the failure of lawyers to reach the top in politics: their prejudices are too lukewarm and, such as they are, are often checked by their legal training and professional conventions. But the failure of the M.P.s of differing parties to dine together is certainly not due to a great divide on principles. It is droll that in our dining room the Tory M.P.s dine at one end and all the Labour M.P.s at the other and ne'er the twain shall meet. If on a crowded night one wanders to a table among the Tories, a frisson is sensed or banter begins;

and indeed it may well be true that all waitresses who at one end serve the Tories, vote Conservative, while our girls certainly vote Labour.

Such paranoic etiquette added to my sense of constraint in my early days in the House. Perhaps I was seeing too much: all my many and worst blemishes were daily flaunted before me in the persons of my colleagues, and such insights as I possessed could no longer be blotted out. I was moving beyond the point of return, and although I knew only too well every pothole in the worn path taken by conventional politicians, I could not without betraying myself take that well signposted, high-walled lane. To repeat oneself is the end of growth: and sooner the dangers of the unknown than to stride confidently to a drab destination. Fitfully there were to be moments of vexation as I was to see lesser men have Ministerial rank; but in the end, fortunately for me, even the feeling of temptation was to die. I made my own way and knew with every step I took I moved away from personal political advancement. By the very approach I brought, by the very areas of controversy I was determined to have explored, I knew I was burning my boats. To be true to myself I had no options. I irrevocably committed myself to the unregretted role of the Private Member.

BOOK I

Assignment with Thanatos

III

Somehow the original strength of aggression contained in every individual has to be limited, modified and controlled. In its primal form it cannot be accommodated within a viable community: if a society is to survive, somehow aggression has to be reduced in quantity and quality. We thrash around for methods to master our destructiveness. But it is not easy to succeed in taming the force we fear most. Within this century man has had the courage to uncover the forbidden components of his love instincts, but still he shrinks from the exposure of his aggressive proclivities. Rather than dare to use insights we cling to the imperfect defences created by our ancestors against themselves. And one of our most important defences is Parliament.

To Parliament we delegate many of our unfulfilled aggressive wishes: from Parliament the army, the police and the judges ultimately receive their instructions. At the behest of Parliament wars can be waged, criminals gaoled, strikers outlawed, taxes wrested. The right to coerce is renounced by the individual and altruistically he hands it over to Parliament. Westminster is the power-house transmitting socially sanctioned aggression. It inevitably becomes the Mecca for all those who wish, even as they did in their nurseries but now without fear of disapproval, to scream with anger, spit at their enemies, bitingly attack opponents, boldly hit out at wrongs, real and imagined. Like moths around a flame, the aggressive flutter around Westminster. Outside Dartmoor and the armed forces, there are no more aggressive men than those sitting in our Parliament.

If such a concentration of aggression is not to lead to a conflagration, strict precautions are necessary. On my arrival at the House of Commons the attendant in the Members' cloakroom pointed out to me the coat hook assigned for my personal use. A loop of pink ribbon was tied around it, as around everyone else's hook. Intrigued, I questioned the flunkey who told me, unsmilingly and with hauteur, that the loops were to hold the swords deposited by M.P.s before they entered the chamber. Thus was I introduced, immediately upon my arrival, to the ritual which the Commons has evolved to defend itself against the morbid aggressiveness of its Members.

Not all our rituals are vestigial. We still insist that Members who wish to address one another must do so not directly but through the Speaker. Even then they must not refer to one another by name: in the House Members are identified either by their office or by their constituency. They also become honourable, honourable and gallant if they are of sufficient military rank, honourable and learned if they are barristers, or right honourable if they are privy councillors. In ensuring that we have no direct confrontations, and by ruling that our most bitter expressed thoughts must be prefaced by stylized courtesies, we seek to neutralize our aggression. And to be certain that our verbal attacks will never regress into infantile musculatory actions, no member is permitted while speaking to cross the red line woven into the carpet of the aisle which divides the two front benches, and the width of the aisle itself is the length of two swords. Any member whose foot does cross this line, if only by an inch, is immediately called to order by angry colleagues in all corners of the House.

Still fearful, however, that these inhibitory rules may fail us, we maintain the convention that no one must lapse into 'unparliamentary language' by investing the Speaker with the authority to insist that no wounding attacks must be couched in other than deliberately protective formalized words. Knowing our well-tried strength, we are unusually sophisticated in dealing with errants who wish to extend the repertoire of their performances by defying our tested and much needed boundaries. If Bernadette Devlin in a carefully prepared impromptu physically attacks the Home Secretary in his seat, the self discipline of a House too wise to over-react leaves her looking and feeling as foolish as a child in tantrums; and even an engaging but rough miner like Dennis Skinner who persistently and defiantly howls abuse in the Chamber lacks sufficiently tough a hide not in the end to feel, by the icy indifference of his colleagues, his own vulgarity.

No one outside the House of Commons understands better the dictum that the man who first hurled a word of abuse at his enemy instead of a spear was the founder of civilization. With the end of early childhood, mitigation and control of the aggressive drives is done by verbalization: from then on words are expected to take the place of muscular action. Dirty words must take the place of dirty actions such as a protesting defecation; verbal abuse must take the place of physical attack. The active politician, far more than most, has incessantly to verbalize if he is to master his own aggression: he dare not stop for his domination of his aggressive destructiveness is precarious, and he fears he will yield, regress, and display his violence in a frighteningly primitive form. Politicians are almost always unusually endowed with aggression, and their capacity to control it has often been impaired by very early experience. The true base for the development of the effective binding and modification of aggressive impulse is known to be found in the essentially non-verbal communication received by the babe, held in love and safety, from the calm voice and reassuring lullaby of the mother; and, lacking that early blessing, the politician later seeks with flawed equipment to contain what is probably in any event a heavy genetic endowment of aggressivity. Only talk can mollify his anxiety; and this defence he uses in all his waking hours.

Prompted by the fear that he may be unsuccessful in warding off his internal enemy, who may drive him to distractions and destructiveness, he endows his defences with magical reassuring overtones: the politician's belief in the wonder-working use of words to resolve all problems is, not surprisingly, the despair of more practical men. And to his eloquence and incantations he oft times gives an accompaniment of revealing gesture and posture. The flaying histrionic gestures of a professional politician, like a Peter Shore, spell out the rudimentary physical accompaniments to anger, hate and rage, such as can be observed in a babe; and sometimes the infantilism of gesture matches the quality of the adult's political thinking. But even among the most weighty of men in the House, like Roy Jenkins and Harold Lever, the extraordinary trembling of their hands as they commence their aggressive and skilled debating forays discloses their anxiety. Such is Lever's fear of his own aggression that his demolition of his opponent's case is invariably accompanied by placatory interludes which weaken the effectiveness of his contribution: he fears to arouse to full pitch his opponent's aggression lest it should provoke him to unleash his own. Indeed, during the Common Market debate, rather than continue to face the unrestrained hatred of puny men, this Member, probably the most intelligent man in the Commons, resigned his place in the Shadow Cabinet. It was not his miserable political enemies he feared: it was the aggression in his own breast which, if he had dared to release it, would have saved the Labour Party from a considerable loss.

But most Members have not such self regulatory inhibitions and our rules therefore are drafted to seek to contain our perversions. The drive of our lust for dominance and power which has brought most of us to our places must be checked if the institution is to survive. The impress of the anal phase, the stage of infantile libidinal development when, accompanied by aggressive phantasies, the child is fascinated by the mastery of his body through sphincter control, is too deeply printed upon our characters. Although most members would fiercely resist any interpretations which hint at the origins of the nomenclature of our institutions and proceedings, the blunt fact is that we take our seats every day in a chamber where we are continuously passing motions.

At the time I arrived at the Commons, even the least perspicacious would have been aware that the secret aggressive fantasies of its members had been lit up as perhaps never before. Gaitskell made me acutely aware of it within a few minutes of my taking my seat. Flanked by two South Wales colleagues I had made my obeisance, moving from the bar of the House at slow pace and bowing three times to the Speaker. Then, after being sworn in before an observing House and receiving a kindly welcome from the Speaker, I moved, as I had been instructed by the attentive Whips, behind the Speaker's chair. By convention, the Leader of the Party stands there to greet the newly arrived member. The greeting was a frigid one: he gave me a wan smile, a less than half-hearted handshake, and a few perfunctory muttered words too strangled even to be heard. I felt his antagonism. I was made to realize immediately how seriously he took my identification in Wales with the Campaign for Nuclear Disarmament which had caused the Press to label my constituency and me as anti-Gaitskell. I was made depressingly aware that I had entered a battleground and not a united Parliamentary Party, and that the Party's failure to come to terms with the ultimate violence, the hydrogen bomb, was tearing it asunder.

Gaitskell's obsessional traits, exacerbated by the internecine Party conflict on the bomb issue, were to prove disastrous for the Party. His determined aim to emancipate the Labour movement from its traditional orthodox ideology was pursued with the fanaticism of the heretic. There are always dangers in any movement which is bound together by common philosophies. The phase of childhood development in which the child alternates between dependence on his mother and the assertion of his own autonomy so often finds echoes in adult life: if the parent group with whom the individual is identified insists upon his total subjugation, then to survive he must sometimes assert his independence. Gaitskell's obsessionalism required that Party lines must be firmly laid down; but papal edicts lead to schisms. Under Gaitskell the rule books of the Party had to be redrawn, no comma omitted and no 't' left uncrossed lest the new holy writ should be ill-defined. His intelligence and, even more, his charm enabled him to assert his authority over large sections of the Party, but his fatal obsessional flaw meant he had to win every battle, never to concede an inch, to 'fight, fight and fight again'; in practice, of course, this meant he won every battle but the last. He himself was never to be Prime Minister, and if he had not died when he did it is unlikely that

Labour would have gained sufficient unity to govern in the sixties.

I found him physically antipathetic, but there were men who were extravagantly in love with him. Frank Soskice once told me, months after the event, that Gaitskell's death had extinguished all his joy in politics, and there were obviously many in Parliament who felt similarly devastated. But despite his Winchester poise he never seemed to me a man with inner security. No doubt his Hampstead Group was the creation more of those who felt excluded from, than of those who were within the magic circle; but his indiscreet favouritism arose from a need to be surrounded by those who affirmed and did not challenge his identity. True, many of them had quality, because he possessed this himself, but this tendency was unnecessarily provocative. His weakness was exposed in his duels with Macmillan: he was for ever under a compulsion to expound and defend his own policies and his own position. He could fight back fiercely, but he could never lead an attack and Macmillan, a meaner man, was forever forcing him to adopt a posture which was to prove electorally disastrous in the 1959 election.

Yet indisputably Gaitskell fascinated many people. In particular, his caressing voice was extraordinarily seductive. In most other species it is the male who possesses the bodily characteristics which are the biological basis of charm used in the service of sexual union. But even if man is one of what Darwin calls the anomalous cases, in which there has been an almost complete transfer of secondary ornamentation to the female, the male is not left totally bereft – and Gaitskell could charm the birds from the trees. Not only men, but women too, would quickly fall under his spell. When I first found myself, some years before I entered the Commons, in the company of both Gaitskell and his wife, I was not surprised to notice the unease, amounting almost to neuroticism, which afflicted Dora Gaitskell. She was totally committed and devoted to him, but on those invariably happy occasions, since his death, when I have worked with her in the Lords, I have found her a much more relaxed, self-confident woman, more attractive and often possessed of shattering insights. It could not have been easy to have been married to a man who possessed some at least of the qualities of a genuinely charismatic leader.

The main asset of the charismatic leader, at once both weapon and armour, is the charm which conveys not only his magic power but also his delicate need for love and protection, and such protection was passionately offered Gaitskell by what the political commentators rightly described as his Praetorian guard. In some ways a leader's command resembles that of the hypnotist – using awe and love, a father-like authority and infallibility, and yet a caressing, maternal tone, which evokes the image of a mother wooing her child to sleep with a lullaby. Gaitskell's attractive voice, so often commented upon, was that of the woman successfully encapsulated within him. The charismatic leader is at once both father and mother and thus fulfils the eternal wish which man expressed in the myth that male and female were originally one. But his own inner balance is precarious, for he must at all costs prevent his active, domineering drives from being overcome by his more submissive, feminine and seductive tendencies. Gaitskell's constant struggle to enforce Party discipline was a symptom of his own inner disorder, and the impolitic rigidity with which he tried to impose changes upon the Party's constitution revealed his lack of inner freedom.

This gave Gaitskell an appearance of operating mechanically and insensitively, and led Nye Bevan to hint devastatingly that he was a dessicated calculating machine. But, for once, Nye's characteristically concrete imagery was confusing, for Gaitskell, paradoxically, was a deeply emotional man. He found the power of the hydrogen bomb far too alluring, for he needed to identify with a powerful father image in order to protect himself from the threat of his own passivity. Perhaps some of that passivity arose from his identification with the coloured nurse who tended him for a short but decisive time in Burma, when he was an infant: certainly her influence was so strong that Gaitskell romantically and nobly imposed upon an uneasy Labour Party a totally unrealistic policy towards coloured immigrants that, electorally, was to make Labour pay a heavy toll even as late as 1970. She was probably only one of a number of early influences that shaped the acquiescence within his character: and his need to ward off this disposition was to have important political consequences. And his extraordinary passion for dancing and rock music may also provide a clue to his constant need to be unnecessarily over-assertive: the dance is said to have its origins in the imitative movements by the tribe of the totem animal which, in turn, was the god father of the primal horde who, in myth or fact, was killed and devoured by the rebellious sons. Gaitskell's need to imitate the heavy handed father, to play so affirmatively the role of leader, was overdetermined and lacked authenticity. But his projection of this psychological need into the Labour Party debate on Britain's retention of the H Bomb acted as a detonator, and when I arrived in the House of Commons, the Parliamentary Party was torn and bleeding.

Only those who proclaimed their passion for peace could have indulged in such continuous and bloody in-fighting. The nature of the main dispute between the factions, the retention or abandonment of the bomb, aroused the most intense anxiety. The most aggressive in the Party were the absolute pacifists, unable to cope with their own violence in any way except by total rejection; but the most determined were those who projected their aggression upon Russia and her satellites. The expressed need for deterrents and elaborate defence systems to protect them from their enemies was too often an ego defence mechanism employed to protect them from their own inner destructive wishes which the excitement of the H Bomb had aroused to fever pitch. I was sickened by the hate the fratricidal struggle engendered.

Any deviation from the Party line at that time on any issue precipitated fierce condemnation. It is not only Christianity which, while exhorting men to love their neighbours, persecutes with a special fervour those who profess a faith which differs but marginally from the current orthodoxy. The role of the Grand Inquisitor in the Parliamentary Party at this time was played by Bert Bowden, the Chief Whip. Bowden carried himself erect, like a Guards officer; severe and uncommunicative he rapped out his orders almost in monosyllables. His silences became him and helped to build his reputation as an intimidating martinet. But he was a sphinx without a secret: when Wilson, whom he had supported in the later leadership struggle, made him Leader of the House, his hollowness became embarrassingly obvious and his banality and impoverished language became a sour joke. Continued parliamentary humiliation was avoided only by his removal, as Lord Aylestone, to head the Independent Television Authority, where the non-communicator was able to take charge of the main communications industry. At the time I entered the House, however, his bludgeoning had helped to reduce the morale of those who opposed Gaitskell to a state of pulp.

The anti-bomb factions felt their helplessness more keenly because they had lost their natural leader. In a bid to present a united Labour Party to the electorate at the forthcoming election Nye Bevan, to the dismay of his friends, had supported Gaitskell's policy at the recent Labour Party Conference. The Left had worshipped Bevan and it now saw him as a renegade. The more forgiving sought to excuse him in whispers about his age and his fear that, if Labour lost the election, he would never be able, as the intended Foreign Secretary, to lay the foundations of a European peace. As the years hurry by, politicians, finding that life has not granted them the fulfilment of their infantile dreams, sometimes impulsively seek reality-denying short cuts to their goals: and often, as they reach and pass their mid fifties their judgments become singularly faulty. Man, too, has his menopause but he is too proud to claim so feminine a mitigation for his extravagances. Enoch Powell at fifty-seven, having made a vain bid for the leadership of the Tory Party, unable to tolerate his frustration any more, ran amok. The other failed contender for the prize, the brilliant Reggie Maudling, at fifty-five, threw all caution to the wind and, in a breathtaking fantasy, acted as a paper millionaire for a while, until the curtain came down and ended the tragedy. Richard Crossman, at the age of sixty-two, unsuccessfully attempted in an election year to put through a mammoth pension bill which was bound to bog down the whole parliamentary session, to be largely incomprehensible to the electorate and, insofar as it would be understood, to provoke many voters. It is exactly the type of Bill which should have been introduced in the first year of a parliament, not the last. But ageing politicians want to construct their own monuments and their clamorous needs can often overcome the protests of their colleagues. Age, in fact, is not a subject dwelt upon at Westminster where death is more usually denied. It was considered outrageously tactless when Harold Wilson, in his reshuffle in the autumn of 1969, sought as a gimmick to create a more youthful party image; an extraordinary wave of resentment swept through the Parliamentary Party. At Westminster, life is eternal. In a sense, indeed, this is true literally as well as metaphorically, for no one is permitted to die on the premises. Men may collapse there, but they always die outside. So intricate and elaborate are the inquest rules of the Royal Palace that medical co-operation can always be relied upon to ensure that no one is pronounced dead within its precincts.

But Bevan's change of mind about the bomb sprang from causes deeper than those suggested by his more sympathetic apologists. From Moses to Demosthenes to Churchill, the eloquent stammerers have always been among the most violent of men. God punished the stutterer Moses for his ungovernable rage by refusing to permit this greatest of men's leaders ever to reach the promised land. Nye Bevan was to share a similar fate. Nye Bevan's oral aggression was feared by foe and friend. Sometimes it could inflict havoc on his opponents and, sometimes, when it recoiled as it did in his notorious anti-Tory 'vermin' speech, upon his colleagues. He feared it himself, and the block in his speech betrayed his fear. In part, his stammer was an unconscious attempt to regulate his intemperate attacks, and often on the occasions when I acted as chairman for his meetings in South Wales I was aware of other bodily gestures deployed for the same purpose. He would, as he warmed up and the Welsh hwyl began, repeatedly take out his handkerchief and wipe it deliberately across his lips. Then I would squirm uneasily in my seat and wonder whether Nye had been successful in smothering the forbidden words, while the reporters below would expectantly hold their pencils and, looking at the platform, hopefully await another indiscretion.

There was no more compelling orator in Britain than Aneurin Bevan; even his most destructive attacks on authority were, however, accompanied by imaginative and healing reparations. A turbulent man, he still yearned for what he called the serene society, and the search for solutions to his own problems brought massive benefits to the nation. Yet the conference speech in which he abandoned his former views and defended the retention of the bomb, and which I heard him deliver shortly before I came to Westminster, illuminated his persistent private agony. Its most striking moment came when he pleaded to have the bomb so that he would not, as Foreign Secretary, be forced to 'go naked into the conference chamber'. The phrase is still remembered. Perhaps it revealed more about his own nuclear complex than about the H Bomb, but it was a complex which he shared with others and some of us who were hostile to his plea were able to sense the way in which many of the delegates reverberated inwardly to it. For his imagery touched upon the castration fears which are common to all men – fears which still, in 1973, cause hundreds of millions of males throughout the world to be circumcised in the unconscious hope that this symbolic castration may avert the actual castration which the awful father gods would otherwise demand. As the great German physician, George Groddeck, put it: 'One fact remains: because every erection is desire for the mother, every erection, without exception, following the law of transference, is accompanied by the dread of castration.'

Nye Bevan's gentle, dreamy father may seem an unlikely contender for the role of castrator, but imperfectly resolved Oedipal situations can make monsters out of the most unsuitable material. The little Aneurin's secret relationship with his dominating mother must have been intense; and, all through his life, fearing his desire to provoke his own elimination, he defended himself against the anticipated retaliation of authority by launching repeated attacks upon authoritarian figures and institutions. If his stammer protected him from the consequences of the outburst which he would otherwise have made against his father, it did not prevent him from releasing his violence as soon as he could find a substitute father figure on whom to vent it.

Inevitably it was upon his first hapless headmaster that he originally fell. Stories are still to be heard in Tredegar of the physical fights which took place between them. If the wretched headmaster was really the bully Nye always maintained this was entirely fortuitous, for Nye would certainly have cast him in this role whether he was fitted to play it or not. No-one who heard Nye talk privately of formal education and of schoolmasters can forget the extravagance of his attacks. One suspects, too, that the further one went back into his childhood, the more violence would be there, waiting to be uncovered. His fateful conference speech was made not by the huge and towering hero whose passion had inspired a generation, but by the frightened little boy sitting naked on his pot. His enemies responded to his infantilism and gave him the vote for which he pleaded but his friends were estranged. He was as naked after the conference as before it: the exposure became not only a personal humiliation. The whole Labour movement was to become a victim of his temperament.

When, despite his uneasy alliance with Gaitskell on the bomb issue, the Labour Party failed in the 1959 election, he returned to the House in a dangerously depressed mood. No longer able with the old freedom to play monarch at his court, no longer surrounded by his old friends and admirers in his special corner of the House of Commons smoke room, he prowled around the corridors engulfed in gloom. His participation in debates became perfunctory and revealed too often a lack of preparation.

Locked up within himself, he could not shift his full attention to the new controversies. His attacks were no longer reserved for the political enemy: they were upon himself, and it was often hard to be physically near him without sensing his melancholic withdrawal. The end was inevitable. To unleash such massive aggression, as was his endowment, upon himself meant cancer and death. He was to die as a result of fall out, as certainly as if the bomb had been dropped.

And, with his death, all hope of a genuinely socialist Britain died too. Only he had the capacity to provide a leadership capable of fending off the temptations of the affluent slavery proffered by an unthinking technology. He alone in the Labour movement could have had the magic to persuade a people to choose the holy land, not the fleshpots of Egypt. However Britain is to be reshaped, his untimely death guaranteed it was never to be in the image of the founding fathers of the Labour Party.

Nye Bevan was not the only protagonist in the nuclear armament debate who went to personal destruction slain by his temperament. For my part I felt even more keenly the death of John Strachey, the great educator, whose books shaped the thinking of a whole generation of socialists. I cannot relinquish the conviction that he, too, fell to the bomb, although my bitter and sad quarrel with him meant that since we barely spoke to each other for months before his death I cannot, reasonably, be so dogmatic.

No man influenced me more in my adolescence. As the years roll on I find I have been to countless and far too many conferences and many become telescoped one with the other; but my attendance at a Youth Conference in Sheffield when I was sixteen, I recall as yesterday. I sat there, a raw provincial boy, for the first time at Strachey's feet and, fascinated by his poise and social confidence as much as by his lucid translation of Marx's knotted and tortuous language into English prose, I became his fervent admirer. As I followed him around from meetings to summer schools I frequently crossed his path and he, becoming aware of my admiration, and flattered, fortunately for me responded to it.

His teaching calmed the time confusions which as an adolescent, enveloped me. Like so many of the adolescents of today, I was at odds with time itself; the alternatives Strachey presented in those days were seductively clear. Fascism and war, or 'scientific' socialism. One or the other was imminent. Other possibilities did not exist. There is, of course, an indispensable temporal aspect to all ideologies, and since a lack of perspective is characteristic of the adolescent some specifically temporal ideologies can have especial attractions. The estranged adolescent of today, mistrusting time, often floats into 'absolute' time by drug taking, or, indifferent to his partner, by dancing to beat music as in a timeless trance. Some adolescents pathologically regress to a period of early infancy when time did not exist: the experience of time arises only from the infant's adaption to initial cycles of need tension, delay of satisfaction and satiation. That is why, as Eric Erikson has indicated, for some of our present day malignantly regressed adolescents every delay appears to be a deceit, every wait an experience of impotence, every hope a danger, every plan a catastrophe, and every possible provider a potential traitor.

But there are more subtle ways which may persuade the young to enter into the self deception that they have overcome the relentless patterns of time than marijuana, or goose-stepping to blaring trumpets in preparation for the Thousand Year Reich. Strachey's literary eloquence held out for me a vision of a stateless socialism with just sufficient qualification to guarantee its credibility: and, of course, it all would happen speedily, in my lifetime. No man, apart from Sir Herbert Read, the gentle anarchist art critic, led me up more intellectual garden paths: although when I once told Read this, he received the barbed compliment wryly.

But Strachey, who periodically, publicly and ruthlessly discarded his past intellectual errors, knew I felt no resentment towards him: I enjoyed his explorations but, for most of his readers hot for a fixed certainty, his intellectual adventures became intolerable. They felt betrayed and dubbed him a traitor: but his arrogance assisted him and he could live, although not without pain, with their abuse, but he could not endure an entrenched existence in a stale intellectual dug-out.

During his early thirties, for three years, he had undergone a therapeutic analysis under the psychoanalyst, Denis Carrol: and consequently he was always open minded, eager and ready to discuss with me the impact of psychoanalytical findings upon political science. He was indeed the only Member of Parliament with whom I could indulge even my most fanciful speculations in applied psychoanalysis, and be met not with resistance but with incitement. Long before I came into the House I remember his excitement when I told him of the contents of an illuminating work on psychoanalysis then recently written by an English analyst, Roger Money-Kyrle. He borrowed my copy, and, uncharacteristically, never returned it: but I was soon aware from some of his later publications that he had well assimilated the contents and so it was for me indeed a case of throwing some bread upon the waters.

His remarkable elder sister, Amabel Williams Ellis, I see each Easter when I escape to Portmeirion, the fantasy village, full of visual excitement and delicious fun created by her husband on the edge of a subdued estuary in North Wales. Now, nearly eighty, she continues to write biographies and children's history books: stately, robed in arresting dress that has no genteel reticence, always possessed with a hauteur that appears to increase her physical height, she carries the world of Bloomsbury with her, a world full of ideational content but often, observing not feeling, hesitant in human relationships. When, with a rare panache, on the green lawn of her manor house facing Snowdon, she authoritatively pours out her own blend of tea – Darjeeling with a pinch of Earl Grey and Lapsang souchong – she talks with all the confidence of her patrician forefathers who governed the ignorant Indians. And, although her comments may sometimes be banal, they ring in and out of the topiary with all the insistence of a prophetess: and because she painfully reminds me of her brother, to whom I owed so much, I would not dream of ever gainsaying her.

The early cultural discipline imposed by John Strachey, Eton and Oxford, masked his heavy aggressive endowment; but like Nye Bevan he was an unusually aggressive personality. It was not, however, in the debates of the House of Commons that he found his release; indeed, I was taken aback when he told me shortly after my arrival at the House that he hated entering the Chamber and found it almost intolerable to listen to the debates. He would read as much or as little of the debates in the Hansard of the following day as he wished and would only enter the Chamber when it was necessary for him to contribute. After more than a decade of enduring debates I now find his diffidence to sit in the Chamber more understandable.

But his battle with his own dangerous aggression revealed itself in his never ending quest for an all embracing philosophic unitary view: always he strove for a *weltanschauung* which would resolve the contradictions, unite the opposites: and as events or facts seeped through the almost hermetically sealed philosophical constructions that he would postulate in one work, he would embark upon another book to explain how the flaws had arisen, and how they could be repaired. A whole generation received the benefits of his vain Sisyphus-like efforts, as books and pamphlets flowed from the man who for a while seemed likely to give British socialism, hitherto always a ragbag of pragmatism and evangelism, a real and divining unitary theory.

It is the erotic instincts which, as Freud has stressed, are always trying to collect living substances together into even larger units. And it is the same process which aims at binding together single human individuals, families, tribes and nations into the great unity of humanity. Repeatedly Freud had claimed that mysteriously under Eros masses of men must be bound to one another libidinally and that necessity alone, the advantages of common work, would not hold them together. Yet the instinct of aggressiveness in man, the hostility of each one against all and of all against one, opposes the programme of civilization. I do not find it as surprising as many that Freud should have concluded that aggression against the external world in general, and other people in particular, was ultimately the result of a death instinct being blocked by erotic and self preservative instincts.

It is, of course, more fashionable and certainly more comfortable to assume that aggression is an impulse which arises as a result of, and is biologically attuned to deal with, the frustration of our other impulses: such a sanguine view comforts us with the hope that, by diminishing frustration, we can diminish aggressiveness and perhaps save humanity from the aggression which, reinforced by the bomb, will destroy all life. But the very vehemence with which the concept of an instinctual drive as the source of aggression is rejected, and an exclusively reactive cause insisted upon, leads to the suspicion that a psychic mechanism of defence is at work. To reject the concept of aggression as an innate drive indicates a certain naiveté in the conception of human nature akin to that held by the 'flower children' of today, who are inclined to the belief that we would all be flower children if away from the environment. Freud's view that aggression springs from a perennial source of energy, deeply rooted in our very nature and ultimately independent of any external thwarting or frustration, more adequately explains to me the unprovoked violence and destruction unleashed in our generation. It is terrible to be compelled to acknowledge that the goal of life is death; but, rather than live with deception, it is wiser to play the game with a zest not born of illusion, and be satisfied with the minor victory of at least prolonging the sport a little. In a man like Strachey the sombre threat of death, of dissolution and dispersal, of increasing entropy, was fiercely warded off as he sublimated his erotic instincts, not only in excessively romantic attachments, but, more relevantly, into his constructive unitary philosophies: but since the self destructive and the erotic instincts perhaps never appeared in isolation, as he sought to turn round the death instinct, and fling it back, one could sometimes be startled by the sadism that, as a result, could bathe even his most quietly spoken and arresting lectures.

I can pinpoint the occasion when I first became disquieted by Strachey's dangerous attraction to violence. He readily had agreed to come to speak on my behalf when I was a parliamentary candidate going through the motions of contesting a safe Conservative seat at Cardiff. Now, as the years move on, by habituation, our biological equipment impedes a realistic assessment of the nuclear danger and thoughts of the horrors of nuclear destruction are defensively avoided. We mask the terrible new weapons under soothing descriptions such as Multiple Independent Targettable Re-Entry Vehicles or Fractional Orbiting Ballistic Systems. But when Strachey then spoke with all the authority of an ex-Secretary of State for War, for most of his audience his quiet unfolding of the facts of even the comparatively unsophisticated nuclear weaponry of those days was a new and challenging experience. He spared them no detail, and the probability of the destruction in our lifetime of the whole of the human race was pitilessly presented to them. The large hushed audience was stunned and dispirited: but as I drove Strachey back from the meeting place to my home he was in high spirits, clearly elated as I remarked on the shock listeners had received. He enjoyed the impact he had made: his address had acted as a catharsis for him, but I found his display of sadism unseemly, and although he was too euphoric that night to notice my disapproval, when I did arrive in the House, some years later, he became aware that my hero-worship was tempered. He was a rare Renaissance man, but his resentment that I had observed his Achilles heel was to flare up.

At first in the House we maintained our old relationship: and both surfeited with ephemeral political small talk, over a meal or in the smoke room we could speculate and philosophize. He significantly was always attracted to the pacific Tolstoy, and every year he would re-read *Family Happiness*, and recount his pleasure. Willingly, I would studiedly avoid any discussion relating to the terrible Party divisions on defence policy, and was content to paddle in his literary pools. But my very silence proved provocative to him. I had declared my witness to the cause of nuclear disarmament but I did little more: I neither spoke in the House nor at the parliamentary meetings on defence issues. I believed that time would reveal the absurdity of the megalomaniac belief that Britain could afford to have the missilery and the bombs. The debate over the independent 'deterrent' and the semantics and self deception involved in the concept of an independent contribution to the 'deterrent' would all ultimately be seen as a grand irrelevance.

I saw the Defence White Paper of 1957 as the last attempt by this country to maintain independent status: and was to see the collapse of the Blue Streak project as the final failure of that attempt. The illusions would persist, and Harold Wilson would still be maniacally posturing in 1967, telling us in the private Parliamentary Party meeting that Britain's frontiers lay on the Himalayas, and Heath would, even later, yearn for an East of Suez defence policy: but time would erode these British pretensions of grandeur. I was not prepared to squander myself in an otiose wrangle over the years. Goaded by Strachey, who wanted to challenge my non-involvement and hammer me into acceptance of his fierce, partisan Gaitskellite attitude, I told him why I opted out: and scorned his waste of talent in acting as defence spokesman for the Party. When he sought to corner me with argument based upon his intimidating knowledge of weaponry, I evaded the trap and insisted upon talking of the dynamics of aggression, of the psychological theory that suggests the use of symbolic gestures as unilateral initiatives to reduce tension before attempting to move on to multi-lateral negotiations. This was the approach President Kennedy was to make in 1963 when he announced the first unilateral initiative, that of stopping all nuclear tests in the atmosphere, a psychological gesture that was to be a starting point towards a détente with the USSR. But such a discussion with Strachey of the psychodynamics of aggression inevitably led to a discussion of personal motivation.

He had, as I am aware, been recently abused by Bertrand Russell who, I was to discover, would, eschewing depth psychology, attribute the most outrageous and the most superficial of motives to those who disagreed with him on the bomb issue. During the Cuban crisis, as I shared platforms at crowded apprehensive meetings with Bertrand Russell, I was made aware how Russell seemed to imagine that he only had to demonstrate man's stupidity in order to overcome it. People, alas, are not made wise by being told that they are stupid. But perhaps Strachey merited Bertrand Russell's abuse, even if Russell only half appreciated the reason for his particular prejudice to Strachey's apologies for Gaitskell's defence policy. I told Strachey that the diminution of his belief in the validity of the theory of the class struggle, to which when I first knew him he was wholly committed, had left his aggression dangerously suspended. The Marxist theory had enabled him to deploy his eroticism in a belief in the brotherhood of the united working class and simultaneously to discharge his aggression against the 'expropriators'. Strachey naturally resented my suggestion that he always needed an enemy: and, worse, that he found the bomb irresistible. But we knew enough – perhaps too much – of each other's life style to speedily tear each other to shreds. And in the end heatedly we dredged up too many of our weaknesses. I told him finally that he was courting death: that his past Under Secretaryship at the Air Ministry, his role at the War Ministry, and his present intolerant involvement, where he was totally ready to cast out of the Party the minority of M.P.s differing from his Gaitskellite defence policy, would prove fatal to him. Addicts should avoid drugs: and the violent should not hang around dangerous fuse boxes.

Doubtless some of the content that surfaced in our furious altercation gave both of us some analytical shock. But I had wounded him beyond tolerance and, for many months after, we passed each other without words, eyes averted. In the end he took the initiative, and we spoke again but our old relationship was shattered. Our conversations became over-circumspect. He was clearly depressed, vexed as ever with his Dundee constituents who returned him to Parliament with ever-diminishing majorities: unable to release his aggression against the voters upon whom he was resentfully dependent, he turned in on himself whenever he was in Scotland and there the local press dubbed him 'the man who never smiled'. I knew the lugubrious moods in which I now found him, even if precipitated sometimes by feelings of rejection by his constituents, sprang from deeper and more poisonous wells. But after the last detonation, out of cowardice, I did not dare again to persist in my warnings against his obsession with military violences.

But I feared for him: he was talking of feeling old and I sensed he was no longer warding off the pull of the death instinct. A few weeks after our last chat he recklessly went sailing in appalling weather and when the boat capsized he narrowly missed drowning. But his last enemy did not have to wait long for his complete and determinedly passive submission. Against the advice of his wife, who wisely never believed in the diagnosis being made of some leg and back pains he was experiencing, within less than a month of his boating accident he unnecessarily insisted upon a major and dangerous operation. The surgeons duly acted as his self-approved executioners and, no doubt, issued a death certificate showing he had died from natural causes. It is not a verdict with which I can concur.

Ironically, and far more obviously, another man who had been extraordinarily generous to me was to pay a terrible price for his partisan involvement in the Party defence policy quarrel. Ron Mathias, whose aid had given me my seat in Parliament, had emerged as the leading Welsh Trade Union leader. Whenever a major strike is threatened or occurs in my constituency, I almost invariably intervene and indeed in these days fortunately it requires little excuse even for the tough and sometimes over-anxious shop stewards of my huge Girling factory to call me in; but invited or uninvited, that I intervene with some confidence is because of Mathias's tutoring.

From my early days in Pontypool Mathias guided me through the issues provoked by the industries in my constituency becoming increasingly highly diversified, mechanized, automated and rationalized. He was a superb trade union leader with considerable intelligence and little formal education always learning empirically, rarely from a book. He spoke, therefore, whatever the occasion, at prodigious length, lacking all economy in presentation; but his men at union meetings amidst the surface ramblings would sense rather than understand his underlying organic approach. They enjoyed his confidence and his authority; and anticipating with sensitivity all their fears, he would obtain their approval of genuine productivity deals long before they became fashionable. He knew every weakness in the worn out institutionalized pattern of industrial relationships but, understanding the essential conservatism of the unions and the men, he understood how to preserve the outward forms whilst revolutionizing the content. He was also, more relevantly, as far as I was concerned, physically a big man. He had no son and his paternalistic feelings were by no means assuaged by his care and concern for the workers within his Union. He liked little men: so tiny Ray Fletcher, now the wry and witty M.P. for Ilkeston, and I were both the beneficiaries of his tireless efforts to place us in the House of Commons. Ray Fletcher for ever philosophizes, muses and psychologizes and can be devastatingly fluent; Ron Mathias had abandoned all his early lay preaching and pacifism and was empty of faith, sustained only by his almost compulsive daily activity in industrial disputes and problems throughout Wales. He, therefore, sought Fletcher's company and mine for anchorage and, since we were unchallengingly small, our theorizing and pithy articulateness did not threaten but rather soothed and complimented him.

But Frank Cousins, then Ron Mathias's boss, is a physically towering man, and could too easily be interpreted by Mathias as a threatening father figure. And, unfortunately for the over-ambitious Mathias, he fell into the hands of Jim Callaghan and George Brown, then bent upon containing Cousins's challenging demand made through his huge Trade Union for unilateral nuclear disarmament. Mathias too was also well-wooed by the American Embassy.

The bait was laid and the ultimate prospect in a future Labour government as the Minister of Labour dangled before Mathias; and there were other possibilities. If Frank Cousins could be successfully forced back, the prospect of his protégé, the able Jack Jones, becoming, as he now has, his successor, would be slight. Other than Ron Mathias there was no other alternative of equal stature in the Union. The prizes were great, and to a man who had been a conscientious objector during the war the issue too seductive and tempting. His was the zeal of the proselyte, the pacifist turned inside out. With the approval and support of the leading figures in the Labour movement, his fear of his own destructiveness could be warded off and he could dare to attack on behalf of the bomb retentionists. I became uneasily aware of the existence of a mounting conspiracy, but Mathias ignored my cautionary advice and, knowing my disapproval, began avoiding me.

On the eve of a full meeting of the area secretaries of the Transport and General Workers in London when, I suspect, Mathias hoped to effect a coup he, under stress, incautiously opened out to me. I begged him to desist and stick to his industrial last but flattery had already enlarged his intellectual conceit, and he was determined to undervalue the strength and the purity of Cousins's candour. At the fateful meeting, Mathias was utterly crushed. On the train back from London to Wales his humiliation and guilt bore down on him. He was seized with a coronary thrombosis and rushed to the main hospital serving my constituency. I speedily visited him. I was to find a shambles of a man. He recovered, but only slowly and partially, and he turned to drink as a solace. When the Labour government came he received the piffling pay-off for his bungled efforts on behalf of the Gaitskell group. Against the wishes of Cousins, who relentlessly had pursued him, he was able to escape from his now intolerable position with the Union and was appointed to a well paid job on the Prices and Incomes Board. For a little while this brought a flicker of life back to him but he was broken and before long a coronary killed him off. His death left us in Wales with no Trade Union figure with the capacity to ease our industrial workers' passage out of the dying traditional industries into the second industrial revolution.

Newly arrived recruits to Westminster are expected to participate, without excessive delay, in the self-destructive political game. There is no shortage of partisan teams to join. The detachment of a non-joiner is easily misunderstood. Some two years after I had entered the House, I had to emit the necessary warning signals emphasizing that my detachment was not to be interpreted as disengagement.

In politics, confrontations are occasionally essential: the weak are brushed aside and no politician will function well unless his peers are aware he possesses a dangerous armour. It is wise that colleagues and opponents should know that there are issues to which your commitment is total, and that they challenge you at their peril. In my case this was especially necessary, for my tepid interest in the baubles of parliamentary life, the Ministerial posts, the possession or loss of which is the sole measurement of success and fulfilment for so many of the thrustful in the House, could have, in my early parliamentary days, led to the facile assumption among my colleagues that I belonged to the drop outs.

There are, of course, many so stigmatized. Sometimes they have arrived too late, and too burnt-out, to endure the fierce competitiveness of the House; a very few are too pure, and, exceptionally, some are too mature to regress into the more infantile pranks of parliamentary politics; more are intimidated and, measuring their skills which they had over-estimated against their more politically sophisticated fellows, and sensing their inadequacy, lapse into lobby fodder, depression and a wide range of psychosomatic illnesses. The lockers of more than one Member I have known have been veritable dispensaries.

The handsome and gentle Llywelyn Williams, for sad example, who represented Abertillery and came into the House renowned for his dramatic preaching throughout the Non-Conformist world, was one such hypochondriac. He could never reconcile himself to his failure to captivate the tough, sceptical Commons as he had his congregants. Not even his appointment as a Governor to Westminster Hospital, which succours ailing M.P.s away from home, allayed his hypochondriacal anxieties: indeed it seemed to provoke them. And lacking admirers and worshippers of God to shore himself up, his religious faith collapsed: running away from his doubt, he became a professional traveller, persistently manipu-lating himself on to every parliamentary delegation all over the world, defying the advice of the doctors who now believed in the illness which he had determinedly created for himself. It was of no avail: he insisted upon me drawing up a will for him in the library of the House of Commons and, although distracted for a while by my successfully waging a libel action on his behalf against the BBC, who had permitted a play carica-turing this good man to be peddled by the sour Welsh playwright Saunders Lewis, Llywelyn too soon collapsed and fulfilled his last testament.

A few, like Robert Davies, the former Member for Cambridge, bravely but desperately and fatally, hurl themselves at the institution. Rigid, ideological, but scrupulous, Robert Davies's rectitude was a personal disaster. He served Cambridge well on the local authority and was accustomed to lead and obtain, as often can occur in local government, speedy and practical results. On the back benches, however, he found himself lacking function and in an ineffectual limbo, despising both the compromises of the 1966 government and those indigenous to Harold Wilson's temperament.

I noticed his dignified loneliness in the lobbies and tried a little to bridge it. We dined together occasionally and, at his invitation, on a few occasions I visited him to speak in his constituency: but his intense hatred of the half truths, shuffles and evasions of Westminster was, I saw, dangerously liable to blow back upon him, and I constantly advised more detachment. It was useless: his fury and impatience with the political charades choked him. Still in his forties, after fifteen months as a Member of Parliament, this gifted man died of his honesty and the House of Commons.

Davies's doom was a rare failure of adaptation. More usually, physical survival at least is ensured but, as ever, since the beginning of time, Bacchus is a great comforter for those feeling defeated. The bars of Westminster are not subject to the licensing laws, although any accusation that a Member in the Chamber has over lingered in those bars arouses hysterical demands for the accusation to be investigated by the Committee of Privileges. Others find consolations in their constituencies: they exchange the anonymity and patronizing they endure in London for a throne at their own parish pumps. For that kingdom they accept their orders, sometimes muttering but unchallengingly; yet if they did but know it, their covetousness for the positions held by others is shared by those holding those positions. The greatest tragedy of the professional politician is his incapacity to enjoy the present: he lives to become a candidate, and then dreams of entering the House where, dream fulfilled, he yearns for a junior Ministership. His compulsions enforce him to resent being a Minister without Cabinet status, and, that achieved, even as a Chancellor of the Exchequer, he wishes to be Prime Minister at which level, it will not have escaped notice, frequently there are visible traces of the assumption of the role of a Deity, against whom, doubtless, envious feelings are focused.

Sometimes the public mask is torn off. Faced with the prospect of being denied the yearned-for office at a seemingly adverse election time, Iain McLeod, losing self control, called the Prime Minister a swine in the

Chamber. Quintin Hogg, one night during the same week in 1970, just after an opinion poll erroneously forecasting a massive Labour victory had come over the tape, bore down on me where I was chatting quietly with another Labour M.P. Screaming like a traditional Shakespearean lead, attracting the attention of nearby Lobby correspondents, quite beside himself with rage, he hurled obscenities at me. 'Cunts, cunts, cunts', he declaimed; the language was poverty stricken but the agony I could see was real. The excuse for his indulgence was a tasteless morning comment from Transport House about Quintin's big boots which, because of some weakness of his ankles, he is compelled to wear. But the anguish sprang from deeper wells. The poll was presaging the destruction of all his hopes: he had relinquished his peerage in a vain bid to become leader of the Party and then, for years, had slogged from the opposition front bench, stretching himself almost beyond endurance as his financial position and his over-anxious attitudes to money compelled him to practise hard in the Law Courts. His remaining prizes, of Home Secretary, or that of Lord Chancellor, a position once held by his father which was reserved for him when the Tories won, seemed to have slipped from his grasp. Suddenly he was aware of all the wasted years and, at sixty-two, he wrongly interpreted the poll as his political death knell. I did not resent this unprovoked abuse: rather I was flattered that he had chosen me as the recipient for I interpreted it to mean that he had a confidence that I had affection and regard for him. We do not abuse those to whom we are indifferent. But he, like so many politicians, had lived excessively in the future, and in this case it was a future which at that moment he felt he never would reach, and for a short while this was his moment of truth.

Living in the present, however, also has its dangers: then colleagues may assume you belong to the drifting political flotsam of Westminster. It was my engagement in the German question that corrected such a false perspective. I had, shortly after entering the house, yielded to the blandishments of Will Owen, the M.P. later to be acquitted on charges of spying, to join a small party of Labour M.P.s invited to meet Ulbricht, the German dictator, in East Berlin. It was, in the late winter of 1958, a drab oppressive world to enter, and the warmth and excessive hospitality of our official hotel an embarrassing contrast to the bleak austere existence of the shabby Berliners. I realized how carefully I was being observed. Caviare is one of my many weaknesses; and occasionally in London I indulge myself, calling in at Fortnum and Masons to collect a pot of

Beluga. My zest was noted in my first meal and I was then plied with extravagant portions on every possible occasion. I interpreted this as seduction, not grace, and strengthened my guard still further.

The usual preliminary rounds of talks with ministers and officials began, and the inevitable offers to show us all followed. I declined a tour of yet more factories and housing estates and, sensing resistance, I almost demanded that I should see Arnold Zweig, the novelist President of the East German Academy of Arts, who I affected I knew was at that time in East Berlin, although, in truth, I had no idea of his whereabouts.

Arnold Zweig, ten years later, when he was to reach his eightieth birthday, was to be the centre of elaborate celebrations in the German Republic. Pompous newspaper stories told how representatives of the State and of the ruling party assembled in order to congratulate him. Over fifty delegations of cultural and political organizations were enumerated, and he was hailed as the Grand Old Man of socialist literature and a favourite of the people. But neither then, nor in the following year when he died and was accorded a state funeral and honoured by lengthy laudatory obituaries throughout the East German press, was his simple but dearest wish granted to him by the inexorable communist state.

I had originally met Arnold Zweig in Haifa fifteen years previously, when I was serving in the R.A.F. in the Middle East. On each leave, I would quit the filth and degrading poverty of Egypt and the bitch city of Cairo to escape to the villa built on Mount Carmel just before the war by my eighty-year-old grandfather, an Orthodox Jew who, having lived most of his life in Wales, went to die in his Holy Land. I discovered that Zweig, having left Germany, was living nearby and, since few modern novels in my teens had enthralled me more than his *Case of Sgt. Grischa* and his cycle of war novels, I called on him, literally to pay my respects. He was a lonely, alienated man, troubled by his own failing eyesight and even more by the narrowness of vision of Zionists who resented his heavily qualified approval of their over-confident enthusiasms. Such resentment is, I am aware, only too easily provoked. When recently I went to Israel with David Frost to have a televised dialogue with a local audience, my tempered criticisms of the shooting down of the civilian Libyan 'plane aroused the Israeli press to fury, and not long ago the Zionists were infuriated by my insistence that the establishment of the State of Israel was Jewry's greatest defeat. For two thousand years, with incredible fortitude, the Jews withstood Christian and pagan cruelty, stubbornly maintaining their Messianic belief in the redemption of all mankind, but in the end, after the final holocaust, in order to survive, they were compelled to capitulate to the mean concept of a nation state. I take no joy in their enforced retreat from their cosmopolitanism. Nor did Zweig, and his impatience with the Hebrew language fanatics of Palestine who resented his continued writing and speaking in German had led to ugly political scenes. In Tel Aviv, as in the fastness of North Wales, it is often necessary to recall that in Babel diversity of language was a curse, and not a blessing, imposed upon mankind for his sin of excessive pride.

Zweig in our slow walks across the anemone-covered Mount Carmel, then free from its present over-development, would tell me of the pre-Hitler Germany literary world of Mann, Wasserman and Toller whose tortuous quests had for me an almost sinister fascination; and we would speak of Nietzsche, whose genius still captivates me, and Zweig would cast a singular illumination upon the prophet; and in return, no doubt, as a young man, I gave to him my faith in the post war world and made temporarily, a little less bitter, his disenchantment and displacement. My political precocity opened a window to him upon the current British democratic scene, relieving the claustrophobia he felt, de-Europeanized, in wartime Palestine.

But when I sought him out in East Berlin, it was to discover how this most committed of Freudians was surviving as the Head of the Cultural Front in the most rigid of communist countries. For I was quite certain that Zweig would never permit any ideology to temper his hero worship of Freud. Zweig had dedicated his treatise on anti-Semitism to Sigmund Freud and a Freudian analysis had, he asserted, freed him from his personal neurosis and released his own creativity; and his gratitude was boundless. A filial relationship was established between Freud and Zweig and for many years until Freud's death they conducted a constant correspondence.

Zweig received me warmly, and, unencumbered by any clinging official interpreter, soon was speaking to me with his former frankness: but his fervent apologia for the German Republic and his catalogue of its achievements was overdetermined, and I told him so. And when, inevitably, we spoke of Freud, the doubts behind the assertiveness became distressingly clear. He showed me some of Freud's letters and while commenting upon the handwriting found me a sympathetic listener. In Vienna, where I had found myself in uniform at the end of the war, an indomitable elderly Austrian woman, who had maintained an oasis of sanity around her family during the terrible years, had, in return for some slight favours I had been able to render, initiated me into the revelations behind our handwriting. She had studied under Professor Klages, the graphologist, and she had made me ever aware how handwriting is a seismograph tapping out the soul. I have placed firmly at a distance more than one of my devious House of Commons colleagues after having received from him a seemingly harmless note; and sometimes, as when the Moors murderer wrote frequently to me begging my aid to permit him to see his killer girl friend, Myra Hindley, I have regretted, for the sake of many young lives, that his school teachers could not have seen the psychopathic madness that dances across every line of his written pages.

I teased Zweig as he told me of his intention to write a book containing his correspondence with Freud and on his relations with the founder of psychoanalysis. My raillery that it would be impossible to publish such a book in a communist state agitated him. He well knew that Freud had asserted that the communist, as the fascist state, would not tolerate the insights of psychoanalysis, and his dogmatic and loud assertion to me that such a book would and must be published in the German Democratic Republic I regarded as a vain rehearsal for the violent arguments in which the issue would eventually be embroiled. Zweig had great courage, and in 1963 he did have published a novel in which he was able to make a tribute to Freud, but the book and the letters of which he spoke to me remained unpublished, and, defeated, the Head of the Cultural Front ultimately had to communicate privately with Ernst Freud in London asking him to edit his father's letters; and ironically, on Zweig's death-bed, they were published in the West Germany that Zweig despised, and later, posthumously, in 1970 in Britain.

Yet I learned more of the German Republic on that visit from Zweig's artist wife than from him. As I entered the house I saw a bowl of anemones and, commenting on their loveliness, I said to her that these were perhaps all that the crusaders had brought back to Europe from Palestine, for I could sense her nostalgia for Mount Carmel. When I was leaving she quietly drew me aside and asked me not to mention that I had seen those flowers in her home: she had obtained them from West Berlin and this was then against the law. This chastening leave taking, after the spirited defence of the State given to me by her husband, prepared me for my session the following day with the East German leader, Walter Ulbricht.

Of all the leaders I have met, only a smiling commander-in-chief of the Indonesian forces nonchalantly telling me in Jakarta the figure of the thousands of communists he had killed or incarcerated, was more immediately unsympathetic than Ulbricht. Perhaps the anemones, Mount Carmel and my grandfather lingered in the interstices of my mind on the morning of our meeting. I found quite intolerable the dogmatic cataloguing of the Nazi connections of the West German Republic leaders with which Ulbricht began his indoctrination. I brusquely interrupted the pedant to suggest that not all the millions of Jews thrown into the ovens were pitched there by those living in West Germany; that the Germans in his Republic must share the guilt even though I conceded that there was at least one difference between West and East Germany on this score: the West Germans were making financial reparations both to the surviving members of the slaughtered families and to Israel; the East Germans had not paid a single penny. My comment was an inauspicious start but it ensured that we had a dialogue, not Ulbricht's prepared monologue. The turbulence increased considerably when Ulbricht attacked the reparations as payment to an imperialist base, and I, showing no compassion to the taut and now perspiring interpreter, retorted that I had never seen British or American troops in Israel but had observed many Russian troops in my few days in East Germany. These pleasantries over, the hour or two then spent with Ulbricht sped along surprisingly productively. But on my return to my hotel I read in the British press that Gaitskell had made clear his disapproval of the visits my colleagues and I were making to East Germany: we should have gone to West Germany and the editorial comments, taking Gaitskell's cue, were treating us as communist dupes.

We should not have been consorting with the wicked: it was, of course, confusing. It is simpler to have a vision of the world in terms of black and white, of gods and devils. It is tough to acknowledge our darker drives, examine and accept them and so subject them to the more rational control which can at least partially be exerted upon them when admitted to consciousness. It is easier to repudiate our aggression and project it upon others: but that is the method that leads to us having no more hope of effectively dealing with the aggression of others than of coping with our own. Ulbricht and his crew certainly needed containing, and it was important they knew the boundaries we set: but it was no less important that we did not feed their paranoia. The distinction between a good lover and a good hater, like Ulbricht, is that the lover is faithful; but the good hater knows no fidelity. He is promiscuous, and is ready to consume with his freely floating aggression anyone who by his action is unwisely showing his wish to offer needless provocation.

I was, therefore, indignant when, not overlong after my visit to East Germany, the Conservative government announced its intention to bring in West German troops for training in Wales. Worse, by collusion with the opposition front bench, this quaint contribution to international understanding was to be acquiesced in by the Parliamentary Labour Party. The decision was ill received in pacific Wales. The placing of

Panzer troops on Welsh soil was widely considered a bizarre method for cementing British–German friendship, and, to many, a grim and offensive heralding of the formal burying of the war against Nazi-ism. I was only too well aware how it would alarm and provoke the leadership in East Germany and the countries of Eastern Europe; and equally aware that the intended token force was a test of British public opinion to see how acceptable a further influx of German forces into Britain would be.

I flung myself unreservedly into the protest movement that, led by the South Wales miners, speedily grew up. I spoke with studied intemperance at many protest meetings, in the Principality; helped to cajole the Welsh Council of Labour, the regional governing body of the Labour Party, into acceptance of my point of view; flanked by hundreds of police, I led a demonstration of many thousands of Trade Unionists to the Pembroke-shire headquarters of the German force; and in the House with a handful of other M.P.s I defied the Party whip. I was, with deliberation, vexatious and provocative. Successful political leadership sometimes must be histrionic and manipulative. One of the psychiatric consultants of the United Nations has shrewdly pointed out the confusions that as a result can arise: unfortunately since the healthy and rational may use such culturally approved methods, it permits the pathological leader who is seriously mentally ill to use the same methods totally unsuspected and unobserved, but there is no obvious way of avoiding this confusion.

Those who undoubtedly had given private assurances of an easy passage to the government naturally found my activities infuriating. The usually well mannered Patrick Gordon Walker was roused to such emotion that, failing to persuade me to abstain and not vote against the Tories, he excitedly pursued me, arguing, into the No Lobby, and I literally had to shake him off as physically he sought to restrain me from passing through the tellers and registering my vote.

George Brown, more characteristically, of course blew his top, and, in his outburst, revealed to me his humiliating awareness of his own in-articulateness, as he sought to scorn what he described as my eloquence. His vocabulary, as was Herbert Morrison's, is limited, and the Tories across the floor have often cruelly mocked his large gestures, booming voice and the portentous and sententious pauses which punctuate his banalities. The sound and fury is his attempt to mask the tortuous struggle for words: and like all those whose violence cannot be ensconsed within a wide vocabulary he can lapse speedily into such obscenity that a squeam-ish churchman like Jeremy Bray, one of his junior Ministers, found it almost unbearable to work with him. But the noise and tumult for which he is notorious, and is his constant aura, springs not so much from his lack of real fluency, as from his unceasing anxiety. His intimates always laughed at his constant fear, over so many elections, that he would be bound to lose his seat in Belper: in the end, wilfully and unnecessarily running away from his more realistically founded anxiety over the changing character of his constituency, he embarked on a national barn-storming campaign, sparing but a few days to his own home ground. He helped to provoke the disaster he courted and feared: but this curious behaviour was but a slight symptom of his burden of anxiety.

Although so many of us in the Commons have maniacal temperaments, no-one more than George Brown, in my judgment, more chasteningly illustrates the assertion of the psychoanalyst, Otto Fenichel, that those who strive passionately for power and prestige are unconsciously fright-ened persons trying to overcome and deny their anxiety. George Brown's friends were his worst enemies for, in his fight for the party leadership, they pushed him absolutely beyond his capacity and equipment, and so increased still further his anxieties. That he is an attractive and engaging man cannot be gainsaid: but this feminine element in him which draws men to him, and which causes the whole nation indulgently to forgive him his many trespasses, is not so acceptable to him as it is to others. I believe that his passivity frightens him, and his bluster and constant assertiveness is his way of working off an inner dependence which he finds detrimental to his self esteem: and of course if he felt anyone politically was getting on top of him, his passivity fears were provoked and he lashed out wildly, to the evident enjoyment of a heartless public which expectantly awaited his next spectacle. At his best he can encourage and reassure others, as I have sometimes seen him do superbly at political rallies: the reassurance and encouragement he gives to others is perhaps indicative of the treat-ment he wishes for himself. But, although now a wounded bull, there have been too many occasions in the past when he has sought to avoid his anxiety by turning on others, seeking to intimidate them, to assume a feeling of great power, and, in the exercise of such external power, by intimidation, to protect himself against his own lurking quiescence. It was no credit to the judgment of the Parliamentary Labour Party of 1963 that in the leadership struggle they almost yielded to the neurotic dominance needs of Brown and his henchmen.

My defiance of the whip on the German troop issue led to me, together with other M.P.s involved, being summoned individually to a disci-plinary committee composed of Bowden, Brown and an embarrassed Gaitskell. My interview was short and pungent, and after it Gaitskell and George Brown were well aware that their Jewish wives would have explained the defiance as well as I could. The recommendation to the

Parliamentary Party that we should be severely reprimanded, but that no further disciplinary action should be taken, was willingly accepted by the Parliamentary Labour Party wishing to close the issue; but I did not intend that the matter should be so ended. Not only was I to march with Michael Foot on the next annual visit of German troops in Pembrokeshire at the head of an even larger demonstration but, meantime, I persuaded my good friends in the South Wales Area Committee of the Municipal and General Workers' Union, where my professional links were strong, to raise the issue at the annual conference of their Union. They did this with effect and, when the Trades Union Congress met, the usually accommodating Municipal and General Workers' Union had been mandated to vote for the protest with the more militant unions. The T.U.C., therefore, lined up with the small number of M.P.s who had been reprimanded. To underline the point, I surprised, by a stratagem, the Tory government and my own front bench on Army Estimates day in the House of Commons. By seizing upon a reference to the money spent on Army recruiting publicity, I raised the whole question of the publicity presented to the nation by the Army on the occasion of the Panzer visits. I elevated the question to a constitutional issue suggesting that the Army was meddling in politics in seeking to persuade the public to accept visits which were abhorrent to the T.U.C. My co-rebels, delighted with my ruse, soon followed me in the Chamber to initiate a full scale debate, and even the staid Chuter Ede, the former Home Secretary, became involved, expressing his misgivings. The Army had had, by the time the debate ended, more than enough: and truth to tell, so had I. From then on the Panzer unit slunk into the western part of Wales without any publicity, and no further German troops were deployed elsewhere in Britain. But I was known from then on in the House not to belong to the meek who, whatever their inheritance may be, will not find it at Westminster. There, if one is to be effective, arrogance must be possessed or affected.

But my declared toughness was rarely to be deployed again into such forays into defence and international issues. Only occasionally, as when after walking on a short holiday with good Joseph Needham, the sinologist Master of Caius had coolly bestowed upon me some of his encyclopaedic knowledge of the East in between his more heated talk of narrow gauge railways in Britain, have I been activated into a parliamentary intervention. Already, in a foreign affairs debate in May 1966, I was saying of the Vietnam war:

In the end, the U.S.A. spitting in the face of history, is bound to lose the war after terrible losses of young American lives. We, in our great maturity as a country should not incite or condone actions which allow this war to continue. Psychologists say that defeat is analogous to death; and the great American people appear to have a flaw which expresses itself in gardens of rest, morticians and embalmers – a whole funereal industry. They appear to find great difficulty – like the Pharoahs – in accepting the fact of death and hence, perhaps, difficulty in accepting defeat.

We should seek to tell them from our experience that anyone can gain from a victory; the great art is to turn a defeat into a triumph, as Dunkirk is now remembered and as de Gaulle achieved for France out of the total loss of Algeria.

We should comfort America with such advice and not sycophantically and with sickening hypocrisy approve with words and never deeds their action.

The admonitions of far better informed and more persistent critics went unheeded so my puny protest was, of course, of no avail. If my wandering ancestors had unhappily settled in the U.S.A., doubtless I would there be marching alongside Dr Spock: but here in Britain we no longer can dare to discharge our aggression in any war. The sun has irrevocably set and Empire is no more for us. We cannot even afford, as the Americans thought they could in Vietnam, local colonial battles: the most the clumsiness of the Foreign Office offers us as a catharsis is Anguilla. And in Ulster our young soldiers alone are involved: the rest of Britain observes, almost bored and indifferent, but does not participate. So our prolonged absence from war, though it may appear a blessing, is in one sense a deprivation.

It is not easy for a nation with a heritage of war-making to suffer such a loss and readily to slough off its inheritance: it is difficult to escape from such a well formed habitude. Since the last quarter of the eighteenth century the intervals between wars fought by European nations and the U.S.A. have been remarkably constant, varying between eighteen and twenty-four years and averaging nineteen-and-a-half years overall – just about the time required for the generation born during or just after the previous war to reach manhood. Then the older generation ensured their dangerous young rivals were either wiped out or matured in the experience of war. But we are no longer able to export our violence by Empire-building: our thugs cannot find themselves in the Black and Tans or the Palestine Police. We cannot transport our criminals to Australia and Kenyatta has ended our using Kenya as a dumping ground for our ne'er-do-wells. For the first time, after a thousand years of wars, we have to live with our aggression in our own land. It is a novel situation,

and our politicians, lacking precedent, flounder in governing a nation
that to survive has to learn the strange lesson of preparing for a thousand
years of peace.

And we have to begin learning this lesson at a time when mechanization
of the production process increasingly deprives the worker of the older
craftsman's creative enjoyment in his task. The worker, however, by
mass production methods, is not only alienated from his work: to the
degree that the sense of belonging depends on a sense of contributing,
he is also alienated from society. The price he is paying for a high standard
of living must, too, include a readiness to submit to mobility of place,
function and social position that adds to his rootlessness. Meantime the
very techniques claimed to be necessary for economic growth and to
endow him with yet more consumer goods, threaten him: dockers fear
containerization, miners fear the new fuels, and all, particularly the
middle-aged, lacking elasticity, fear redundancy. Anxiety is abroad, and
anxious men make for aggressive men. Private protest increasingly
expresses itself in an increase in delinquency, vandalism, child cruelty,
violent crime and divorce petitions based on unreasonable conduct;
ideological protest expresses itself in symptoms like industrial strife, violent
picketing, rent strikes, lawless self-styled nationalism in Wales and the
sadism on our television and cinema screens. It is not surprising that M.P.s
return to Westminster from the headlong plunge most of them take during the week-end into the problems of their constituencies increasingly
disturbed by the turbulence in the community.

But the ancient secular unifier, patriotism, which formerly acted
as the ultimate guarantee that every warring element in our society
could be bound together against any selected external scapegoat, no
longer dare be used: war, for our little island, in an atom bomb age is
ruled out. Our worried legislature, however, is aware that the growth of
violence within the State, even if it has some special feautres here, is not
peculiar to Britain: and that similar pressures to export domestic violence
are operating elsewhere, and, understandably, there is apprehension that
some State somewhere will, under some pretext or provocation, yield to
those pressures and the fatal conflagration will begin. Even as our status
as a great power declines, and our weaponry becomes obsolescent, our
M.P.s, hoping their words will smother their fears, demand more and
more debates on foreign policy and defence issues.

My increasing non-involvement in such debates, since my initial
involvement in the German question, is not because I do not share my
colleagues' apprehension. Nor is it because I mock at the conceit of those
who act as if their speeches, no longer delivered with the coercive force

of a world power, can still influence world events. It is because I scorn this illusion that by some more treaties, some more disarmament conventions, some more international constitutional changes, we shall necessarily gain relief from the consequences of our aggresivity which indeed has deeper roots in less tractable circumstances than most of my colleagues are prepared to acknowledge.

There are two ways of adjusting to reality, by means of adjusting reality to make it fit one's needs or by means of changing oneself to fit in with reality: the psychoanalysts, following Ferenczi, call these reactions alloplastic and autoplastic adjustments to reality. The autoplastic method of adjustment is unpopular with contemporary Western man: intoxicated by his progress in controlling the environment, he lacks deference for the wisdom gained by the autoplastically orientated civilizations of the East and by the antiquity of our own civilization. Robert Waelder, in his admonitory overview of the history of man, has spelt out how the post-Renaissance civilization of Europe has been characterized to an ever increasing and dangerous degree by an alloplastic attitude. Technological progress has caused man to believe he can by external changes conquer everything: but I do not share the utopian view that merely by tinkering with external institutions, by new combinations in or out of the United Nations, or by the heralding of new governments committed to new social systems, man can conquer himself. The wonders of technology have added to the evolutionary optimism of the typical progressive; it led to a General Election being fought and won in 1964 on Wilson's prognostications of the boons to be gained by the 'white heat of technological revolution', but disenchantment was soon to follow. Reinhold Niebuhr's Christian criticism of the moderns cannot, in the shadow of the bomb, be gainsaid: human history is not so much a chronicle of the progressive victory of cosmos over chaos, but a story of an ever increasing cosmos creating ever increasing possibilities of chaos.

And, if the ultimate chaos of the exploded bomb is to be avoided, it will come about only if sufficient of us have mastered, through insight, the worst consequences of our aggression and deflected it into more constructive tasks. Perhaps in one sense I am more pretentious and more conceited than my colleagues who expect, through the decisions that flow from the usual defence and foreign policy debates, peace to be maintained. For I believe it is possible to lever to the surface our buried fear of our violence, confront it, and so overcome the most destructive excesses of our aggressivity. If we try to deal with our aggression by denial, by repression or by projections, we are heading for disaster: then we have defence debates that are really aggression debates, in which by projecting our aggression on others, or indeed identifying ourselves with aggressors, we invariably come to the conclusion that our only possibility of survival lies with the piling up of still more weapons: we unwisely then depend upon hardware, not ourselves.

It has been shown that the provoking of continuous national debates on issues like divorce, illegitimacy, homosexuality and family planning has helped to end some of the distortions of human spirit which were caused by the cruel repression of our libidinal drives: in these fields perhaps I can make a small claim to have helped a little in making our country a little more civilized and more humane, more at ease with its sexuality. Similarly, we need to seek the issues which, if continuously talked through and debated, may help us to be more comfortable with our aggression. The issues that can provide us with the insights that may lead us to greater maturity, more equipped to deal with our smouldering violences, are more elusive; the problems they present more refractory than those presented by our sexual instincts. These we may be ashamed of, but our aggressive proclivities we fear. But although to the impatient this way to peace may be too devious, it is more likely in the long run to make even our judgment on defence policies less clouded, more adult.

It was, therefore, with deliberation that I turned my back on defence and foreign policy groups in the Commons. I wanted to use my energies to compel the community to wrestle with its own violence, with the eternal adversary of all those who wish a more civilized society. Our aggression must be stared into: we must not run away. The expressed aggression with which we have empathy, which possesses all of us, is the violence of suicide, of infanticide, of murder and armed robbery. If we dare to attempt to master such outbursts, we may bring therapeutic relief not only to those who cannot control their violence and to those who are its direct victims, but to all who are fated to live in our tension-ridden society.

IV

A murderer whom I was defending and who, for no apparent reason, had cut his wife up almost to shreds in the bathroom of their suburban home, once courteously and gently explained his savage conduct to me. 'It was absolutely necessary for me to kill her,' he said. 'If I had not killed her I would have had no choice but to have killed myself.' And for good measure, with the attendant prison officer fortunately within sight but, in accordance with the prison rules, out of hearing, he explained insistently that he had also killed a young man some years ago in the north of England for exactly the same reasons. His mad frankness may have been unusual: but his motivation for murder was sadly orthodox.

The lure of self-destruction, the attraction of death, are often warded off only by turning outwards the aggression which is threatening to destroy the potential assailant. The terrible injuries wreaked upon his wife by this murderer were a measure of the destructiveness from which, at another's expense, he had just saved himself. Suicide or murder is often the option: and the conscience, temporarily stilled or undeveloped, the deed balanced on a razor's edge, becomes, by chance, murder, not *felo de se*.

The ultimate consummation may, however, only have been temporarily staved off, for a third of the murderers of Britain commit suicide before being brought to trial, and many more make determined attempts: sometimes indeed with a high sense of occasion, as I have found on arriving at an interview in prison with a murderer client who so timed the appointment that he was able to receive me with a freshly cut throat and slashed wrists.

The Janus-faced suicide demon is directed not only towards destruction and death but also towards human contact – and more often those clients of mine possessed by the demon turned their gaze, at the very last moment, towards life. Then they would find themselves in the dock charged with the crime of attempted suicide, leaving me to seek to mitigate their felony as, listless and depressed, they sat wondering why they should be punished for their yearning to stop living while not wanting to die. They were part of the long procession of 7,000 attempted suicides who were, during the ten years from 1946 onwards, convicted by the courts; more than 300 found themselves thrown into prison without the alternative of a fine. My quota of desperate melancholic clients inevitably included some doctors: one in every fifty male doctors kill themselves, having failed in their attempts to ward off their own death-wishes by keeping their patients alive. And builder clients, too, were particularly prone to despair. I sympathized especially with them, for, in my dreams, sometimes I create wondrous towns full of domed, capricious and unattainable buildings, rivalling the impossible Renaissance cities painted by Carpaccio. My builders built, it is true, only semi-detached horrors: but their reparative need to build, and so divert their aggression from being turned against themselves, was not dissimilar from my own. Yet, sometimes, their manic zeal to cover their corners of Wales in ugly bungalows and 'chalet-type' houses spent itself: and in the trough of despair they hanged themselves outright or, more fortunately, pleaded for help by way of a suicide attempt likely to be discovered.

And sometimes, since I acted for many bookmakers, more exotic suicides crossed my path. The punter often compulsively gambles desperately, hoping to prove to himself that fate loves him: his original uncertainty of parental love leaves him with a gnawing doubt. Fate must be continuously tested, and many a game of Russian roulette is being acted out by the shabby worker slinking furtively into a corner betting-shop. His sad 'loves me, loves me not' sport can be accompanied by odd and fatal tantrums. Once a football-pool director, a client of mine, con-fronted by a would-be suicide 'phoned me in some agitation. A defeated commercial traveller, refusing to accept his rejection by fate, was at the pools offices renewing his ill-founded accusations that he had been swindled out of a substantial prize. During the parleys between the pool representatives and himself, he was threatening that, unless his demands were met by that evening, he would immediately post letters to all the national dailies proclaiming that the pools company was responsible for his death, and inviting the dailies to send representatives to a macabre press conference for the following day at the hotel room where his body would be discovered.

The pools chief was seeking my reassurance that those who threaten suicide, never do: when I insisted that, on the contrary, such warnings were ominous, he found my advice to call the police to cajole the wretch to the local mental hospital quite unacceptable. I insisted that in some cases the publicity that follows a violent death is an additional attraction to the suicide: but he brushed aside my admonition. Pools millionaires do not achieve their wealth by yielding to blackmail. My client could be wooed, but threats inevitably provoked his stubborn, anal, character traits and he would then become more retentive; and my advice to bring in police and doctors offended all his secretive characteristics. He possessed some of the traits with which my sojourn at Westminster since has familiarized me. Early interference by mother or nurse with private faecal or urethral indulgences can mean that the adult politician, thwarted too soon, may now not only have a desire for secrecy but also a revengeful passion to be privy to the secrets of authority, currently symbolized, not by a martinet nurse, but by the Establishment, from which knowledge he often derives an inordinate feeling of superiority. Simultaneously with this compelling wish to be on the inside, to know every secret involved in the ruling of the community, which has been one of the drives propelling him to Parliament, there still remains, however, the intemperate resentment of any violation of privacy with which he personally empathizes. Such violation evokes all his early humiliation. I admit that I have sometimes consciously stirred these glowing embers in Parliament for what I regard as desirable goals, such as ending the need for private guilt to be exposed as a prerequisite to a divorce, and I have never failed to sense that the response in some parts of the House comes from the bowels rather than the brain. The temperament of my pools client was too similar to that of some of my colleagues not to make the rejection of my advice inevitable, for he feared it could lead to inevitable publicity. I, therefore, cancelled my arrangements to go away for a few days, sensing that I was to be needed at an inquest. And so it proved. The reporters duly arrived at the hotel room the following morning to find that the man had certainly filled in his last coupon: he had poisoned himself in the night.

Involvement in such incidents made me uncomfortably aware that the law had categorized as criminals more than half a million of our fellow citizens who have made suicidal attempts. The possibility of life imprisonment was the riposte of an enraged society, still governed by a cruel rule – a late, relatively sophisticated invention of Christianity more or less foreign to the Judeo-Hellenic tradition – which made suicide a grievous felony. Equally jealous of murderers and suicides, divining the same motivation within the murderer and the self-slayer, society declared them both criminals. Killing is too attractive, howsoever performed. As Ferenczi has noted:

The criminal dares to do something which we all unconsciously have the greatest inclination to do. The punishment will not infrequently give those who carry it out an opportunity of committing the same outrage under cover of an act of expiation.

Punishment of the suicide and the attempted suicide was therefore irresistible. And, irrationally, in order to punish ourselves for our own impulses, as well as for our own misdirected penalties, we need to punish even more the acts we have labelled as criminal.

It is not surprising that suicide should attract such hostility: what is termed schizoid suicide is said to be the result of apathy towards real life which cannot be accepted any longer. All the available energy goes into a quiet but tenacious determination to fade out into oblivion. Such a depreciation of society is evidently felt to be quite intolerable and such *lèse majesté* predictably has received punishment throughout the ages. More, depressive suicide, the result of angry destructive impulses, is too insufferable an insult to the puritans: the perpetrator not only has the pleasure of self-murder but, symbolically, the murder of someone else, such as the man for whom the suicide's fiancée has jilted him or, indeed, the faithless fiancée herself. And, to add to his triumph, the suicide, at a deeper level, is often symbolically murdering the parental figures to whose behaviour can perhaps be traced his unhappiness.

It is as if he fires a gun at the real objects of his hatred only to have his conscience act as a shield which protects them and deflects the shots back upon himself in fitting retribution for his own murderous impulses. Indeed, it is the tyrannical conscience which is the object of the aggression so often inherent in suicide as well as being the cause of its inward-directedness: and it is to this extent, doubtless, too successful to be acceptable to the prim who are dismayed at seeing the conscience perish along with the rest of the personality.

But when I entered the House I found that pressures were building up, largely prompted by Kenneth Robinson, to enact that suicide and attempted suicide should cease to be criminal offences: and I soon became involved in the campaign. Clearly only when society abandoned its confidence in the spurious deterrent of imprisonment would preventative measures be taken to save those tempted by suicide. We need not be passive observers each late spring, when life affirms itself in all its glory, and the lonely ones amidst the joy of others can no longer tolerate their isolation and, more than at any other time of year, choose in their hundreds to die.

For thousands of years man has been aware of those who, unless helped, are likely to anticipate their deaths. Homer in the *Iliad*, through Andromache's lament, long ago told of some of the depressive effects of orphanhood. When a child loses a parent, the State should be unashamedly interventionalist to ensure that the remnant of the family has support. In Britain today the loss of a father, particularly between the age of ten and fourteen, trebles the possibility of that child becoming an adult depressive.

And even later there are constant altering signs: a survey made of 800 suicides in twelve counties of Wales found that four out of five of these defeated men and women had seen doctors with warning symptoms, but only one in five had been referred to a psychiatrist for aid. Few issues were ultimately to take more of my time in the House than battling for aid to the children who by death, desertion or law are deprived of a natural or legal parent: and for an improvement in the quality and availability of psychiatric and social work facilities. And these involvements began when I joined in the efforts being made to change our suicide laws. Indeed my participation in these efforts taught me what role I could play as a Member for, from these efforts, I learned that, if my work was to be meaningful, I had to become engaged ceaselessly in what the American political scientist, Harold Laswell, has described as the politics of prevention, the most difficult of all politics.

It required a political scientist, like Laswell, who had assimilated the implications of psychoanalysis to the study of politics to depreciate the usual political methods of exhortation and coercion and to mock these methods which assume that the role of politics is to solve the conflicts when they have happened. Rarely do political demands which spring from such techniques produce permanent reductions in the tension level of society: the ideal of a politics of prevention is to obviate conflict by the reduction of this tension level in society, and this means an insistence upon a continuing audit of the human consequences of social and political acts. My antipathy to instant politics is not founded merely upon a personal prejudice against the practitioners: it is because I concur with Laswell that the problem of politics is less to solve the conflicts than to prevent them; less to serve as a safety valve for social protest than to apply social energy to the abolition of recurrent strains in society. The threadbare thinking of those who so eagerly describe themselves as pragmatists, be they Tories or socialists, leads them so frequently to deal with symptoms not causes – and inevitably they scramble in unseemly disarray from one crisis to another. Quite often the 'solutions' that have emerged are 'magical' ones: they are often semantic and incantatory ones deliberately presented as a manipulation designed to drive a controversy out of the public's mind. Too often all that happens is that the community is distracted by another set of equally irrelevant symbols, and politicians have often deliberately created new controversies as a part of the technique of distraction. I have seen too many pretentious statutes pass through the Commons, which in fact change nothing in the permanent practices of our society, not to be keenly aware of the role of magic in politics.

It is understandable that so many of the thinking young in our universities have contemptuously turned away from this shallow pragmatism, but the banners and the slogans of the ultra-left to which they are sometimes attracted lead equally to a cul-de-sac. So far the socialist has primarily concerned himself with the effects of the social system upon man as a worker, and the stress has been on his devaluation as a human being at work. But exploitation and alienation of man does not only take place in the capitalists' factory: we must be concerned with human beings, as babes, children and adolescents, at home, at play, in the High Street, as sons and lovers, as mothers and fathers and indeed as grandparents. 'Our problem,' Laswell has written, 'is to be ruled by the truth about the conditions of harmonious human relations.' But this is not the problem faced by the politician, preoccupied with the belief that politics is about office, about power, rather than about people. Our total aim should be the creation of a society which improves the quality of human relationships. We must not permit the maladoption of the professional politicians, panting for deference, and only capable of endowing vitality to a political movement provided it is sufficiently loaded with a displacement of their private affects, to confuse us. Nor must we allow our impatience to mislead us. The politics of prevention are slow and laborious, but at least no shoddiness is attached to their aim.

In practice such politics always meet strong resistance, and our efforts to have a new Suicide Act were no exception to the general rule. The Home Office, under Rab Butler, was holding out against our suggestions. They were too controversial, for some people would take the view that what in law is permissible is free from objection; and belief in the sanctity of life, and the duty of the State to uphold its responsibility to seek to preserve the life of every person, necessitated no weakening in our criminal law. The determination to harry the wretched man or woman who had bungled a suicide, or had made the attempt as a dramatic plea for help, was hidden behind inimitable displays of self-righteous sententiousness.

No one could procrastinate with greater grace than Butler: that is why when he became Leader of the House he was such a success. The Leader must each Thursday advance reasons to importuning Members explaining why the business they regard as urgent and vital cannot be discussed the following week. With his face puckered by a poignant pierrot smile, Butler would pirouette with a devastating elegance, expressed as much in the grace of his bodily movements as in the feints and parries with which he seductively eluded his pursuers, so that in the end the House would yield to the gentle wit of the choreographer/dancer and wonder at the charm of ballet possessed of such an exquisite form, and so devoid of content. His rococo performances made every other subsequent Leader of the House appear incredibly vulgar.

The winds, however, were blowing in favour of the reformers. A committee appointed by the Archbishop of Canterbury eventually cautiously recommended that the offence of suicide should be abolished, provided that a second class burial service could be used in those cases of suicide quaintly described by the Churchmen as 'manifestly selfish'. And then, ultimately, after long persuasion, and the inevitable tardy reference for review of the offence to the Criminal Law Review Committee, the Judges came back with recommendations sufficiently tough upon the survivors of suicide pacts to enable the proposition, without loss of face, to be put to the House, by way of a government Bill, that attempted suicide should no longer be a criminal offence. The government's ambivalence towards the Bill was nicely expressed in the affectation that so little time was available that it must, if it were to be passed, be rushed through almost unnoticed in the fag end of a Friday afternoon. I did not find this impressive: time had recently without difficulty been found for an esoteric Indecency Against Children Act which pruriently created new and unusual Lolita-like offences but made no effort to emancipate those miserable characters who compulsively practise the bizarre aberrations which the Act adumbrates. There is always time to be found for the creation of new criminal acts: but, once we have labelled conduct as criminal and thus made enemies of those who practise it, the label can never be removed without a fierce and prolonged struggle.

Now the wish was to enshroud the Suicide Bill with the same shame-faced secrecy as formerly by law was a suicide's body which, almost to the end of the last century, was only permitted to be buried between the hours of 9 p.m. and midnight. Kenneth Robinson, understandably anxious to see the Bill through, was ready to collude with the government and was perplexed and angry with me when he realized that on the fateful Friday afternoon I was bent upon taking the risk of talking the Bill out, calling the government's bluff, and so, if successful, gaining a full-scale debate to complete the Bill. I did not then seek to explain to him what he would have regarded as an absurdly Olympian view that I would rather lose the Bill than corroborate in the morbid stealth of the government.

For it is not the passing of a civilized act by an interested cabal in Westminster that makes a nation more humane: it is the public affront to evil history that must, with anguish, be metabolized by the whole community if a nation is securely to move forward. The past, with the authority of the law, must be defiantly rejected and the Act must not only be on the statute book but must press upon the internal conscience of the citizen. Such Promethean efforts fail if performed in whispers: the desire of society to have criminals to punish has been concealed with cunning sophistication by the Benthamite and Kantian theories of punishment. Depth psychology undermines the utilitarian justification of punishment for deterrence and retribution: for suffering lures as well as deters, and the primitivism embedded in the Talionic concepts of retribution can now be exposed. But the subversive role of psychoanalytical doctrine is of no avail if cribbed to consulting room and couch: the reformers must be the true revolutionaries, and through the hearts of men compel understanding. The hearts of men are not reached, however, in clandestine chats held between Whitehall and Westminster and, although Kenneth Robinson vowed my wilful eccentricity would wreck the Bill, having been called by the Speaker a few minutes before 4 o'clock, when the House must rise, I talked the Bill out.

I disliked being so vexatious to Kenneth Robinson, for he is a good man with a worthy record whose dedication over many years to health affairs well deserved the ultimate accolade of Health Minister. He was intended by his parents to study medicine, but his father, a doctor, died when Kenneth was a boy and financial difficulties thwarted the young lad's ambition: he was compelled to take up a job in insurance. He remained, however, a consultant manqué, and this was his strength and his weakness. On Hospital Management Boards, as Opposition Health Spokesman, and, later, as Minister, he moved with ease among the consultants, but one suspects too much of the desired manner and approach rubbed on to him, as must have been his wish. He was hardworking and earnest as a Minister, but too controlled, cautious and unimaginative: and his lack of adventurousness was reinforced by his sense of insecurity with Wilson who excluded him from the Cabinet, for Robinson was never one of Wilson's favourites.

But Robinson is possessed of dignity, a quality for which he was to pay dear. When Harold Wilson attempted to present a new image with the age gimmick of 1969, although older men than Robinson, still in his fifties, were retained in government, he was dismissed. As Robinson told me, he had not run sufficiently frequently to Harold Wilson for help in solving departmental difficulties: such independence was unacceptable to a Prime Minister who needed flattering dependency relationships. Fortunately for my future relationship with Robinson my judgement that the Tory government, having presented the Suicide Bill, were too committed to draw back proved correct and more time was found to complete the Bill, so that I was able to talk at length on the issues, right indeed into the early hours of one morning.

I used the occasion to suggest, to the vexation of the press, that newspaper reports on inquests should be severely limited. Durkheim, in his classical work on suicide, long since emphasized the imitative factor in self-slaying. The point indeed has been made on many occasions since the time of the proverbial and fateful tree of Timon of Athens. There is a notorious story, hopefully apocryphal, that when an English peer in the nineteenth century threw himself into Vesuvius several of his companions followed his example: but there are many better documented illustrations. Indeed in South Wales some years ago, where there had not been such a form of suicide for some fifty years, there was a minor wave of suicides by tinplate workers jumping into vats of sulphuric acid precipitated by zealous inquest reporting of the first case. Only too often the frail, overwhelmed by real or imaginary injuries of life, or the suggestible, who have perilously kept at bay their lurking death wish, when they see the example of others vividly and excitingly portrayed, are incited to follow the grim example. Self-immolation as a form of suicide was rare but more recently the monks who burnt themselves alive, nominally in protest against the regime in Vietnam, soon had disciples in every country of Europe, proffering a variety of justifications for burning themselves.

I once raised the issue with Lord Thomson, the press peer, when he invited me to one of his luncheon parties. Thomson was in the habit of gathering small groups of people active in one or two spheres, likely to have different views, and then, flanked by his executives, would encourage the controversialists to engage in battle: but I was not prepared to act as a court jester and, knowing his compulsive interest in crime novels, challenged him personally for the irresponsibility of the press presentation of crime and criminals. I deplored the correspondence between the reported content and the infantile fantasy images of the readers, and the manner in which the journalists, under the guise of freedom of the press, peddled thrills and justified the punishments their readers wanted to inflict, determinedly blocking out any insights which, if acknowledged, would temper the satisfaction of their readers' perverted desires. His executives came to his aid: but when I deployed inquest reports as an illustration of how crime reports could spread crime, they fumbled. I felt the engaging Thomson was discomfited, since he possesses conscience: he gave me a book for my daughter when I took my leave, perchance to appease me for his own unease, but his executives never invited me to another lunch.

But, during the Commons suicide debates, my main concern was to express the fear that society's grudging good-will would be exhausted by the reluctant removal of attempted suicide from the category of criminal offences. Those brought before the court had at least compelled society to mobilize and be aware of the agony of their condition: now the attempted suicide's cry for help could go unheard; and the danger of the offence disappearing from public view was that only the grim annual announcement of statistics of suicide would be made the occasion for comment. This consequence would slyly accommodate our society; already out of fear the community averts its eyes from the suicide fatalities which, despite the availability of anti-depressant drugs, persist.

But the government spokesmen were of course impatient that I should so prolong the discussion, for it needs a rare statesman like Masaryk, the first President of Czechoslovakia, who found in his thesis on suicide that it was a rough index of the value strains in a culture, to face the real life and death issues of a society: these blinkered front bench spokesmen had none of the insights of a fasting Gandhi who, by his suicidal threats, so entangled his enemies in guilt feelings that, to free themselves, they were compelled to free India. The Church committee's recommendations absolved the government spokesmen from any longer having to condemn suicide out of the fear that since suicide, faintly disguised as martyrdom, was the rock upon which Christianity had been founded, it may prove to be too attractive. But, in some ways, the government approach was more unfeeling than the Christian attitude: the Churches' brutal condemnation of the self-slayer was based at least on concern for the suicide's soul.

The perfunctory approach of the government implicitly meant that having removed suicide from the State penal code, the attempted suicide's fate was no longer to be a matter of political concern.

I was aware how unwelcome the House found my intervention: but if I did not have any of my political colleagues on my side I imagined, in those early hours when the debate was concluded, I could hear the faint applause of the English poets and writers, John Donne, Robert Burton and David Hume who, in more dangerous times, had dared to insinuate heretical and compassionate views on behalf of the suicides of their centuries. The debates, in the end, did at least ensure that the informed community knew of the passing of the Suicide Act, and its rationale: and the government did agree, following upon its passage, to issue a memorandum advising all doctors and other authorities concerned that an attempted suicide was to be regarded as a medical and social problem and that every such case ought to be seen by a psychiatrist. But my fears, in 1961, that the needed abolition of the criminal offence, without much more positive preventive measures being taken, had grave dangers were proved well founded. Although the highly toxic domestic gas, which was the most common cause of death by suicide has now been replaced by detoxicated or natural gas, suicidal acts by drugs now ominously mount. About 90,000 self-poisoning attempted suicides are taking place each year, and not long ago, the Cambridge Professor of Medicine recounted that in his region attempted suicide is the commonest cause of admission to medical wards of those in the 15-40 age group. Among women in this age group half of all the medical admissions in his area are now for attempted suicide and these figures are similar to those revealed in widely disparate regions of Britain. Considerate coroners are distorting the suicide returns, in attempts to ease the relatives' hurt pride and pain, by increasingly giving verdicts of misadventure rather than suicide. In reality suicide is increasing not diminishing. Despite the claims of well intentioned, inadequately skilled, interventionist voluntary societies, we can take no comfort from our false suicide statistics. Each year in Britain, making a sham of our declared belief in the sanctity of life, we are abandoning thousands to their unnecessary death. The reformers' task is to continue to make society guilty and ashamed, so that a wealthy community invests more in saving life than in missiles to destroy it.

V

To change the public attitudes and those of the Press, which yields to and reinforces them, shame must continually be interjected into the dialogue. Guilt can be provoked for good as well as evil ends and, by proceeding elliptically, a dramatic presentation of seemingly peripheral issues can force a community to look into a mirror, see a Caliban and then, out of self esteem, revamp itself to gain assurance of a more flattering image. I comfort myself, therefore, that my so far unsuccessful attempts to alter the law relating to infanticide have not been entirely in vain.

Infanticide is a curious offence to remain within our criminal code. It is the only offence known to our law where the prosecution, in order to gain a conviction, has to establish the absurdity that the wrongdoing was done wilfully and at the same time the wrongdoer was not responsible for the deed. Upon the prosecution falls the task of showing not only that the mother killed her child under the age of twelve months, but that, at the time of the killing, the balance of the mother's mind was disturbed because she had not fully recovered from the effect of the birth or because of the effect of lactation. Having proved the tumult of mind of the unfortunate mother, in defiance of every canon of criminal responsibility and with a rare sadism masking the affected mercy, the law decrees that the punishment to be meted out shall not be that accorded to a murderer, but that the woman should be treated as if she had committed manslaughter. In theory this means that the sick woman could be sentenced to life imprisonment.

It was a long and hard struggle in the teeth of overwhelming judicial opinion before the law was changed to give, as it does now, a grudging acknowledgment that babes can be slain, not out of criminal intent, but out of mental illness. The main reason why these changes were made was not because of increasing insight that came with expanding psychiatric knowledge, but because of the robust common sense of nineteenth-century juries. They, despite many admonitions by many judges, refused to bring in a verdict of guilty that could send a temporarily insane woman to the gallows. Those juries knew that, at or about the time of birth, dogs, cats, sows, white mice, rabbits – all of them – sometimes kill their own young. The jurymen were not prepared to extend less compassion and concern to a mentally sick woman than they would to an excitable bitch. So they defied the judges by refusing to behave as it was often said to be their duty to behave.

My attempts to modify the existing law in 1964, and again in 1969, were made not only out of concern for the two-score mothers who each year are unnecessarily hauled to trial at the assize courts to face the charge that in theory can attract such a severe sentence. Rather I was seeking to illuminate the dark forces that lie behind and are responsible for the distorted and bizarre legal elements that constitute the present offence: and, by obtaining implicit acknowledgment of those forces from the community, summon it to have the courage to roll forward the front-iers of compassion within our criminal law. We can go beyond the point reached more than thirty years ago when the compromise was struck in Parliament between those who were still tenaciously holding on to the punitive attitude and those who wanted the law to be informed by in-creased medical understanding of the post-natal mental condition of the mother. But in the attempted reform I was moving into deep and troubled waters for, as every picture gallery reveals, not all the idyllic paintings of the Madonna and Child camouflage either the troubled demeanour of many a Virgin or the murderous stance of many a violent Lamb. There are, however, neurotic compulsions, social and psychological, to resist the unmasking of the overdetermined, coy and sweet image of the mother and child. In our fairy stories we may reveal ourselves in tales of killing and devouring mothers: but expounding changes in the law of infanticide is, nevertheless, a little different from retelling the grim tale of Red Riding Hood.

I did not attempt the impossible task of spelling out such subtleties to Alice Bacon who unfortunately was Minister of State at the Home Office when I brought in my first Infanticide Bill: but even a much less sophisti-cated approach brought about little understanding of the points at issue, and her initial response only revealed to me the inadequacy of her advising officials and her flaccid hold over them. The letters they were drafting for her signature showed a complete misunderstanding of the law of infanti-cide. The Home Office officials were totally confused between the laws relating to diminished responsibility in homicide cases and the offence of infanticide. My modest aim was to end the rite of the present long-drawn agony which compels the woman to be brought before magistrates in preliminary proceedings two or three times for the taking of depositions, and then to endure the strain of many weeks waiting before being brought for trial to face all the pomp and paraphernalia of the assize court: I wanted a Magistrates' Court to have the power to dispose of the whole matter speedily and finally; and for there to be restriction on press reporting of the essentially private tragedy. But the officials, resisting any change, began irrelevantly and desperately plumbing the depths of the Homicide Act, which deals with the degree of impairment of mental responsibility that a defence must establish to gain a reduction in a charge of murder. Even the Infanticide Act of 1938 had avoided tackling the problems arising from puerperal psychosis in such an obtuse manner.

As I insisted, in exasperation, to Alice Bacon, that this was a discreditable display of bad law, she arranged a confrontation between myself and the officials in her room at Whitehall. It was easy enough to win the argument with the ill-informed officials. Alice Bacon did not grasp all the details of the dialogue but it was clear to her that the departmental view was ill-considered. Yet, under the department's surveillance, she could only look at me with despair and could not come a whit nearer to meeting my demands.

Her original advancement had come under Gaitskell and the gossip of the House was that he had done so to have an untroubled base at Leeds, where she was a neighbouring member. She was, however, certainly not without private qualities, ready to make unusual efforts of sacrifice for the elderly and ailing of her own family and her developed sense of service found expression in her politics: but she had suffered the disadvantage of having left teaching to become a full time M.P. at a comparatively early age. Entries at a young age are now becoming even more frequent and this will add to the problem of M.P.s becoming Ministers totally lacking in experience of decision-making: too many young men who now come into the House have nothing to proffer but a second class degree and a considerable verbal facility. All their decisions have been taken for them by their parents, the state or the university. More, some of them are demanding that Members should be paid more and treated as professional full-time workers. A back bench M.P. has, however, no right, if he wishes to make a real contribution, to be a full-time M.P. absolutely bound to Westminster: and certainly not when he is in his thirties and forties. As the years roll on, the successful back bencher increasingly provokes his own punishment. The lobbyists, those in trouble, the importunate, turn to the known doers in the House and the post bag becomes a crushing burden. When the *Times* did a survey of Members' mail a few years ago Nabarro and I, both with many extra-Parliamentary interests, were found to receive more letters than any other back bench M.P. But the demands made upon an M.P. cannot be adequately met if the M.P.'s working life is spent wholly in the Palace of Westminster. The life of a busy M.P.

involved in outside work is almost but not quite intolerable. For an M.P. with a Welsh seat the burden must always be greater for he is expected to be part lover, part father of his constituency; and this notorious expectation, if not met, as it sometimes has not been met by a non-Welsh representative or by a detribalized Welshman, has led to the loss of seats to both parties in Wales. But even the cooler family life of England, leading to less passionate demands towards father-surrogates by constituents, does not mean that any member who wants to live the full life of an M.P. can escape the fate of being stretched on the rack: and the cruel physical demands and disorder of the peripatetic life between Westminster and constituency must be added to the work load. But those who evade any extra responsibility, outside the minimal role of an M.P., face the danger of degenerating into what Chaim Weizman, who created the state of Israel as a part time job between his sojourns as a chemist in the laboratory, used to describe as the '*luftmenschen*'. At the worst the full-time M.P.s, lacking abrasive challenges from outside, become increasingly slothful: and even some of the most energetic are in danger of living off press reports and then, sometimes, between them, the journalist word-spinners and the Westminster wind-men create a fantasy world which both the M.P. actors and the voyeur correspondents are foolish enough to believe is reality.

It is not surprising that businessmen, seconded to the civil service in the last government, shocked by the impracticability of some of the Ministers, sometimes urged a school for decision-making for their masters. But I doubt whether wise choices can be learned except in the deed: the label of experience which we conceitedly attach to our mistakes should be learned outside the House where error does not usually lead to such widespread disaster. When governments plead a run of bad luck and M.P.s gather to bemoan how accident-prone some of their Ministers appear to have become, they are attributing to the stars the faults within themselves. Plato's absorption with the connection between knowledge and choice led him to believe that the only science which is valuable is the science of choice, which enables us to make the right decisions: and young men, untutored in that science, so often ultimately, when older, reach office supported only by top civil servants whose role is conventionally regarded as complete when they have presented to the Minister a range of choices. There are exceptional civil servants like Sir Dennis Dobson, Permanent Secretary to the Lord Chancellor's Department, a man who is impatient with the weak and ready to debate with the strong, who fortunately for the nation does not so strictly interpret his duties; and the civilized Ian Grey, Regional Head of the Ministry of Technology, did

more in an unconventional manner to bring industry to Wales, before he was finally squeezed out of the civil service, than all the Secretaries of State for Wales put together. But these regrettably are rare men in our increasingly diluted civil service. More usually, the terrified inexperienced Minister is presented with a bewildering multiplicity of choices. Only too often in his anxiety he cannot tolerate delay, and instantly plumps for one of the deceptively easier partial choices suggested to him.

Elliot Jacque has, in his fascinating analysis of differential of wages in industry, shown how the capability of carrying responsibility depends upon an individual's capacity to sustain doubt, as he ponders over the alternatives before yielding, over-speedily, to the growing tension forcing an active decision upon him. It is only the man who can wait who can carry the heaviest load of decision-making: and I have often found the validity of Elliot Jacque's method of measuring responsibility in industry corroborated in my work in our criminal courts, where it is demonstrable that the really skilful defending lawyer can, in the early hours of a prosecution case, so cross-examine witnesses that he leaves himself ample elbow room at a much later stage of the trial, when he has fully heard the prosecution, to decide the exact nature of his defence. The bad, over-anxious lawyer rigidly cross-examines at an early stage in a form which reveals a defence that so often crumbles as the prosecution, before long, brings evidence which undermines the nervous over-prepared position.

The low threshold of tolerance of delay made the later years of Wilson's administration so notorious an example of instant government that the Tories came to power avowing such an era was to be ended. But they are not avoiding the trap: they have been in many respects more precipitate than their predecessors. Every big employer of labour knows, however, that high intelligence, as is possessed by many of the present Ministers and the Socialist ex-Ministers, does not in itself compensate for emotional instability and impulsiveness: and it is surely clear that there are inbuilt factors within the temperament of many of the politicians of all parties which particularly mitigate against their capacity to tolerate uncertainty. The capacity to suspend judgment, to exercise patient discretion, is an outcome of the capacity to anticipate the sequence of events that will flow from any particular action: and the length of time into the future that any likely consequences can be traced is related mentally to the ability to organize previous experience. But the capacity to organize such experience can be inhibited by unconscious anxieties, and Elliot Jacque, following Melanie Klein, suggests that the babe's reactions to the duration of gratifying or frustrating experiences, such as those arising from the periods in between feeding, may both be the source of such anxiety and the foundation upon which there grows the capacity to tolerate doubt for greater or lesser periods of time.

Those who would impatiently dismiss the speculation that faulty decision-making can be founded in such sources, and would doubt the impress our early oral explorations have upon adult character, should at least ponder on the origins of the recurring democratic error of over-estimating the contribution dialectical experiences make to our scale of values. There is a chasm between the resolving of problems by debate in the House and their actual solution. Ministers take decisions upon the basis of their being able orally to justify them in the Cabinet and Chamber: but Stafford Cripps was only one of many statesmen who could out-argue the whole Cabinet, and be absurdly wrong. I have dealt with too many protestors, received too many petitions, and too many requests, not to be aware that what people verbally demand is not what they necessarily need. There is insufficient scepticism among the politicians, victims of their own prolixity, about the efficacy of the techniques of discussion as a means of handling social problems: and, bound by the conventions of West-minster, Ministers' decisions can sometimes lead to glorious triumphs in Parliament, granting a catharsis to all the participants that is at best irrelevant to the actual needs of the nation.

Nor is it reassuring for the future when I enquire of the fluent young men in the universities of their choice of career that they blandly and so unashamedly reply that they intend to go in for politics, as if being a politician was a professional and separate role. Those of us brought up to regard a politician who was a careerist as odious are inevitably shocked: but the worst consequence is that such young men can arrive at West-minster so ill-equipped, lacking the experience of maturating exposure to the real world. A disproportionate number of members are now enter-ing the House from a life that has been lived only in school, college and junior common room. Society, however, is too complex for vital decisions to be left to men and women, some of whom, when they become Members, have never taken a decision outside a classroom. My encounter with Alice Bacon's ministerial incapacity was one of too many that I have been compelled to endure.

Happily when, some years later, a generous Welsh colleague, successful in the annual Private Members' Bill ballot, offered me the opportunity to reintroduce my Infanticide Bill, the decisions were no longer to be influ-enced by Alice Bacon. She had been succeeded as Minister of State at the Home Office by Shirley Williams. No-one would doubt her capacity for decision-making. She is an engaging woman, outside the group of intelli-gent hysterics who make up an uncomfortable quota of women M.P.s.

Her femininity belongs to her: it is not a façade, and, because of this, she does not dress in the vulgar exhibitionist manner of some of her colleagues. It is not their garish colour schemes or even their sometimes ridiculous attachment to clothes that they could have suitably worn when they were young, some twenty or thirty years ago, which proclaim their difficulties: rather it is the droll display of nudity in low necklines and sleeveless dresses worn by women far too old, big, tall or fat for such caprices which is startling. Karen Horney's conjecture, that the woman who feels keenly that, unlike a man, she has no genital organs to display regresses to the stage at which the desire to display still applies to her whole body, receives not a little corroboration from the clothes some women M.P.s wear. Yet perhaps it is because Shirley Williams, as her careless but modest clothes reveal, is more confident of her femininity that one feels this is a racked woman. To be a father, a husband and an M.P. is a difficult enough task, but to attempt to be a wife and mother when you are endowed with a commanding intellect sufficient to equip you to be a Prime Minister must set up an almost intolerable conflict of aspirations and ambitions.

The publication of my second Infanticide Bill, the widespread and sympathetic press notices it received, and the encouraging responses coming from M.P.s and the public interested in social problems, led me to hope that some progress could now be made. But it was not to be. Shirley Williams was not capable of being deceived by any banal arguments proffered by officials; but the real sticking point between us was reached when she supported the departmental view that the insuperable defect within my Bill was that it reduced the penalty of infanticide to less than the maximum of two years' imprisonment attached to the offence of neglecting, assaulting or ill-treating a child. Shirley's passionate Catholic conscience came through in every gap in her argument; it was in vain that I sought to show that even at present the law acquits the mother found guilty of infanticide of responsibility and that it was a false analogy to make comparisons with the 'wilful' offence of assaulting a child.

The Catholic Penal Reformers will always cling on to the doctrine of retribution; they will not accept that guilt can be an illusion. For them it is an awful reality, even if not the final reality, and it is not in law but in grace, which dwarfs all calculations of individual merit and demerit, that the master concept governing responsibility must be found. Lord Longford, Shirley Williams's colleague in politics and faith, has artlessly sought to persuade agnostic penal reformers that no rehabilitation can come to a delinquent until he has achieved redemption by recognition of his sin: and that this recognition comes when he sees his punishment as an act of love from the community. Shirley Williams may not be as well schooled as Longford in Pope Pius XII's classical discourses on punishment, but her attitude to crime and punishment deserves Rome's full approbation. After several discussions with her, it was clear to me I was not able to obtain government support for the Bill. And thus, seeing that masochism and metaphysics were temporarily too much for me, I accepted her helpful offer that in return for my dropping the Bill she would have the whole offence referred for particular attention to the Judges' Criminal Law Review Committee, from which in God's good time, as occurred with the suicide issue, a stammering proposal for some reform will doubtless emerge.

Thus must the reforming legislator advance, with patience and cunning, always selecting the issues with guile if his charity is not to be speedily overwhelmed by the vengeful or the Christians, or indeed sometimes an alliance between them. He must possess the historical sense to be aware that such alliances have always overcome brave and candid attempts to eliminate criminal responsibility from the penal codes. In the draft Italian code of 1921 and the former criminal codes of Mexico and Cuba, and in the first adopted by the Soviet Union, for a brief period, the idealists won: but all have now yielded to the counter revolution and only in glacial Greenland, away from the searching eyes of the moralist, is there a criminal code insistent that criminals are not 'responsible' and that they must not be 'punished'.

The infanticide issue, therefore, is not dead: and there will be occasions again in the future when, by placing this offence of infanticide under scrutiny, it will be possible to undermine yet a little more the doctrine of criminal responsibility, and compel further recognition of the role society, nurture and nature, play in creating our criminals. For, as Barbara Wootton has wisely contended, only if we forget responsibility will we ask not whether an offender ought to be punished but whether he is likely to benefit from the punishment. Meantime, as often happens, even before the law is changed, the clamour of the reformers is heard in the courts, and, tentatively, the Judges adjust to a strong public opinion. Despite the maximum penalty infanticide can attract, in practice, in very recent years, only once has a woman been sentenced to more than twelve months' imprisonment. Grudgingly the Judges are conceding that perhaps responsibility should not be added to the terrible anguish of a woman who emerges from the trauma of childbirth to make the discovery that she has not a living child to suckle, but one she has strangled, suffocated or decapitated.

VI

It was the danger that murderers could cheat society out of its bland desire to fix responsibility that brought forth such a fury against the zealous abolitionists battling for the end of capital punishment. The frontal assaults, over-frank and passionate, of the abolitionists, banked up such hatred that my hostile postbag to this day unfailingly reveals the unremitting detestation felt towards those of us who ended hanging in the land. I was often discomfited by the tactics of my fellow campaigners, and frequently reminded of that friend of Sir Lewis Namier who on being presented with a perfect case in support of a political thesis replied: 'I should be convinced of the argument if I did not know the passion which is behind it.'

Freud has written:

If one person succeeds in gratifying the repressed desire, the same desire is bound to be kindled for all other members of the community. In order to keep the temptation down the transgressor must be deprived of the fruits of his enterprise; and the punishment will not infrequently give those who carry it out an opportunity of committing the same outrage under colour of an act of expiation.

No longer to be able to kill the killers, is grief indeed, as my postbag testifies. Every time a murder is now committed, the sense of deprivation is renewed, and I am again overwhelmed with obscene and abusive letters sent by the frustrated who, with extraordinary accuracy, cite my comments, torn out of context, made during 1969 on television and radio when, with poor Sidney Silverman's death, it fell to me to write the last few sentences of his long, tortuous and successful polemic.

At long last the parcels of shit, carefully wrapped and sent to me from all parts of the country when I put through the homosexual act, are now rarely received; and the House of Commons cleaners emptying the waste paper baskets of our library no longer need to muse on the perplexing lavatory habits of their rulers. But, although resistance to the reforming homosexual act has died away, every major criminal act of violence is still a sign for the hymns of hate to be sung at me.

However, after Sidney's death I had, of course, no choice in the matter: the communications industry, reflecting public need, cast me in Sidney's role and as tiny Jew, a socialist solicitor, reformer and declared abolitionist, I was in their view perfection itself as an understudy. But, although I played it out, I had no illusions about his campaign which, in immediate practical terms, perhaps at most meant that each year two or three wretched psychopathic killers were to be saved from the gallows: the campaign was simultaneously backing up such thwarted hate and aggression that the penal reformers, concerned with the thousands of inadequates in our slum prisons, were bound to be struggling against a murderous tide for years to come.

But in any event, in the House of Commons, the campaign was, as long as Sidney Silverman lived, a one man affair: only after his death when the five year pause in hanging, which he had achieved, had to be converted into a permanent ban did some of the main burden in the House fall upon me. In the final stages of Sidney's campaign it is true some of us had to prop him up, for he was so spent and burned-out that occasionally he fumbled: but the ultimate triumph belonged to this wilful, irascible man.

Sidney Silverman was the most quarrelsome man in the House: he never quarrelled with me, but that certainly was not through lack of effort on his part. Whenever his temper escalated, by careful teasing and, more importantly, by a display of genuinely felt deference, I warded off the explosion. But with most of his other peers his persistence would be rewarded by an altercation. He quarrelled of course with his professional partners; he quarrelled with the Law Society; he quarrelled with the attendants in the House. No opportunity would be missed: when he sold his home in Swiss Cottage, though socialist slogans of brotherly love were worked into the cement path of the house, the hapless purchaser found that he had acquired not a home, but litigation, as Sidney deftly managed to complicate a simple conveyancing transaction into a labyrinthine ordeal. His great quarrels were, however, reserved for the Chamber, and there was no happier man than Sidney when he succeeded by an intervention in bringing down upon himself the wrath of the whole House. These were his finest hours: and they were many. As the whole House fumed he would, weaving his way through all the procedural checks that should have contained him, disrupt the whole business of the afternoon. Oft times his insistence gradually would erode the confidence of the House and, as his logic dented the seemingly self-evident proposition, the whole Chamber would be thrown into a mood of self doubt. Such arresting performances, played with such elan, were, however, too often repeated not to betray an element of compulsion: his daring provocations, even if seemingly justified, made the diminutive Sidney appear as a puppet controlled, not by himself, but by forces compelling him to act out defiances for which the transitory debate was but the occasion, not the cause.

He was determined to be attacked: he revelled in the retaliation which enabled him to release yet more hostility against the conspicuous conventional authorities in society. But, to permit such indulgences in venom, to ward off the punishment which he deserved for his excessive hatred of others, he always set the stage so that players would speedily emerge attacking him illogically and unjustly: and then almost always his secret playwright gave him the lines to enable him, without guilt, to release an orgiastic outpouring of language upon those whom he had provoked to act as his tormentors. His attachment to the House, which made him such a great Parliamentarian, was understandable: it was his own special theatre and since there, with all the familiar props at hand, he could act all others off the stage, breaking every rule whilst wearing the mask of some precedent, he protected the institution with a fanatical passion.

Doubtless the role he assumed satisfied a powerful unconscious homosexual need: he wanted, as so many agitators, to be forced into a passive, feminine, victimized role, and some of these repressions were illuminated to me by the squeamishness that I sensed when discussing with him my own reforming aspirations. But the dominant drive was his hatred: for Sidney was a killer. Perhaps only a killer could have fought with such fanaticism and with such stamina for the abolition of capital punishment.

The community may perhaps owe the formation of this over-determined reaction, which had so many benevolent side effects, to Sidney's criminal brother who spent many years in gaol; and who maliciously, in the fratricidal struggle between them, involved Sidney, even using stolen House of Commons note paper to buttress an exposition of a fraudulent scheme.

Not a few of my socialist colleagues who expound brotherly love have disastrous relationships with their own brothers: it is a case of Cain and Abel at home, and the brotherhood of man on the platform. I have, with care, been compelled to maintain a more distant relationship with some M.P.s with whom I have worked effectively, since I observed warning symptoms that I was becoming a brother-surrogate to them, and was therefore in danger of becoming a target for their displaced hostility. And I have wryly observed some of those on the right wing of the party who are not satisfied with the doctrine of from each according to his ability, to each according to his needs, but must continuously stress that socialism is above all else about equality, a doctrine that is not conspicuous in their own style of life. There is an odour of envy pervading some of their writings and speeches and one suspects that in their early battle for love of their parents they feel they lost out: a guarantee of equality means no one else can be the favourite son.

But the fierceness of brother hatred can lead to a heavy burden of guilt; and then the load is lightened by a generalized prohibition against brother hatred upon all society and by displacement of fraternal affection upon more remote social objects. The socialist dreams of a brotherly state and the abolition of fratricidal wars can draw its inspiration from the most murderous impulses: it is not surprising that, from the point of view of modern personality research, the characters which are achieved by such elaborate processes of balanced defences are viewed as less dependable and enduring formations than those which evolve more directly.

Some of Sidney Silverman's sources of hate were drawn from yet more primal sources: some scenes I witnessed, revealing how low was his threshold of tolerance if thwarted over any demand for food, were heavily suggestive. I came upon him once in an almost empty Commons tea room involved in a furious row with a good and long suffering woman employed in the cafeteria. Some beverage or titbit normally available had been denied him, and he had turned his formidable fury upon her: but this time he had met his match, and, her patience overstretched, she had counter-attacked with such effect that he was fleeing, literally trembling with rage, when I came upon him. I strove to settle him down, and deflect him; and later remonstrated with the woman, praying in aid of Sidney's growing age and fragility, but she was unforgiving. The incident was evidently no isolated one, and the waitress, displaying more insight than she appreciated, kept insisting that whenever he came to be served by her he behaved like a little baby.

Hate is love grown angry because of rejection: and the clamorous, insatiable babe at the breast has his early temper-tantrums directed against the hostile, actively refusing, bad mother-breast. Our society undoubtedly benefits from the Silvermans of this world whose early anger and rage in these primal situations compel them later to make aggressive attacks on a newly discovered bad object, to attempt to make it good and no longer frustrating, even as a small child who cannot wrest what he wants from the mother flies into a temper and hammers on her with his fists. Not all who carry on their way to adulthood powerful feelings of hatred select, however, with such happy discrimination as Sidney the bad within our society: but such unselfconscious campaigning, however well directed, must have its dangers, and dangerous extravagances must often result.

Victor Gollancz, the publisher who led the extra-parliamentary campaign for the abolition of capital punishment, often betrayed such extravagances as he, too, wrestled, ever publicly, with the destructiveness of his own hate. He was to attack the German Nazis with unrestrained zeal in the thirties and then to lead the 'let's be kind to the Germans' campaign in the immediate post war years; his Zionist sympathies were to be followed by emotionally charged appeals for the Arab refugees. Only by massive and public reparative displays could he expiate his guilt for his aggression: and in the end so loathsome and repulsive did he find the deep hate in his soul that, unable to smother it within a secular socialist creed affirming the brotherhood of man, he must needs become a Christian too. Not since another Jew, Paul, saw the light on the road to Damascus, was there such a well publicized conversion: nor would one more easily find one more replete with hysteria. A conversion of a Jew, brought up within a Jewish tradition, to Christianity, must always be suspect: and for a man with Gollancz's temperament doubly so.

In these days when ecumenicalism is fashionable, emphasis on the profound difference between religions is often resented: but the Jews did not go to the stake for two thousand years rejecting Christ because of some minor shibboleth. There is a great divide between the two tradit-ions and not least on their injunctions to man telling him how to cope with his hate. The Rabbinical adage is to do unto others what you would have them do unto you: but such a realistic and anambitious admonition is far removed from the Christian calls both to love others as yourself and to love your enemies. The narcissism of man is too unlimited to be capable of such Christian commands and the history of Christendom bears witness to their pretentiousness. Such impossible demands upon man lead not to Jerusalem, but to Belfast. But Gollancz was obviously in need of more affirmative commands to restrain him than Judaism provided. His Christian attachment, however, never really freed him from his earlier shackles. When I shared a table with him at a dinner held in the Tate Gallery to precede a private viewing of a Picasso exhibition, appropri-ately a paella was served to mark such a Catalan occasion, and immediately Gollancz was offering rationalized reasons why he could not eat the proffered meal. Others in the vicinity accepted his emphatic explanations but I realized my Christian companion was on the side of the Pharisees and that he was responding, as he well knew, to the ancient Hebrew taboo against the eating of shell fish.

The reaction formations of Silverman and Gollancz to their killer syndromes provided much of the dynamic to the abolitionist campaigns: but their regression to pregenital fixations in their emotional life and its concomitant, a lasting burden of guilt, which so evidently illuminated their enthusiasms, clearly suggests they met a barrier which they but imperfectly surmounted when confronted with the Oedipal situation in their last phase of infancy. I know nothing directly of Silverman's early relationships with his father and mother: and, not surprisingly, he showed considerable prickliness when once I sought to draw him out. But the earlier ambivalences to his mother and father that must have existed brought a verve to his campaigning that is now rarely seen in Parliament. After his death, as the experimental five year period of abolition of capital punishment was drawing to a close, I was uneasily aware that, inside the House, the steam had gone out of the demand: and matters were not made easier by the economic blows which were to be sustained by the Labour government which had more than enough burdens without viewing with any enthusiasm the task of taking upon itself the final unpopular step of abolition.

But procrastination, I knew, would be fatal. Already in 1968 I had warned and reminded many in the Cabinet that the experimental five year period of abolition which Sidney Silverman had pushed through Parliament was due to end in a probable election year. Both Houses, before July 1970, needed to pass affirmative resolutions making abolition final. Jim Callaghan, the Home Secretary in 1969, was too shrewd a political operator to require any second reminder of the need at all costs to avoid capital punishment becoming an election issue: for taking away the death penalty for ever would be interpreted by so many as a severe and intolerable deprivation. I knew in 1969 it was then or never. I was, therefore, dismayed to find that the Lord Chancellor, the most committed of abolitionists, was contemplating another view. The over-objective honesty and the lawyer's scruples of Gerald Gardiner were almost to thwart his own passionate desire to be the Lord Chancellor who presided over the final abolition of capital punishment.

Gerald Gardiner had sent for me within an hour of the Cabinet decision that the abolitionist resolutions were to be put without delay to Parliament. I arrived at his private rooms to discover he had invited from the Commons the energetic Liberal whip, Eric Lubbock, and Geoffrey de Freitas, and from the Lords the Chancellor had wisely summoned Barbara Wootton, and a couple of sympathetic Bishops.

The Lord Chancellor proffered us the same reasons why an immediate decision must be taken as he had obviously put to the Cabinet an hour earlier. He pointed out that if the resolutions were not affirmed, as he believed might well occur at least in the Lords, the present experimental Act would end in 1970 and then the provisions within the previous compromise Act of 1957, which categorized a restricted range of murders attracting the death penalty, would come into effect. Everybody, hanging Judges and political opponents of abolition, was agreed that the short lived provisions of the 1957 Act were senseless, unfair and unworkable. However, if Parliament refused total abolition, the restoration of hanging would have to be accepted but the 1957 Act, the Lord Chancellor explained, could not be allowed to come into effect and would need to be overhauled and a compromise rationalized Bill would have to be presented. Time would be needed to draft and pilot this rationalized Hanging Bill through Parliament before the 1965 Bill lapsed, and this was why he wanted the resolutions to be taken immediately: and this evidently was the public reason which he would offer if he was criticized for asking for the resolutions to be taken long before the intended five year experimental period had been exhausted.

I listened to the handsome Chancellor's quietly spoken, cool and objective piece of political lunacy with increasing disbelief. He is totally incapable of guile: and I was aware, therefore, this was no piece of sophisticated chicanery deployed to evade a coincidence of election and abolitionist campaigning. Gardiner's proposition was a genuine piece of contingency planning: but there are occasions when contingency planning invites and provokes the contingency, and this was certainly such an occasion. It is vitally important to recognize those rare moments in politics when to stake all means victory, and when the hedged bet means certain defeat. One whisper that the Lord Chancellor was contemplating drawing up a rationalized compromising Hanging Bill, and there was the certainty that the whole hanging campaign would be concentrated on a demand for such a Bill.

The more pusillanimous M.P.s would with relief yield to such a compromise, the Tory abolitionists in order to assuage their hostile constituency parties and the restless Trade Union M.P.s to defeat the charge of excessive permissiveness. And even if we nevertheless succeeded in wresting the necessary abolitionist affirmative resolution from the Commons, the strategic skills of opponents Lord Dilhorne and Henry Brooke and Robert Mortimer, Bishop of Exeter, would almost certainly guarantee that the Lords would falter and refuse the resolution, certainly until they had seen the proposed Bill. Time would then be against us and I feared what in fact did happen, that an election would be called early and that the Tories would win: with the Tories in government, as was to be proved when an abortive attempt to reintroduce capital punishment in 1973 brought support from an overwhelming majority of the Conservative M.P.s in the House, there would have been little possibility of ending State strangulation. I knew in 1969 that we could only win if we presented a clear-cut alternative between an absolute end to hanging and the reactivation of the anomalous 1957 Act, which we could deride. The 1957 Act had created a situation where if a man raped a girl and then strangled her and stole her handbag it was a capital offence, but if he did not steal the handbag it was non capital; the slow-poisoning premeditating murderer would escape hanging, but not the man who shot his wife in a paroxysm of jealousy. No present day House of Lords would accept such an act replete with such anomalies, and the way to compel the House to yield to the abolitionists was to insist there was no third way. Yet here was a Lord Chancellor, who for years had eschewed all judicial advancement because of his refusal to sentence any man to death, apparently naively offering signposts to that third way.

Gardiner presented his view, as ever, with his curious and characteristic detachment: the determined will catch glimpses of this man's passionate inner world, but the conscious ego of our greatest ex-Chancellor translates his interior drama like a diplomat's interpreter, neutral and uninvolved. He bewilders those who, on approaching him, first are captivated by his commanding appearance, graceful welcome and arresting pale blue eyes and then soon feel rejected and intimidated by his non-involvement and remoteness. As Lord Chancellor, possessed of what he has described as disgraceful patronage and living largely in a world of lawyers, inevitably deference to him became exaggerated and corroborated the distance his temperament had already set between himself and the external world.

His inner attraction to rich fantasy is displayed in his love of the theatre: but his thwarted ambition to become an actor reveals his determination to remain on stage, divided by the footlights from the audience. The world is kept at a distance and, even when engaged in a joint enterprise with him, there are moments when one feels only that an extraordinarily intelligent and faintly interested press reporter has joined you in a social gathering of which he is not a part. His type of political commitment, his legendary capacity for work and his assimilation in the impersonality of law books, one suspects, enable him to attenuate his personal relationships, but, nevertheless, ward off the ultimate temptation and danger of retreat into total abolition of human contact. His own formidable departmental civil servants, well adapted within the idiom of British public service to work at a distance with the Minister, worshipped him abandonedly for his integrity and intellectual genius; but many others, even those bereft of gaucherie and possessed of limitless social fluency, have found he has reduced them to tongue-tied mutes.

Even Frank Soskice, possessed of an elegant wife to whom, with wisdom, not a few raw M.P.s' wives have turned for instruction in the social etiquettes, would beg me to accompany him to Gerald when complex discussions were needed, as Frank Soskice, in the Lords, was steering the Divorce Bill which I had sent to him from the Commons. Then I would find myself in grotesque, Pinter-like situations with the ex-Home Secretary and the Lord Chancellor, two of the most publicly articulate men in Britain, failing, despite my bridging efforts, to communicate with each other: despairingly, Soskice would look entreatingly to me as in a soft voice, insensitively not raised to meet Frank's slight deafness, Gerald Gardiner would release some comment which seemed to Frank Soskice totally irrelevant and removed from the query he had just been raising. These sessions were not dialogues but discordant fugues, lacking counterpoint; and after they were over, alone with Frank, who as an M.P. had moved with rare ease and understanding among all social classes, he would sadly ask what had been decided as if we had just returned from Mars together, and I alone had held the key to the astral language.

Frank Soskice and I would gladly forgive such a man; but some of the Chancellor's Cabinet colleagues, after they had overcome their initial awe but still resentful at finding the gulf Gardiner has placed between him and them, gleefully discovered that the aura of distance surrounding him inhibited his ability as a politician. This was unfortunately true, for the poverty of effect in his relationship with the external world left him ill equipped to master other people by manipulation, a talent in which some of his Cabinet colleagues were only too liberally endowed.

The detachment enveloping Gerald Gardiner protects his integrity: but the schizoid-like dissociation that was placing a gulf between himself and the contingency Hanging Bill which, on that fateful morning, he was contemplating, angered me, and when he had explained his strategy I fiercely reacted. The explosion was short, but I carried the others present with me and visibly unnerved Gardiner. He rarely moves from the position he has struck, but I had crashed through his normal defences and he capitulated. We left his drawing room on the clear understanding, which he, naturally, punctiliously later observed, that no public mention of the possibility of a contingency Bill was to be made.

But I left with disquiet. We had a leaky Cabinet, and if the significance of Gardiner's original strategy had been sufficiently grasped and discussed in the earlier morning Cabinet meeting, then one hint from a Cabinet Minister to the press, and the abolitionists could be undone. I, therefore, dashed down the red carpeted corridor of the Lords into our more decorous lobby to drop a hint to a passing press man that I had been at a private meeting with the Lord Chancellor concerning the hanging resolutions. Within minutes the lobby correspondents were chasing me.

I deliberately deceived them: it is the only occasion that I have ever attempted to deceive the lobby and I recall it with distaste. It is possible to build up with this corps of elite and shrewd journalists an absolutely frank political relationship and on this occasion I took a grossly unfair advantage of their trust. Only a little time before the inner core of twenty-one lobby correspondents constituting their Guinea Club had invited me to be their guest of honour at their annual end of session dinner, when they select one M.P. to whom to give praise. I had been moved by their generosity. Praise and thanks usually make me restless: but when it comes from discerning peers whom I respect, then I yield to flattery as do all men. Espousing unpopular causes leaves one too often bruised not to appreciate balm. I felt, however, I had no choice but to mislead my lobby friends. I told them the choice before Parliament was unequivocally clear, and that if the resolutions did not move us to complete abolition the government were definitely going back to the old anomalous situation: and for good measure I provided them with a long and lurid list of the types of anomalies the 1957 Act would breed. In the days that followed the anomalies were inevitably heavily publicized, and the stark alternative was put before the nation.

The choice, so presented in the Commons, gave us a comfortable majority with Edward Heath, to his credit and to the pain of many of his back benchers who wanted to collect hanging votes in the coming election, joining us in the voting Lobby. Wilson, of course, gave Heath no credit for his courage: as I was shepherding my flock past the tellers, the then Prime Minister came up to tell me that I could thank him that Heath was not abstaining but was leading so many of his followers into the abolitionist Lobby. It was all due to the manner in which for the past week on the floor of the House he had been taunting Heath for his total indecisiveness: now Heath had been provoked by him out of neutrality. Wilson's capacity to appropriate credit is infinite, as the doleful tales of his former Cabinet colleagues so often illustrate.

But in the Lords the battle was tough, despite our well organized marshalling of our supporters. The efforts of Lord Brooke and Viscount Dilhorne to postpone a decision were well supported: and if it were not that Gerald Gardiner from the beginning of his opening speech hammered home that postponement meant the reactivation of the old homicide Act, and that there was no question but that that would be the result of any postponement, I have little doubt we would have lost the day. If I had been more frank with the lobby or less brutal with sweet Gerald Gardiner, the work of poor dead Sidney Silverman would indeed have been betrayed, and still today we would have had the gallows in the land.

VII

The insistence in Christian civilizations upon the immaculate conception stands witness to our deep sense of betrayal. Each man resents his own conception. The denial in the Christ myth of the intervention of the human father reveals the true agony of every son: and Judas, the betrayer, is but the scapegoat for the parents who dared to love exclusively. The injunction of the Catholic Church, still not eroded, that lovemaking must only be for procreation is the penalty the sons of God have imposed upon the parents, forbidding them to revel without thought of children. Within a Christian culture, haunted by the betrayal theme, the role of the spy, the voyeur, who fulfils the buried wish to view and discover the secrets of the coupling authorities, assumes a sinister, loved and hated, significance.

Nor can our James Bond stories, our ceaseless flow of television spy tales, and tedious outpourings of cold war novels, act as a sufficient abreaction. The spies are endowed with beauty, evil, heroism and cunning, and all their neurotic compulsive symptoms blotted out: but still the aching heart yearns for vengeance and the real world spy, hero and villain, always part of ourselves, must triumph and suffer. But doom always follows the success; and the wages of his sin must be death or imprisonment. Only thus can we dare to enjoy, secondhand, the betrayal of the betrayers.

A wild and senseless avalanche, therefore, hit the Home Office when the Russian intelligence service succeeded in the easy task of prising out of the leaky Wormwood Scrubs the obsolescent spy, George Blake, who had already served more than five years of his sentence and who possessed not a scrap of contemporary information that would have harmed Britain. The escapes in the previous two years of the train robbers Charles Wilson and Ronald Biggs had, of course, aroused some concern, but the political consequences of the escapes were slight. The train robbers had become folk heroes in the community and, but for the official they had injured, they would have fallen into the long line of immature thugs who have in Britain been elevated to martyrdom by the masses: if prevailing conditions did not allow the populace to cheer and applaud them, as did hundreds of thousands of Londoners when the notorious housebreaker Jack Sheppard and, later, the highwayman Dick Turpin were hauled to the gallows, that was because of lack of opportunity not of desire.

But the escape of Blake stirred emotions at volcanic level: nowhere more, of course, than among the more authoritarian Tory M.P.s. Their repudiated hostility to their overvalued fathers made it intolerable for them to accept that anyone could successfully betray the fatherland and yet escape punishment. In the House the initial scenes that the escape provoked plunged me into despair. I immediately sensed that penal reformers were to fail to resist the onslaught. The demands being made for greater security in the prisons could only be achieved at the expense of the constructive and rehabilitative elements which feebly struggle to gain a place within the regimes – only by making prisons still more primitive, still more destructive, and, in the long view, still more useless. The real truth may well be that men can only live as men in a prison if they believe there is some hope of escape, as I have often been told by ex R.A.F. prisoner of war friends of mine.

Reason was, however, to be stilled. We had just begun to reach the point where the House and nation could have reluctantly accepted that it was impossible to contemplate an indefinite expansion of the prison population when prison sentences neither deter nor reform those who receive them: and that the only alternative was the rapid building up of strong supportive services within the community committed to re-habilitating criminals in a non-custodial setting. All hopes that we could edge our way to such reforms were dashed by the furore caused by Blake's escape. The Russians triumphed: and by a rare irony it is upon Kosygin's hirelings that the 14,000 men, today rotting three in a stinking cell in our gaols, can lay a large measure of the responsibility for their grim fate. I was to be strategically placed to play a small part in limiting the boundaries of wild fear the escape occasioned: but penal reform in this country has nevertheless been set back by at least a decade by this one unimportant escape and, for this, I bear a grudge against the British Secret Service whose obtuseness led them initially to use Blake as a secret and double agent. In my professional capacity I have had, by some unusual combination of circumstance, the opportunity to penetrate the inner sanctum of our security services and to observe their interrogations of some of those Englishmen who have been trapped by Eastern European agents operating in this country. I do not doubt the stamina of our security service: but I question their insights.

It required no special prescience to evaluate Blake as far too vulnerable a man ever to be employed in our intelligence services. His whole early

life was punctuated by events calculated to make him, at least unconsciously, yearn for revenge upon Britain. His father Behar, an
Egyptian Jew holding a British passport and living in Holland, was an
ostentatious British patriot who probably acted as a British intelligence
agent in the First World War. In honour of King George V, young Blake
was burdened by his first name, and like everything else that was to
associate him with his determinedly British father, it was to bring him
little but misfortune. His father, poisoned by German phosgene gas in
the First World War was, from the effects, to die prematurely when
George was only thirteen. His father's death would not only be interpreted
as a desertion in itself, as children irrationally interpret a death: it was
also to wrench George away during his adolescence from his mother, a
Lutheran Protestant, from his sister, from his ambition to be a priest
and from his settled Dutch home. For Behar had left a fiat, submitted
to by his wife, that on his death, the son George had to be sent to an
uncle in Egypt. It needs no special imagination to relate to the feelings
of the young adolescent who found the consequences of his Egyptian
father's love for Britain was to make him an orphan exiled in a strange
land.

Worse was to follow. When eventually George Blake returned to
Holland, the tenuous British connection was to precipitate the break-up
of the family home, with the Dutch mother and daughter compelled to
flee to Britain and with the British George Blake arrested by the Gestapo.
When the young man did finally succeed in making his getaway he came
to a Britain where his foreign descent barred him from ever feeling fully
accepted. Certainly holding the right of a British passport was no blessing
but a curse for George Blake. With a father who had betrayed George by
his choice of nationality, by his unnecessary death, by condemning his
son to exile, and with a father whose allegiances had provoked his son's
arrest in Holland and alienation in Britain, it would indeed be astonishing
if the son's deep resentment was not to be worked out against his father's
first love. Only our secret service could have been so accommodating as
to provide full facilities for George Blake to commit posthumous parricide. He was to attack his father's land with such devastating effect that
the Lord Chief Justice felt compelled to pronounce upon him the longest
sentence of imprisonment ever recorded in modern legal history: forty-
two years. Yet the scantiest psychiatric screening of Blake by the intelligence service would have saved him from himself, scores of our agents
from falling into Russian hands, and penal reformers in Britain from a
tragic set-back.

The syndromes presented by these compulsive spies are wearisomely monotonous, and their deceits surely easily divined. When I later was to meet the spy Kroger, he displayed the predictable character traits. He had insulated himself from his austere prison surroundings and from his long sentence by play acting a part in a debased Dostoevski story. It was an easy role for him to assume. He was a half-educated man with embarrassing literary pretentions and a self-conscious love of books and, despite the absurd press glamorization of this spy, as of every spy, the only identity he was capable of attaining was of a second rate hero in a shabby novelette. The stilted literary language and the vulgar brummagem of sentiment in which he artificially described to me his predicament trivialized the real tragedy of his position. Yet, from the interstices of the droll and over gentle lines he had assigned to himself, there welled up a great hatred against authority.

He shared, with all the murderers and violent robbers by whom he was surrounded, a hatred and fear of all the parent-surrogates, from the Home Secretary to the prison governor responsible for containing him in the maximum security block. He was clearly at home with all these rejected men and, with barely concealed conceit, used his slightly superior intelligence to act as priest-confessor to them and become a presiding chairman between the rival gang groupings within the security block. The game became him. He could empathize with his outcast prison colleagues and at the same time play the father: simultaneously he was betrayer and betrayed, and although the fear of dying in the prison sometimes overwhelmed him, the satisfaction to be obtained from his fantasy as a gaoled romantic hero shored him up.

Kroger's defences were immediately alerted if any attempt was made to probe his relationship with his parents: it was of his beloved Lona, separately gaoled, of whom he spoke and yet I found his importuning, asking me to intervene and obtain for him a right to meet her periodically, couched in adolescent terms. He addressed me not as man to man: he seemed to be more concerned to assert his rights under the prison regulations, and persuade me of the tyranny of the authorities, than to meet his woman. The shadow of assertive antagonistic parents thwarting his claims enshrouded him.

Kroger's fellow spy, Gordon Lonsdale, has given us even more explicit documentation of his own motivation. Whatever ambiguity there may be about his birthplace, it is established that Lonsdale's parents' marriage broke up and the deserted mother, living in Russia, unable or unwilling to keep the twelve-year-old boy, sent him far away to a state institution school. Lonsdale has explained the position in a letter discovered in Kroger's bungalow. 'I did not wish it and I did not seek it, but it turned out to be. I have thought very much about it – why all this? The answer is it all started in 1932 when mother decided to send me to the nether regions. At that time she could not imagine all the consequences of this step. I do not blame her.' His protest that his mother did not bear any responsibility may be too much: but the significant lack of acquittal of his deserting, betraying father cannot be denied: in all his life he worked out his revenge by creating a life totally dedicated to betrayal.

Sometimes these unhappy men, who, as Lonsdale poignantly declared, do not freely seek their fate, are propelled a little off the more usual spy trail. There is a character type that originates in a childhood picture of the father as a figure of almost unlimited power who sets a problem in loyalty because the child does not know how to dispose of the hostility which grows up together with his strong feelings of love. This ambivalence is sometimes imperfectly resolved by distinguishing between a good father who is loved and a bad father who is repressed and displaced. In adult life the less integrated may recreate a representative of the good father as the head of the country: and the bad figure is in the world outside. Out of such material can spring blind patriotism and great hatred of alien authorities. But sometimes the primal loyalty of the child to a father who was himself an outsider causes a reversal in the pattern.

The original love bond prompts an alliance between son and a father in the wilderness, a father who never belonged to the compact majority, like the Arabist St John Philby who played the part of a Moslem eminence grise to oil chieftains. Then the fractured son, when adult, remains alienated from his own establishment. 'To betray you must first belong', was Kim Philby's apologia: and he, like many spies, found his good father in Russia and the bad father at home in England. He betrayed his bad father, and so followed the same course as Tangye Lean has, with insight, shown to have been precariously walked by many displaced Englishmen who in other days eulogized Napoleon and loathed the British government.

However, perhaps those who direct our intelligence service dare not use the insights which could protect us from such double agents, for their own personal motivations may then also be over-illuminated to themselves. Certainly all the spies I have met have presented obvious symptoms of their unsuitability to assume any security role. Vassall, for example, an agent for the Russians for seven years, was positively vetted by our security service before being sent to Moscow and again positively vetted before being attached to the Naval Intelligence Division. Yet he is as obvious a passive homosexual as I have ever encountered. A few minutes' conversation with such a man, and an awareness of his style of speech, manner and posture, would surely have alerted any worldly person, unless of course the interviewer was so anxiously trying to obscure his own homosexual component that he blotted out any symptoms of his buried drives in everyone else.

The worthy judges and lawyers who conducted the Vassall enquiry and came to the conclusions that no one could be held responsible for failing to detect Vassall's homosexuality as a security risk, and, further, that the senior members of our Moscow Embassy could not be blamed for failing to notice his effeminacy were, however, bound to record that the more robust members of the junior Embassy staff referred to Vassall amongst themselves as 'Vera'. And whatever assessments our ambassadors, the Under Secretaries of State for Scotland and security chiefs may make, I have no doubt he would have been so described by any group of factory workers within my constituency with whom Vassall may have spent ten minutes.

I suspect the fastidiousness that fails to recognize a raging homosexual after months of associating with him. Those who have come to terms with their own homosexual component, possessed as it is by every man and woman, are not terrified to see and sympathize with a man whose homosexuality has overwhelmed him and left him emasculated. The wretched Vassall for many years languished in his cell after being thrust into roles by men of superior rank and intelligence that, given his character, provoked his nemesis. The over-civilized Radcliffe Tribunal acquitted his superiors of responsibility for the resulting breaches of security: but I doubt that all his superiors can all be absolutely free from responsibility for this miserable man having found himself in a maximum security prison.

There is, too, within the Radcliffe report, an assumption that the real danger to our national security comes from a homosexual's vulnerability to exposure and prosecution, not from his homosexuality: but although the Russians have been able to use the antics of heterosexuals with equal effect, in the light of the history of spies strewn across British history, it is too jejune and orthodoxly liberal a view to be maintained. From James I, of whom it was said he gave his money to his favourites and the secrets of the state to everyone, down to Guy Burgess, treachery is uncomfortably linked with disturbed homosexuals unable to come to terms with their sexual destiny. This is a harsh judgment: but from Elizabethan times until today the names of notorious homosexual traitors and spies ring out. Vassall, Burgess and Maclean are but the end of a long line stretching out from Lord Henry Howard, Francis Bacon, Christopher Marlowe and Antonio Perez. In this century, two of the most notorious traitors, the Austrian Colonel Redl and the tragic Roger Casement, were compulsive and bizarre homosexuals. Those acquainted with contemporary clinical research into the aetiology of homosexuality will not find this correspondence between irreconciled homosexuality and treachery so surprising. Increasingly the evidence mounts that it is a hostile father who takes away the manhood of his son. It would be more surprising if the emasculated son sometimes did not grow up feeling compelled to seek revenge upon the state, the symbol of all authoritarian and interfering paternalistic qualities.

Such musings, however, even if they could lead to more effective methods of preventing the Russians infiltrating our intelligence services, were not, of course, acceptable at the time of Blake's escape. The Home Office, a department forever on the defensive, lacking confidence and philosophy, was ill equipped to contain the storm and to give support to Roy Jenkins, then Home Secretary.

Jenkins was unpopular in the department, which was to his credit: he did not disguise his impatience with its rule-bound mood, its reverence of precedent, all showing an almost obsessional need to ward off the anxiety which forever lurks around the corridors of this section of Whitehall. The Home Office bureaucrats are always, even in the midst of sunny political days, fearfully waiting for the lightning to strike: and, of course, it does. For as Kierkegaard has taught us, in a psychological sense what a man most dreads he yearns for, and what one fears one desires. Fear of death itself, the unbearable tension of expectation, can become a motive for suicide, and fear of pregnancy can become a motive for conception. The Home Office's fears always guarantee their realization: the moment comes, and panic stricken, it almost always over-reacts, particularly so when the issue affects security, be it a Blake escape or a Rudi Deutchke deportation.

Faced with no real support from the department, and a vote of censure from the Tories, Roy Jenkins yielded to the poor advice tendered to him, and pre-empted the demands of the Tories by announcing the appointment of Earl Mountbatten to conduct an enquiry into prison escapes, and to make firm recommendations to strengthen prison security. The strategy was to prove disastrous: the immediate tumult was stilled but all those of us who had fought for our prisons to have a therapeutic rationale were doomed to suffer a grim defeat.

The Admiral of the Fleet's conclusions and recommendations were predictable. He found that there was no really secure prison in the country: physical defences had to be strengthened against enemy attack from outside. Horizontal barriers such as barbed wire, together with moats were needed; concrete stubs arranged in series around outside walls should be erected to act as barriers to attacking vehicles; walls should be high and smooth; early warning systems including geo-phones to detect ground movements were required; ultrasonic acoustic radar could give perhaps too many false alarms but ideally each cell should be designed as a separate unit mounted on pressure transducers virtually converting the cell into a weighing machine giving built-in alarms if the prisoner without authorization left his cell; electric capacity or contact devices and the use of bandit glass sandwich windows were needed; hot air systems to blow away fog at the foot of outer perimeter fences were essential. And a new fortress, the first of two, to incarcerate what were to be described as Category A prisoners was to be built on the Isle of Wight. A totally uninhabited island off our coast would be preferable like the Calf of Man or Muck Island, but reluctantly the Admiral conceded this might make for staffing difficulties: and he had to be content with Spithead and the Solent as providing further barriers to a getaway of prisoners. The Admiral, as Governor of the Isle of Wight, meticulous to the last detail, announced with evident relish that the fortress should have, as indeed it deserved, a nostalgic name, 'Vectis', the old Roman name for Wight.

To match and sustain these new security measures, prison officers should receive greater emphasis in their training on security, a proportion were to receive specialized training in modern security devices, more prison officers were to be enlisted for night work and head office was to have an Inspector General with command functions; more staff officers were to be created so that inspection of the security arrangements in prisons should be constant and continuous. The whole report inevitably would effectively reinforce all the paranoid traits within the community; and many despairing penal reformers privately asserted that the only security measure omitted was a proposal to keep prisoners locked up within the cells for twenty-four hours each day.

I found the report an affront. From the earliest months of my member-ship of the House I had sought always to proffer illustrations that would dramatically reveal the folly of believing that either security or therapy could be achieved by excessive containment of the prisoner. The ultimate restriction on movement that can be placed upon a human being is, of course, the strait jacket and this weapon, under the benign euphemism of 'loose canvas restraint jackets' was, when I first raised its use in the Com-mons, being placed upon hundreds of men and women in prison each year.

I had discovered that a schizophrenic client of mine had been bound, while on a charge, in a strait jacket on two occasions for twenty-one hours continuously: and I permitted my anger at this display of barbarism to overspill into the House. So many Members loudly assert their powerfulness to cover their fears of defenceless helplessness, that my indignation speedily lit up these and even deeper anxieties.

When I was soon able to show that men had been kept in strait jackets for more than forty-seven hours the House shared my concern and, after forcing an adjournment debate, the use of the strait jacket in our prisons nose-dived dramatically. Now it is used on less than ten occasions a year and then only for short periods. But such interventions of mine, revealing the primitive responses sometimes made to violence by the prison service in our gaols, enabled me to pin-point the inadequacy of psychiatric qualifications within the prison medical service, and eventually assisted me to demand, with success, the appointment of a working party to enquire into the prison medical service and its relationship with the Health Service. The recommendations of that Committee, under pressure from the House, were first published and later substantially implemented. The gains so made were not without effect. A special prison where treatment of some selected psychopaths could be attempted came into existence and group counselling with prisoner and staff participation was commenced at two of our prisons.

These tentative advances were now to be blocked. Once the prison officer is relegated to the role of a turnkey, the slender hope of effecting any rehabilitation of a prisoner is snapped. It is not enough that the prison worker is a custodian, even a guardian; he must be someone who cares too. Certainly the criminal, and particularly the young criminal, needs a guardian, a stable non-delinquent figure with whom he can identify, and under whose aegis there can be some physical and emotional security. But he needs, too, a continued ongoing relationship of long duration with an understanding person who can contain his communications, especially his fears and anxieties, and can do some work upon them and then return them in acceptable form. The guardians protect, provide a framework, constitute boundaries, and are in fact performing a paternal role. But those who care, accept what is put into them by the prisoner, clarify and return it.

It is possible for both these roles of guardian and carer to be fulfilled in one person: I have seen prison workers who by their geniality, tolerance, firmness and understanding act as a container for communications without reacting by rejection or by excessive punitive measures or by becoming excited or seduced by the criminal. There are, of course, others, whom I have observed, who are insufficiently stable to withstand what the prisoners put in them. There are too many who see their own criminality in the prisoners and punish it there; and some whose latent criminality through their experiences with criminals flares up so that they are incapable of dealing with their charges and become either unduly rejecting or, frequently, ill themselves.

For many prisoners the custodial experience is capable of being made into a growth period; but during such a growth period turbulence is bound to occur precisely at the time when meaningful character changes are occurring. A safe static situation for long periods of time can be found no doubt in a conventionally secure prison: the prison officers can become institutionalized and the prisoners confirmed in their criminality. It is a deceptively easy and utterly useless way to administer a prison.

When constructive measures are attempted, the Mephistophelean part of the criminal will often begin operating at the very moment when those measures promise to be most effective. This is when the criminal provokes the guardian into making mistakes, and then the criminal tenaciously holds on to those very mistakes as a defence against the growth of his personal responsibility from within: they provide him with the excuses for a paranoid attitude against the establishment. This makes tough going for the prison staff and, when a trigger-happy incontinence of violence characterizes many of their charges, it is no doubt safer to leave bad alone and not attempt to build up the interpersonal relationships without which the drift into confirmed criminality can never be arrested. The Mountbatten philosophy was too easily misinterpreted to mean that the efficient prison officer was to be a gaoler: and that interpersonal relations were to be superseded by new technological devices that would automatically create a secure prison. I have seen the absurdities of such a doctrine made explicit inside the most modern gaol in Europe, at Kumla in Sweden, where the prisoners, utterly cut off from the staff in their gleaming electronically controlled cells, had become depersonalized and their custodians almost dehumanized. Such a prison indeed was no real improvement on the ancient wing of another Swedish gaol, the Langholmen Prison, where I found the Soviet spy Colonel Wennerstrom and others incarcerated under horrifying conditions. The Swedes' pretension to being zealous penal reformers is a fraud: and I have no desire for Britain to follow Sweden's example.

Given my views, it was ironic that within a few weeks of the publication of the Mountbatten report, when asked by Roy Jenkins, the then Home Secretary, to become a member of our newly created Advisory Council on the penal system, I found the first task assigned to a handful of colleagues and myself on that Council was to frame a regime under which the long-term prisoners were to live in the fortress-type prison Mountbatten was demanding.

Whatever openness of mind my colleagues may have had in their approach to this problem, I had none. I was totally prejudiced. To concentrate a group of evil men, who felt themselves finally rejected by society, in a repressive custodial atmosphere was to invite disaster. Such men would have nothing to gain by co-operation and nothing to lose by revolt. All their energies and ingenuity would inevitably be expended on plans for escape or on conflict with authority, and the strains on a prison staff, engulfed in anxieties about the attitudes and activities of scores of the most dangerous prisoners in Britain, would be intolerable. From the start I had one objective in mind: how to use our terms of reference to circumvent the implementation of the Mountbatten recommendation.

Contrary to my expectations, I was fortunate in my three committee colleagues. I knew only one, and he and I had met in bitter television confrontations over the divorce issue. Dr Robert Mortimer, Bishop of Exeter, spokesman for the Church of England on social affairs, no doubt approached me as warily as I approached him. A few years later, secure in the friendship which we had then forged, he was to tell me that at one time there was no man in Britain whom he had hated more than myself. Certainly we had conducted our controversy on the divorce issues with rare acrimony; yet it was to be an odd fact that our alliance on this penal problem, more perhaps than any other single factor, was to prepare the way for considerable changes in the divorce law of Britain. I never discussed theology with the Conservative Bishop and, with metaphysics eschewed, we were to find ourselves, as we travelled through the United States and Europe inspecting the maximum security prisons of the Western world, almost always in agreement on our assessments of the regimes under which they operated; and as to how, if at all, some of their features could be deployed in Britain.

I would not have found such agreement, as I know from other experiences, if I had been working with some of our swinging but ineffective Bishops, forever peddling their doubts and exhibiting their anguish with unseemly immodesty. It is true that one can be forgiving, as when the wife of the former Bishop of Woolwich told mine, as they complained to each other of the prolonged absences of their husbands, that she had devised a method which enabled her to see her husband for at least fifteen minutes of the day: they took their bath together and fortunately for her the Bishop took a bath every day.

But more usually I am impatient with these egalitarian priests, and I have sometimes over-reacted to their abdications, as in more than one encounter with Lord Soper I have poured scorn on his declared suspicion of leadership. Organized religion is authority or it is nothing.

The Jewish culture from which I spring is anti-Christian: it is essentially antithetical to the denial of sex and the elevation of celibacy, to the doctrine of original sin, to the manic pacifist denial of aggression, to the emphasis upon individual as against collective redemption, and to the Christian yearning for personal immortality. The idealization of the zealous Christian lacks the realism and compromise which is my habit of mind and I cannot work well with true Christians. But with Churchmen I am always happily engaged: and in my many skirmishes with the Church I have had no unease. Benjamin Disraeli, commenting on the number of Jews who are revolutionaries, once shrewdly remarked that 'If you scratch a Jew deeply enough you will always find a Tory.' Old institutions always attract me, and, if they are ramshackle, I do not assault them as an iconoclast; I am ready to help refurbish them. The Right Reverend Lord Bishop of Exeter and I understood each other.

The chairman of our committee was Sir Leon Radzinowicz, a Pole and cosmopolitan who loves England with all the exaggerated affection of the step-child. I had often used his magnum opus, the extraordinary *History of English Criminal Law*, as a reference work, but I knew of him as a man only through other jaundiced eyes. The precursor to the Advisory Council on the penal system was the Royal Commission on crime, upon which Radzinowicz had served. It had been set up by Henry Brooke and, having become after almost three years' work a complete shambles, had the rare distinction of being wound up in despair, with no report issued, with the members possessed by a frenzy of disagreement and recrimination and with the fumbling chairman, the ex-Chancellor of the Exchequer Heathcoat-Amory, suffering from a stroke. Crime is over-attractive to all of us: it can be an incendiary bomb causing the most rational to light up and certainly on this unique Royal Commission the members failed to place the criminality they were examining at a sufficient distance from themselves. At another level, the essential pragmatism of Radzinowicz clashed with the restless perfectionism of my friend, the present shadow Solicitor General, Sam Silkin. These formidable protagonists became locked in a fatal struggle: over the corpse of the Commission they were to continue to view each other unforgivingly.

I approached Radzinowicz with an unnecessary circumspection, because in fact he was evidently determined to avoid the previous disaster. He is, of course, a great organizer, at his best manipulating international criminological conferences and, preferably by conspiracy, manoeuvring in the corridors of Whitehall for his Cambridge empire. Britain owes a considerable debt to this dynamic outsider whose doggedness led to the establishment of our first Institute of Criminology. He commenced our immediate task with a great show of programme planning and procedure: and since I accepted this unchallengingly from the beginning, I did not provoke his persecutory anxieties which, when evoked, can distort his relationships. I have been too long in the Commons in any event to elevate importance to procedures and rules. Members in recent times have squandered years of effort devising changes in our procedure and rules in the magical belief that this will improve our government. Procedures, however, are man-made and can be man-avoided. I have never found any rule or procedure in the House which effectively obstructed me from obtaining my objective: rules, however, must be shyly dodged and of course, simultaneously, elaborate overt genuflections must be made to them.

Thus settled down, our little committee proceeded merrily. Radzinowicz's zeal for work more than matched my own and, of course, I admired his boldness except, when abroad, he would expect me to join him as he plunged recklessly into the swirling traffic, gripped by a fantasy of omnipotent control, and triumphantly reached the opposite pavement. In vain did I lecture him as a driver to a non-driver that he was overestimating the capacity or the will of motorists to avoid a pedestrian: he would persist, albeit alone and not with me, in indulging his infantile megalomania, for, as Ernest Jones and others have repeatedly pointed out, a child has such ideas of omnipotence at his anal stage when he ascribes magical power of this kind to his excretions. Mastery of the body and particularly the sphincter induces such illusions of power. And some of Rad's other mild classical anal traits would drive our accompanying civil servants to despair. He would put off catching a train or plane to the very last minute and, whatever pay-off this may have been to those who had injured his primary narcissism by demands of strict regularity in his infant toilet habits, it was an irregularity barely tolerable to the painstaking bureaucrats split-timing our itinerary across the United States and Europe. But I admit to great delight in his gamesmanship as, eluding his watching Whitehall men, he would slip off to buy strawberries with one minute to go before the train left the platform: sometimes however he lost the game with himself and he was left to hire, at great personal expense, a car to chase the Bishop and me across the continent.

It is not, of course, such whimsies in criminologists and in those employed in our corrective institutions that alarm one. The elaborate, ordered and frequently meaningless tables beloved of many criminologists, like the excessive concern for rules and order in so many prison custodians, can be comparatively harmless reaction formations to their coprophilic tendencies. Imperfectly sublimated anal erotic endowments in themselves may be innocent enough: what is far more threatening is the convergent action of anal and sadistic instincts in the obsessional characteristics of too many professionally interested in crime and in those who are frequently employed in the control of prisoners. Gamekeepers turned poachers may be acceptable but sadistic gamekeepers are another matter. Radzinowicz can unselfconsciously indulge his anality by giving to his last volume of his formidable historical work the title *Grappling for Control* and the contents of the book reveal how a thinker may ward off his sadism constructively. But lesser men do not loosen their own desire for domination by expounding, as Radzinowicz does, revealing historical descriptions of the growth of policing in Britain in the eighteenth and nineteenth centuries. Too many of those professionally engaged in searching for causes and treatment of crime, like those involved in its detection and those controlling prisoners, use elaborate techniques bathed in a raw sadism.

The continuing slopping out system, for example, that is insisted upon in Britain's prisons, provides ample corroboration for any who may still doubt that expelling a man out of society to a prison can be treated by the community as an act of defecation. The primitive idea that removing an object is equivalent to defecating may be a remote notion to many grown up people: but the child psychiatrists know that according to the child's view the way to get rid of a person one no longer likes is by means of defecation. The prison authorities get the message from the outside world: the prisoner is shit, must be treated as shit and must live and sleep amongst shit.

Our committee was to urge that in the new prisons a screened flush lavatory should be attached to each cell together with a wash basin with running water: but officialdom proffered the most extraordinary rationalizations to persuade us not to make such a recommendation. And the insistence that prisoners could not be trusted to possess a toilet of their own was irrationally insisted upon despite our assurances that we had seen such facilities provided without difficulty to the most dangerous criminals of Europe and America. It would require a Swift, whose excremental vision long preceded Freud's exposition of the sadistic fantasies that accompany the stage of infantile libidinal development in which the anus and defecation are the major sources of sensuous pleasure, to savage adequately the elaborate defences of those resisting change. In the current rearguard action upon which prison officials are now engaged, electronic unlocking, by which, at night, one prisoner at a time on each landing can be released to go to the lavatory, has commenced in some new prisons. Under the pretence of security, a cunning control of the prisoners' motions has been gained by the authorities as the demanded price for giving up the stinking chamber pot in the cell.

American prisons, on the other hand, have their own especial cruel refinements. An uncouth governor of one state prison regaled me with stories of homosexuality rife in his prison, and, in particular, told me how today the imprisoned black gang leader, as a matter of prestige, not of affection or desire, must possess as a bum boy a white man: and in another prison, where the visitors' book contained the signature of Charles Dickens, the same ambience prevails as in his day. In a solitary confinement cell a prisoner under sentence of death for eight years, and still appealing, under the coaxing of the Warden, rose from his now habitual crouching position to greet me through the grille, as would my little dog, albeit with less responsiveness and intelligibility. My status as a man was reduced: and the diminution of human dignity is felt more keenly because of an absolute lack of confidence in the administration of American justice.

It is true that our administration of justice is not impeccable, but our faults, as I know from experience, are capable of remedy. Thus in 1963, whilst visiting Mauritius, in a small parliamentary delegation, I called in at the Seychelles, British ruled islands in the Indian Ocean, hopefully expecting in the luxurious home of the Governor, the Earl of Oxford and Asquith, and on the dreamy beaches of those beautiful tropical isles to gain some rest. But I was persistently importuned by a cranky old settler who constantly waylaid me to tell me of two fishermen who, he claimed, had been wrongly sent to prison on a squalid murder charge. His allegations against the police, the bar, and the courts were extravagant and my two parliamentary colleagues understandably shook him off: but I found I could not lie peacefully sunbathing and my swims were uneasy as I failed to dismiss from my mind his story which, like his tortuous method of presentation, had a certain surrealistic logic. In the end, impatiently I yielded to my guilt, visited the courts, interviewed some witnesses and became more disturbed.

It was the beginning of a long saga: for three years I questioned and pressed the Colonial Office and built up a mountain of relevant affidavits. The government, to silence me, decided to appoint a leading Silk privately to review the evidence; he became as disquieted as I was. Ultimately a special permanent appellate court was established in London to supervise not only the Seychelles but the other small island remnants of the Empire. The first case to be referred to the new court was that of my two wretched fishermen. Three years after I had begun my agitation and ten years after they had been convicted, their sentences were quashed. I do not believe blemishes in the American administration of justice could today be so remedied.

But our committee was able, nevertheless, out of the American prison scene, to extrapolate considerable helpful evidence to establish our thesis that no satisfactory regime could ever be found for long term maximum security prisoners concentrated in a fortress-type prison. The Alcatraz experience was usefully on our side, and the abandonment of that disastrous island prison, both on penal and financial grounds, and the successful dispersal of the inmates of Alcatraz throughout the American prisons reinforced our view.

The penal regime we were spelling out was, I realized, becoming dangerously liberal, for it could explode in our faces if the community believed we were out to pamper men: for a vengeful community the deprivation of liberty for twenty years or more was not enough punishment. Yet we even insisted upon considering the issue of conjugal visits, much to the consternation of the Home Office and, more strangely, to the equal consternation of the possible beneficiaries. These men were, for the most part, professional criminals, thoroughly committed to a life of crime, who had mixed freely among the criminal underworld, and most of them were physically tough and vigorous and under thirty-five years of age; they had committed homicide or near homicide in pursuance of robberies and were violent and ruthless. Most of their crimes were ambitious and daring: jewel thefts and massive wage snatches were part of their way of life. Yet these desperadoes, including some of the train robbers, beneath their bravado, quivered like jellies when one discussed with them the possibility of conjugal visits.

It is not easy to discuss sex, within a prison environment, with an inmate. Apart from the obvious difficulty that the prisoner discerns speedily the sexual viewpoint of the enquirer, and so gives distorted but acceptable replies, there is also the danger that genuine confidences in this domain can become a sort of sexual complicity between the subject and the investigator. The complicity can be experienced as embarrassment or pleasure and, in either event, the confidences may bear little relation to reality. The investigation, insensitively conducted, can indeed falsify its object, and I fear initially, unaware upon what dangerous ground I was treading, I proceeded most clumsily.

I was, therefore, taken aback to find that most of these men proffered to me all the arguments against conjugal visits that I had heard less skilfully assembled by their gaolers. All the practical difficulties of arranging conjugal visits in conditions that combined security with decency were elaborated upon to me by these prim thugs: and they were certainly not slow to damp down my liberal reforming zeal by pointing out the consequences of many fatherless children likely to be born. But the tension I sensed when the matter was broached, and their eagerness to shift the conversation to other minor grievances, when seen as a recurring pattern, put me on guard and eventually gave me more insight into their problem.

I was, in fact, cheating, and they did not like it. The rules of the game were well understood by them and the prison authorities, and I was not observing well established regulations. A conspiracy existed between gaoler and gaoled: the prisoner was reduced to his desired level of a prepubertal child and, in return, he received tranquillity. The pretence that it was his confinement, not his fear, that prevented an adult sexual attitude was, under no circumstances, to be commented on. While in the maximum security blocks, with their walls covered with pin-ups, these gangsters swaggered and boasted of their past criminality; they had the excuse that only the prison walls prevented them from being great lovers. The truth was otherwise: the overwhelming majority of them had no regular relationship with any woman at the time of their arrest.

In the prisons they were back in childhood: even as, when infants, the father was the law imposing his will upon them, so now an adult, on the occasion of his transgressing, was subject to an all-powerful authority. And they were accepting their quiescent sexuality with relief, for these were flawed men. All of us must, after puberty, break through parental authority to become sexually mature; but to achieve such adulthood means a revolt against the father.

We rebel successfully only if we can do this without excessive fear: but these were men who feared freedom. They yearned to shelter behind an authority, behind their prison walls, renouncing their maleness in return for protection even as they had, out of terror, subjugated themselves to parental authority. For all these killers and brutes came from rejecting, disordered and deprived homes, and these miserable men had received no love to temper the fear all must overcome to replace our own fathers. It was not surprising that the talk of conjugal relations disturbed them: they knew it was not sex of which we spoke, but of the constrained freedom of adulthood limited by obligations of family, friends, work and society and this was a type of freedom which frightened them out of their wits.

They wanted to be left to their childish sexual activities. As the French psychoanalyst Lavie had said of onanism among prisoners:

Masturbation will come into its own again, and being considered a compensation it will be laden with less guilt and be regarded as less defiling in spite of the adult age. An imaginary dimension of the woman will be evoked in which she will appear infinitely more satisfying than in reality, the more so because there is no question of her accessibility or her inaccessibility either. This means that the gap between the dream and the reality no longer brings the virility of the man into question, for he no longer feels responsible for the poverty of his sexual life in comparison with the richness of his imagination. Masturbation, therefore, is all that remains licit.

But understanding the predicament of these heroes, although compelling caution, was not to deter us from stressing in our report that the aim of a prison should be to help a man to mature, and not to reinforce and encourage regression. We of course had no illusions that our cautious recommendations, when published, would escape the fate of headlines. The combination of sex and prison in one headline is irresistible to sub-editors, but at least we were to succeed in wresting out of the prison authorities a little more generosity in the granting of home leave to some prisoners under sentence.

I pondered upon how we could not only make such recommendations but also have them substantially accepted, and implemented. To thwart the Mountbatten Report, we were to affirm we could not discharge the assignment set us by the Home Secretary without examining the framework of security within the intended fortress-like prison in which all maximum security prisoners were to be concentrated; and that, as a result of our examination, we were to assert that no satisfactory regime could possibly be established within such a prison and would proffer the alternative of these lifetime prisoners being diverted to live with hundreds of other prisoners in three or four prisons, where a liberal regime could be introduced provided it was accompanied by a high degree of perimeter security.

But I knew that the community and the House of Commons would reject the real fact that insofar as prison security can be achieved at all it can come only from a regime that fosters good relationships between prisoners and an anticipatory prison staff. The public would want to know far more about the physical perimeter security: and I came to the conclusion that public anxiety about security would have to be allayed by some tangible and emphatic innovation, if we were to succeed in our aim of dispersing these Category A prisoners into liberal prisons rather than concentrating them into an oppressive fortress that would cast a shadow over our whole prison system.

I cynically decided, therefore, to embark upon a diversionary tactic: to shift attention from the real issue of dispersal or concentration to another issue which would rouse the hostility of all the liberals, and place me on the side of the devils. It would provoke great controversy and, by riveting attention upon an irrelevancy, enable our sabotage of the main Mountbatten proposal to go unnoticed amidst the clamour. I put to my committee colleagues that perimeter security should be enforced by the use of guns.

There were, of course, strong arguments for this to be done: we had received evidence which made it quite clear that at least one attempt by outside members of a gang to rescue prisoners, involving the use of a helicopter, had been contemplated. Although efforts from outside to 'spring' a prisoner are almost unknown in America, there is a different sociology of crime in Britain as the classic escapes of the train robbers Wilson and Biggs revealed. Yet in the Federal Prison system in America the observation towers on prison perimeters are manned by armed officers, and there can be no doubt that confidence by prison officers in perimeter security does make possible a more relaxed regime within the walls. It was arguments such as these that persuaded Radzinowicz and the Bishop of Exeter to concur in the need for armed tower watchers: and I would acquit them entirely of my political deviousness. I was pleased, however, to find that the kind psychiatrist who was the fourth member of our committee, refused to go along with us, and I knew he could be relied upon to write a fierce minority report against the use of guns that would precipitate the storm I wished to burst. For I knew there would be an articulate minority who would declare that my proposal would pander to the public's fantasy image of the criminal, as in a sense we had represented him as someone who could justifiably be gunned down and thus as someone more dangerous, more unworthy, and more deserving of society's aggressive condemnation. Radzinowicz, the Bishop and I would be dubbed as toughies: and indeed it was not long before leaks appeared in the press stigmatizing me as gun-mad.

It was an easy martyrdom to endure, for I knew that only by a compensating show of toughness would our real aims be achieved. The full Advisory Committee of the Penal Council, on receiving our report, divided almost down the middle on the silly issue of guns, with the present Lord Chief Justice supporting us and this was not surprising for in August of 1972 he was to tell a *Times* interviewer 'I love guns'. And most of my friends in the committee fortunately opposed me. Almost the whole Council, however, agreed on dispersal and rejected Mountbatten. I was even more shamelessly pleased with my misbehaviour when I saw the Press concurring in our view of dispersal, and, with the ambivalent Prison Officers' Association, demurring against our reactionary plea for guns. The Home Secretary, by now Jim Callaghan, ever with sensitive antennae to majority opinion, picked up the mood and with the approval of Parliament, accepted most of our report, except the guns. Not for the first time in politics, wickedness triumphed. Painfully slowly, but nevertheless in accord with our recommendations, the grim temporary maximum security blocks are now being closed down and their inmates dispersed to new prisons like Albany and Long Martin where, hopefully, if reformers are vigilant, our recommended liberal regimes can be implemented no less effectively than our security suggestions. Mountbatten's fury that his plan was rejected was evidently boundless: even four years later, at a conference in 1971, in a highly publicized attempt to re-write history, he was still attacking the Radzinowicz Report and seeking to minimize his earlier obsession with security. In subsequent public exchanges with him I bluntly accused him of responsibility for putting back penal reform in this country by a decade. Doubtless Mountbatten's arrogance is his strength: he clearly takes unkindly to his views not only being questioned but rejected.

But I would not exaggerate his defeat or my victory. Winston Churchill once said a country's civilization could be judged by the way it treats its prisoners, and by that standard we are almost barbarous. But this little triumph taught me once again to resist, in mad seasons, the temptation to accept defeat. It was the temptation yielded to by a man upon whose fate I have oft times pondered, Sir Samuel Romilly, the greatest lawyer reformer in the Commons in the nineteenth century.

No-one understood better than he that if the criminal law was ever going to be administered with humanity in this country, the key lay in reducing the number of offences that attracted the death sentence. Yet, after ten years of unstinting work, all he apparently succeeded in doing was to persuade Parliament that it should no longer be an offence punishable by death to pick pockets or to steal from bleaching grounds. All his manifold efforts did not in his lifetime reduce further the sentences of more than two hundred offences for which death remained the penalty. Despite the acclamations he was receiving from many towards the end of his life, his legislative successes were painfully few: and when personal tragedy supervened he lacked the type of success which was alone meaningful to him and that perhaps could have shored him up, and he could fight no longer.

Romilly, it is true, was unfortunate in his rejecting mother who, after his birth, became an invalid and, on her recovery, remained affectionless to her son who yearned for her. He was in her thralldom and could not marry until she died, over eighty, and he had already passed his fortieth birthday. When his wife, at forty-five, died, the primal situation was evoked. He could not tolerate his wife leaving him as had his mother, and rejected and dejected, the man who hated capital punishment and had condemned the guillotine, within hours of his wife's death, cut his own throat. Yet within a comparatively short time of his suicide, so much for which he had so rationally and eloquently pleaded came about.

Private Members, if they wish to die from natural causes, should learn the lesson. We do not need to echo Heath's maniacal declamation that he was elected to change the course of British history; but, with detachment, stoically we must strive to see ourselves only as part of an historical process, and never interpret our defeats as wounds to our unimportant personal narcissism. We must reconcile ourselves to our inevitable graves and, looking at our children, dare to hope that perhaps we shall have some little posthumous success.

BOOK II

Tryst with Eros

VIII

It was not long after my arrival in the House that I became aware of Richard Crossman's unrelaxed parental attitudes. When the House rises for Christmas or the summer vacation, the members do not, after the final late night vote, rush off: in an end of term spirit, in the members' lobby, they linger and among the banal statuary of Churchill, Lloyd George and other dead Prime Ministers, amidst a hubbub of gossip, last minute arrangements and partings are sorted out. I was in a small knot of members that included Richard Crossman: he said he was off abroad with his wife. Since I was aware that very recently she had delivered a baby, without malice I responded by asking if the child was going along too. He was enraged, fiercely interpreting my casual query as a reproach corroborating his guilt over his intended temporary desertion. He acknowledges he is a bully, albeit an intellectual one. And I am not slow to wrath, so I retorted that he was talking like a man brought up by a nanny and not by his mother. Although I did not know it at the time, this was a true account of his upbringing and inevitably my remark added much fuel to the fire. I observed with pleasure many years later that one of the reasons he publicly proffered for leaving the front bench after the 1970 Labour defeat was his need to give more time to his young children; but he did not relish my robust and no doubt impertinent expression of views on such needs years before.

He was a man always at war with his own father. He has said that even now, if he could meet his father again after more than thirty years, the conflict would start again. In fact the conflict, although it has been internalized, has never ceased, and certainly did not end with his father's death.

The older Crossman was an obsessional and able Chancery Judge: his passions were strong and temptations inordinate, for he lived in constant fear that one of his family would be involved in litigation or scandal: he would lie awake if his children were out late, his inflamed imagination conjuring up situations in which they would become hopelessly involved in breach of promise actions. Such masked jealousy of and hostility to his young sons could not leave them unscathed: and Dick, fated in any event as a second son to the probability of rebellion, so over-reacted that Attlee, a friend of the Judge, carried his disapproval of Dick as a youngster so far that he impugned Wilson's judgment in ever appointing Dick as a Minister. The father was a conservative: so the son was a socialist. The older Crossman was an unquestioning Christian: the son today remains a belligerent secularist. The father loved the law and lawyers: it is difficult for Dick Crossman to be civil to any lawyer, and he never resists devaluing them. The father in terror of his own criminality removed himself to the branch of law which would guarantee he never saw or judged a criminal: his son, knowing his father's Achilles heel, threatened him that if forced to choose law as a profession he would become a criminal lawyer, upon which prospect the father in panic and despair encouraged Dick to become a don. The father was notorious among lawyers for his indecisiveness in his adjudications: the son is overdecisive, one decision quickly succeeding and oft times contradicting another. The father, by inheritance a comfortably-off man, preached thrift: his son enjoys earning well and spending freely. The father taught worldly success brought only unhappiness: the son has fought for his happiness on the path his father despised.

Dick Crossman's personal account of his father is a picture of a dragon: but Attlee and all the Bar who knew him attested to his attractiveness and charm. It is difficult not to believe that the image of the father presented by the son is overdrawn: and one's suspicions grow as we find the idealized picture Dick presents of his mother whom he affirms was really much cleverer, finer, more generous, more courageous and, forsooth, of better breeding too than her husband. It hardly needs to be added that Dick claims that his mother's married life was a life of long submission alien to the spirit of a woman who was really able, strong willed and passionate. Flugel long since pointed out how boys seek to come to terms with the agony of the preferential love of the mother for the father by portraying the marital relationship as a forced and reluctant one: and Flugel too has found the origins of the old myth within the story of St George and the dragon in the fantasy life of the boy who dreams of rescuing the enslaved woman from the predatory father dragon.

Dick Crossman, to the good fortune of the nation, has oft-times played St George tilting against the stale values of the Establishment with great effect: but he is not content to play one part. The bond between the attentive father who patiently coached his son in Latin to enable him to enter Winchester is by no means broken: and his identification with the father punctuates his thinking and conduct. Fluently and brilliantly the interior dialogue between father and son is carried on further in Dick's speeches, hectoring and arguments. He infuriates his parliamentary colleagues as he first devastatingly proceeds to proffer one argument and then no less urgently destroys it. The essentially schizoid mode of thinking which causes him to put two contrary views to a Parliament that, by the very nature of its party system insists upon bias and the black and white, arouses extraordinary hostility. He is unfairly dubbed double-Crossman simply because he find it difficult to be possessed of single mindedness.

His approach sometimes has droll consequences. When the question of allowing the proceedings of the House to be televised was in issue, a free vote was allowed to the members: but it was well known that the government wished to have the cameras introduced. It was not a vanity that I shared: in Solomon's temple of old the mystery of the holy of holies, which was of course empty, was much enhanced by forbidding all but the High Priest to enter, and there are lessons to be learned from that precedent. However, Dick Crossman was put up to manoeuvre the decision through, albeit it was intended with a neutrality towards the outcome, as befits a Leader of the House.

The terms of reference were fatal: faced with the opportunity of presenting two views, Dick commenced his speech with all the conservative arguments against change, and the Judge was in fine form. He persuaded not only the House, but also the son: by the time Dick came to present the reforming arguments he found he had out-argued himself. Despite the discreet work done for the government by the whips, by one vote the proposition was defeated and the House has ever since maintained its refusal. But it is to good Judge Crossman that we owe our freedom in the House from the prying television cameras.

Sometimes Crossman's unpredictability nevertheless has led to more positive results. And while he was Minister for Housing, Wales had an especial reason to be grateful to this highly intelligent ever-unresolved man.

An Englishman's home may be his castle: a Welshman's home is his fold. Freud more than once has reminded us that one of the first acts of civilization was the construction of a dwelling, and that the dwelling house was a substitute for the mother's womb, the first lodging, for which in all likelihood man still longs, and in which he was safe and felt at ease. The Welshman's frank and unashamed attachment to his Mam, which many an Englishman would regard as unmanly, makes it inevitable that there are special overtones in the relationship between a Welshman and his home. The loss of a mother, or the loss of a home, can in Wales unite a whole community.

When in the early summer of 1972 the shadow Secretary of State for Wales, George Thomas, lost his ninety-year-old mother, the chief Whip, Bob Mellish, was shocked to find that, despite an important three line whip being called, almost all the Welsh M.P.s without any hesitation abandoned the House for Wales for the funeral. In vain did I, as chairman of the Welsh Parliamentary Labour Party, seek to justify and explain their priorities and their departure to an irate chief Whip: there was too vast a gulf between the cultures of the London Irish and the Welsh valleys. There was no less a gulf between the nature of the election campaigns fought in Wales in the sixties and those fought in London. In South Wales there was almost only one issue: the demand that every leaseholder's home should be protected by giving him the right to purchase, at a reasonable price, the land upon which his house stood.

In Glamorgan and Monmouthshire a higher percentage of the population than in any other part of Britain own their own houses but, by an historical quirk, few own the freehold. Almost all their homes have been held under leases with small ground rents granted by the landlords and coal owners at a time of industrial expansion some eighty years ago for ninety-nine years. As the expiry date of the leaseholds approached, anxiety mounted. The leaseholders feared that their homes could soon be wrenched away or that they would, in order to remain in them, be forced to pay a ransom price to acquire their freehold. The behaviour of some of the big corporations who had over the years acquired the ground rents meant that in too many cases their fears were well founded. The leaseholders were certainly not reconciled to the argument that they knew, when they had purchased or inherited the home, that the tenure was not an indefinite one: and they were no less contemptuous of the argument that the sanctity of contract had to be maintained and that it would be a breach of the rule of law if, ninety-nine years after the contract had been entered into, the landlord should not now be able to obtain his agreed pound of flesh.

No-one was more sensitive to the anxieties of leaseholders than George Thomas. To the aging leasehold house of Wales, this bachelor displayed the same well publicized attachment, as, with his constituents' enthusiastic approval, he always showed to his ageing mother. And the resentment that, as a youngster, he must have felt when his beloved widowed mother married his feckless stepfather could have been no fiercer than that he displayed against the interfering parasitical authoritarian landlords who wished to snatch a South Wales home from its rightful possessor. For years by active and sustained campaigning he whipped up the apprehensiveness of Welsh leaseholders: no one could dispute, particu-

larly since he was not overburdened with much other distracting ideational content, that his considerable and old-style eloquence was directed
with remarkable effect to the one demand. Even Welsh Tory M.P.s who
had huge and hitherto impregnable majorities were to fall to the dynamism behind his insistence for leasehold enfranchisement. Unfortunately,
however, he did not excessively trouble himself with the manner of its
accomplishment, even although past legislative attempts had foundered
and at least one Royal Commission had inconclusively quarrelled over its
practicability. George, as he makes well known, is a fighter for the Lord,
and I felt he expected the deity and Harold Wilson, to whom he accorded
similar obeisances, to deal with the more sophisticated problem of
executing the promises he freely gave. We came to power without an idea
in our heads as to how the pledge was to be implemented.

As time went on I was dismayed, as were many of my Welsh colleagues,
that we were in danger of returning to our electorate empty handed: and
we vigorously pressed Harold Wilson for government action. In the end
an exasperated Dick Crossman, by now Housing Minister, pressurized by
Wilson but already overstretched in his attempts to implement rent
control promises given in the Labour manifesto, sent for me and for Sam
Silkin, one of the most able Silks in the House, whose constituency,
Dulwich, was also, by a particular circumstance, plagued with leasehold
problems. In front of a team of his top permanent officials he told us
gruffly that if we wanted to get a bill, since we were lawyers, we would
have to get on with it ourselves: his own officials could do no more than
they were doing. I was only too well aware that many of them for years
had provided Sir Keith Joseph, the former Tory Minister supervising
Welsh affairs, with all the reasons why enfranchisement could not and
should not be granted and that their present burden was yet another
excuse for inaction. Despite Dick's inevitable ambivalence in dealing with
us as lawyers, it was however clear he wanted to help: he offered Sam and
me a small secretariat, and access to all information already gathered and
available within the department, and any other help required. His subdued
officials remained almost silent as he put to us his unorthodox proposition
that, in effect, we metamorphoze ourselves into temporary unpaid civil
servants. I found the tough proposal unattractive. I had, however, no
alternative but to accept. Although I had sought to do so with caution, I
myself in Wales, during the elections, had been compelled to underwrite
some of George Thomas's promises. To tell the people of Wales again
that it was impossible to shape an equitable law that could bring them
relief would have made me feel, as a socialist lawyer, ashamed and
devalued.

For the afternoons of many months, therefore, with the occasional aid of some outside Labour lawyers, Sam and I struggled with the task. It was a labour of duty not love for me for I am no land lawyer: but Silkin was superb. Sometimes, however, it was necessary for me to restrain this staid lawyer, with a reputation for being on the right wing of the Labour Party, from excessively radical conclusions which at first sight appeared to me to be the presentation of obsessional perfectionist traits. As we wrestled with the complex leasehold problems I felt, however, that the caveats I occasionally had to enter against his masterful but too detailed schemes arose from what I regarded as his tendency to intellectualization, an over-valuation of thought processes that can occur amongst those Jung has delineated as introverted types. Such types can search for intellectual solutions for what are properly emotional problems. Their thought processes can become highly libidinized, and their predominant sphere of self expression is in the world of thought. This may make them splendid lawyers, but because ideas tend to become substituted for feelings, and intellectual values for emotional values, they can make imperfect politic-ians lacking facility to relate to others. Silkin's father, who was the architect of the Town and Country Planning Acts of Britain, despite his massive contribution in the 1945 Labour government, when he was not readopted in his slightly changed constituency in 1950, could not be found another seat and constituency parties rejected or avoided him as he failed to connect emotionally with them. Sam has many of the consider-able strengths of his father, and a few of his weaknesses.

Yet it was perhaps easy for me to work with Silkin: there was a cultural rapport between us, for his mother and mine were born in the Swansea valley and, as young girls belonging to almost the only Jewish families in the area, had commenced a friendship which lasted until his mother's death. In the end, largely due to Sam's ingenuity, we produced for the government, a practical and reforming departmental brief upon which the Leasehold Reform Act of 1967 was slavishly drawn. Sam Silkin certainly repaid in this work the debt his grandfather may have owed Wales when he had been generously received there as a refugee from the Russian pale. But it was from Crossman's essential irreverence toward established civil service procedures that the work had sprung, and he can have the full satisfaction of knowing that this was an Act, involving as it did a fundamental interference with the rights of contract, of which his father would have thoroughly disapproved.

Leo Abse at nine years of age.

(*Above*) Leo Abse with Michael Foot, Aneurin Bevan and George Thomas. (1955)

(*Below*) Leo Abse and the Bishop of Exeter. (1967)

Some members of the British Humanist Association. Seated: Brigid Brophy; standing, from left to right: Kingsley Martin, Leo Abse, Ludovic Kennedy, Lord Francis-Williams, Professor A. J. Ayer. (1967)

Mr and Mrs Leo Abse and Se

Mrs George McGovern. (1973)

'As a great reforming Government, Abse, we'd like to sponsor it, but we feel that acts committed in private should be dealt with by a Private Member's Bill.' Cartoon by Trog.

Leo Abse on Budget Day, 1969.

(*Above*) Leo Abse with his children and Mr and Mrs Roy Jenkins and their son

(*Below*) Leo Abse leading an anti-abortion demonstration at Manchester. (1973)

IX

The 1959–64 Parliament was overwhelmingly opposed to the recommendations of the Wolfenden Report urging that homosexual acts in private between adults should no longer be criminal offences. I had witnessed the reactions in the House on the one occasion, in 1960, prior to my attempt, when a move had been made to approve the proposals. I had concluded that there were inherent difficulties within the temperaments of Members barring the way to reform. The resistances I was to meet in the field of divorce reform came largely from pressure on Members from outside the House: the resistances against homosexual reform arose largely from the imperfectly resolved homosexual drives of some of the Members themselves.

Competitiveness in the House of Commons is incredibly intense: it has to exist side by side with loyalty to a Party or to a group. Naked jealousies run parallel with declarations of comradeship and of common objectives. The hostile wishes felt by those competing for acknowledgment and advancement are suspended but never extinguished, as, interdependently, they work together to obtain power for their Party. From time to time, usually on the excuse of differing policies, the hatreds overflow and internecine Party strife breaks out: the Labour Party has public brawls, the Conservatives have the nights of long knives, and the public then are shocked at the violence exposed by the professed comrades or the gentle gentlemen.

The surprise of the public would be less if they had a greater understanding of the compulsive drives which prompt these oscillations between brotherhood and fratricide. Edward Glover has stressed how sibling rivalry, giving rise to intense unconscious hostility, can later lead to a positive homosexual attachment to brother-substitutes. The banding together of men holding hands at the end of Party Conferences, singing *Auld Lang Syne*, after they have been savaging each other to their political depths for days, must be understood in the light of the mechanism to which Glover has brought attention.

Childhood impulses of jealousy derived from competition against rivals, usually with older brothers, for the mother's love, leads to hostile and aggressive attitudes towards those brothers which can reach the pitch of actual death wishes: but these dangerous impulses cannot maintain themselves. Under the influence of upbringing, with the awareness of his continued powerlessness, the boy's impulses yield to repression and undergo a transformation, so that the rivals of the earlier period become the first homosexual love objects. The process as Freud has explained is

a complete contrast to the development of persecutory paranoia, in which the person who has before been loved becomes the hated persecutor, whereas here the hated rivals are transformed into love objects. It represents too an exaggeration of the process which, according to my view, leads to the birth of social instincts in the individual. In both processes there is first the presence of jealous and hostile influences which cannot achieve satisfaction; and both the affectionate and social feelings of identification arise as reactive formations against the repressive aggressive impulses.

The repressed aggressive impulses of so many politicians are, however, so violent that the feelings of identification created with other members of their Party are not invariably powerful enough to contain them. The Parties break open and we witness the Bevan-Gaitskell or Powell-Heath struggles. Living in the House, plagued always with intrigue and rumours of intrigue, means that the more sensitive must ever be aware of the homosexual rivalries that express themselves in rationalizations about political policy.

With homosexual impulses inadequately desexualized and contained, any mention of a change of law meets resistance. There was too much uncertainty among too many in the Conservative Parliament. Permitting more freedom to homosexuals was interpreted as a personal threat: unknowingly they equated relaxation of the law with the relaxation of the control which they were anxious at all costs to preserve over their own repudiated feelings. It was fitting that repeatedly my opponents should have taken as their rallying cry the assertion that 'the floodgates would open' if the law were to be changed: for the flood they feared was the flood of their own desires, and the gates for whose security they were so concerned were really those of their own repressions.

I thought on my first attempt to calm their anxieties by putting forward a compromise measure which would give effect to some of the subsidiary recommendations of the Wolfenden Report but which made no attempt to implement the main one. Accordingly I introduced a Bill with three principal objects. First, to ensure that all prosecutions for offences between consenting adults in private were authorized by the Director of Public Prosecutions before they were launched; this was intended to act as some slight kerb on police enthusiasm and to impose some uniformity upon police practice. Secondly, to provide that prosecutions for offences of this kind must be commenced within twelve months of their commission; this was intended to minimize the likelihood of the prolonged blackmail of homosexual offenders. Thirdly, to make it obligatory for the courts to obtain a psychiatrist's report before sentencing a man who had been convicted for the first time, since attaining the age of seventeen, of a homosexual offence: this very modest proposal was intended to let a little of the light of understanding into the darkness of the judicial mind.

Nevertheless my private negotiations with the government, through Fletcher-Cooke, who was then Under Secretary of State at the Home Office, to accept this Bill, were of no avail. Fletcher-Cooke was wholly sympathetic but the figure of Lord Kilmuir, then Lord Chancellor, loomed in the background. He refused to sit at any Cabinet meeting where this 'filthy subject' would be discussed: such is the disgust and horror which some men need to express as their defence against admitting the existence of their own homosexual feelings. And Kilmuir's reactions were reflected in the mail which from then onwards poured upon me: with but thinly disguised delight my disapproving correspondents described in crude anatomical detail the homosexual acts which they professed so strongly to abhor.

With the government hostile, there was no difficulty in ensuring that my Bill was talked out. If, by chance, there were insufficient Tory back benchers present to kill the Bill, the hapless Fletcher-Cooke was there on the front bench ready to make a long speech to indicate why the government found my proposals unacceptable. It was ironic that, some few months after he had undertaken this distasteful task, he felt compelled to resign: a Borstal boy, on licence, was discovered committing a motoring offence, and it was revealed that he was driving Fletcher-Cooke's car and was living at his home. Fletcher-Cooke showed singular courage, braved the storm, insisted upon the innocence of his motives, and carried his constituency with him: but it proved to be the end of his political advancement.

My failure on this occasion was, however, not complete. The first of the objectives of my Bill was largely achieved. When, soon after, a new Director of Public Prosecutions was appointed, he requested Chief Constables to consult him before starting proceedings against those who had consented to homosexual acts in private, and this led to some discrimination and at least a little curb upon the excess of zeal of some Chief Constables. But, more important, the very defeat acted as a greater spur upon those wanting reform: and it kept the issue alive. The more it was talked about, the more the repressed material was levered into public consciousness, the more the tabu on discussion was weakened. When after the return in 1964 of a Labour government with a dangerously small majority I made another bid to bring the matter before the House, it was to be received still in a tense but undoubtedly less taut atmosphere than before: homosexuality needed no longer to be spoken about in sanctimonious whispers. And now, when I sought the leave of the House to introduce a Private Member's Bill, it was with the object of implementing all the main Wolfenden recommendations. My main protagonist, self-styled Victorian, Sir Cyril Osborne, encapsulated all the vociferous prejudices of my opponents, and it was he who led the attack upon my proposals.

I rather liked Osborne. He lived under the restraints of a rigid puritanical code, unselfconsciously elaborating his needed personal prohibitions into generalized prohibitions for all society. Even when I would find him at his worst, debating with me at a university on some aspect of the permissive society, wringing his hands, pleading and begging the students not to yield to the temptations he claimed I was to present to them, I still felt compassion for him. Such a severe conscience was, I have no doubt, to be traced to unusually strong repressions in infancy; and judging from a bizarre conversation I once had privately with him during one of our university visits, the curbs placed on his infantile masturbatory activities were so intimidating that he thereafter was compelled to protect himself from further danger by removing all temptation from the British scene. This was a formidable task, but such was his self-punishing strain of insecurity, that he was compelled to maintain his sexual repressions by forever preaching a public creed of self-control and self-discipline. But his capacity to cope with his own desires and to maintain self-mastery was uncertain: doubtful of his own control, he was incessantly controlling others. He was the active director of nine companies; and since his insecurity demanded daily evidence and reaffirmation of his importance, he was ceaselessly on his feet in the House, distracting himself and others from his internal war by didactically pontificating on industrial relations, on China, or whatever the issue of the day may have been, all to the accompaniment of jerky, rapid, almost desperate, movements. The battle he fought against the evils in society being a projection of his own repudiated sensuality, was, however, inevitably an uneven one: and the denied body hit back, and one coronary after another was to send him to his grave.

He was an isolated man in the Conservative Party, and this was certainly not only due to his humble origins and to the fact that he was very much a self-made man: there was a deficiency in the intensity of his feeling for other people, and this strangulation of affect, leaving him without sufficient warmth, meant there was a distance between him and his colleagues. But such men, as Ferenczi has pointed out, often value their capacity to produce words, and Osborne certainly was the most talkative of men. His orgiastic indulgence in language was an effort to heighten the affective intensity of his own emotionally impoverished life. When I pleaded with members in the 1964 Parliament, Osborne could not resist the opportunity to pour out his condemnations. But he opened the lockgates too far and, to an astonished House, the fears and anxieties that poured out became so extravagant, themselves so clothed in sensuous titillation, that their neurotic content could be seen even by the least perspicacious. I witnessed the scene as first the House became irritated, then amused and finally, as more and more of his repressed fantasies surfaced, seized with laughter. Many of the new intake of young Labour M.P.s came from the more relaxed world of university common rooms and were bringing their children up on Spock, and this droll apparition of yesterday's distorted fears was period burlesque: their amusement infected many others glad to be released from the tensions my pleading had already provoked, and their loud laughter was the explosion of the tabu. The press looked down upon a House convulsed with paroxysms of laughter. Manny Shinwell, then Chairman of the Parliamentary Party, was furious: he had stalked the tea rooms whipping in his Trade Union acolytes to defeat my attempt, making known, as ever, his contempt for the intellectuals who would bring disastrous opprobrium upon the Labour government soon to face an election. Such political jeremiads, of course, matched his prim temperament: it is quite extraordinary how many Jews who have lived in Scotland become overdetermined Calvinists. He intervened to beg Osborne to sit down and save the vote, but not even he could stop Osborne's torrent.

In the event, my supporters were narrowly defeated. Manny's opportunism was supported by Edward Heath and other bachelors who ostentatiously went into the No Lobby to demonstrate to their constituents their hostility to extending any relief to homosexuals. But the majority against the reformers was wafer-thin, and I knew that the bizarre and unpredictable events of that afternoon, well reported to a bemused nation the next day, meant that never again would homosexual law reformers be on the defensive in the Commons.

Meantime, the Earl of Arran had begun his educational campaign and had introduced in the House of Lords a reforming Bill which passed its second reading. The issue of course could never be finally decided in the Lords; peers do not face constituents. But the continuing affirmation of the lords and bishops, under Arran's prompting, of the need for reform was to play an important part in shaming the equivocating Commons into action. I was naturally soon in touch with this new unexpected and indefatigable ally: and although a disparate pair, we worked together in complete harmony.

For some time I could not understand Arran's persistence: he had no history of reforming zeal, and his views on many other matters I frequently found wilful and eccentric. He was certainly not possessed of the usual liberal syndrome and I could not unravel why this heterosexual man, lacking formed philosophy, should so relentlessly pursue this path. A man may be much more cocooned in the Lords than in the Commons, but to become a major protagonist in this cause was nevertheless to invite opprobrium: innuendo and insults had to be lived with, and the strain was keenly felt by Arran whom on more than one occasion during this time I had to visit at a clinic where he was very ill. His choice of role, so clearly distasteful to him, perplexed me until by chance, through my wife, I met a man who for many years had been the lover of Arran's older brother: then all was clear. This older brother, who over many years had received psychiatric aid, died tragically only a matter of days after becoming the Earl. Arran succeeded to the title: it must have brought him much guilt. But it brought him, too, the opportunity to make a massive and brave act of reparation. Arran's was a considerable contribution to making Britain a little more civilized, and, by his courage, was indeed to make a fitting memorial to his ill-fated brother.

With a new session came the good fortune that in the annual ballot for Private Member's Bills, Humphry Berkeley, then a Conservative M.P., had drawn a high place. It was reckless for a bachelor representing a marginal constituency to sponsor a homosexual reform Bill: but the very risk, I suspect, attracted Berkeley who has to live his public life amidst never ending tumult and controversy. He has arrogance, and the intellectual ability to match it, but has not learned that he is too old to continue to play the part of the *enfant terrible*. He has had his triumphs, and could no doubt claim that the democratization of the Tory leadership contests is among them. But the quarrels that have led him out of the Tory Party into the Labour Party and with which his tireless work in the U.N.A. are associated reveal a rare talent for provocation: he indeed suffers from the handicap of being a son of an M.P. He is certainly not the man whom I would choose to accompany for a skate on thin ice: and this measure of reform was just that.

Nevertheless no one could fault him in his steering of the second reading of the Bill through the House: the dangers, I felt, would come later. A Private Member has to coax and cajole his Bill through its committee and report stages; lacking official Party support and no enforceable whipping, he is entirely dependent on the goodwill and the relationships he is able to establish with his colleagues if the Bill is to be completed in the limited Private Members' time available. He must be ready to yield on inessentials and be firm on points of substance, but he must allow his opponents to believe they are winning a war when they have gained a little ground in a minor skirmish. He must never fall into the hands of a partisan lobby, and must maintain a constant and sensitive but non-manipulative relationship with all the press and TV communicators. He must maintain sufficient passion to mobilize his supporters, and constantly, at least formally, consult with them while presenting a front of reasonableness to doubters and opponents so as never provocatively and unreasonably to estrange them. Whether Berkeley's talents would have been overextended in such an exercise remains unproven. After the successful second reading the dissolution of Parliament was announced and the incomplete Bill fell. In the General Election of 1966 with his Labour opponent pointedly marrying in the midst of the campaign, Berkeley lost his seat, and the House lost a valuable member.

I returned to the House with a majority of 20,000. I was able to taunt my opponents and encourage the more pusillanimous of my colleagues by declaring that every time I introduced a sex Bill my majority increased. I disliked the suggestion that Berkeley was a victim of the Bill: it would spread fear amongst the vacillators. Although ultimately he cultivated this story, when we exchanged correspondence at the time and I commiserated with his loss, he wrote to me that, although in his view the Bill cost him a thousand votes, it had not cost him his seat which was in any event to be lost.

Whatever the circumstances in his constituency, I had always been aware that taking on controversial Bills impinging upon human relationships meant a re-doubling of constituency efforts. I was blessed with a political agent, Ray Morgan, a wise Girling's shop steward, who was my anchorman in the constituency and I had half a dozen Labour Party men and women living throughout the valley upon whom I could absolutely rely, and who always had direct communication to me. However perplexed they must have been in the early days of my activities, they stood loyally by me and contained any constituency murmurs. The constituency, pleased with my efforts on their behalf, far beyond those usually given by Members in big majority seats, at first indulged me in my law

reforming activities, regarding them as unimportant personal idiosyncrasies taking second place to my real interest in the local hospital. Later,
as the significance of my work became understood, my activists shared in
my victories: what I was doing related to other people, and there is no
part of the kingdom more than Wales where people are regarded with
greater wonder, curiosity, concern and understanding. Thus my base
was well secured when I returned to the Commons in 1966: and I was
now determined at an early stage of a new Parliament, when no electoral
considerations could be pleaded by the weak-kneed, once and for all to
dismantle our barbaric homosexual laws.

While Arran yet again started a Bill in the House of Lords, the Commons was at a disadvantage: because we had reassembled in March,
there was to be no ballot for Private Members' Bills and, therefore, no
opportunity to gain time for a Bill in the conventional manner. Nevertheless I was convinced that, with the new intake of Labour M.P.s I could
muster enough support to force the government to give me the time to
put through the measure. I therefore gave notice of my intention to
introduce a Bill in the Commons. Immediately, on his own initiative,
Roy Jenkins, then the Home Secretary, sent for me and assured me that
if I could gain a decisive vote when, under the ten-minute-rule procedure,
I was to ask leave to introduce the Bill, he would insist at Cabinet level
for government time to be given to me. He was to prove as good as his
word, and my friendship with the chief Whip John Silkin was to guarantee
that Jenkins's private undertaking to me was able to be fulfilled.

The government stance had to be one of neutrality: but Silkin's
assurance to me that, whatever procedural obstruction I was to meet,
provided I could maintain a decisive majority, he, by hook or by crook,
would find the parliamentary time, was to prove decisive. Silkin was the
most gentle, and probably the most successful, whip in Labour's history,
and the result of his regime meant that the Parliamentary Labour Party
would never again submit to the rigid martinet discipline which has
provoked so many unnecessary fissures. Silkin was an unusual whip:
he still has retained some stardust on his shoulders and his freedom from
cynicism, and his capacity to empathize with minority groups in the
Party, meant that by wooing and coaxing he was to succeed in maintaining
a unity that never could have been achieved by edict and threat. He was
to suffer the fate that so often falls upon bearers of bad tidings who insist
upon realism and will not yield to sycophancy. When he told Wilson that
no Industrial Relations Bill containing a penal clause would be accepted
by the Parliamentary Party, Wilson, foolishly and peremptorily, dismissed him. But these events were in the future, and in the earlier years

of the Labour government John Silkin was to give me unfailing assistance.

Nevertheless, even with good allies, in order to succeed the argument had to be presented in a form which violated my private beliefs; the dispute about means and ends is, alas, not as simple as is sometimes presented. I accept wholly the Freudian belief in the universality of bi-sexuality: but to have pleaded Freud would have alarmed too many in the House, insufficiently secure in their own heterosexuality to acknowledge their homosexual dispositions. Freud said:

By studying sexual excitations other than those that are manifestly displayed, it is found that all human beings are capable of making a homosexual object choice and have in fact made one in their unconscious. Psychoanalytical research is most decidedly opposed to any attempt at separating off homosexuals from the rest of mankind as a group of a special character.

But, of course, it was only by insisting that compassion was needed for a totally separate group, quite unlike the absolutely normal male males of the Commons, could I allay the anxiety and resistances that otherwise would have been provoked. Homosexuals had to be placed at a distance, suffering a distinctive and terrible fate so different from that enjoyed by Honourable Members blessed with normality, children and the joys of a secure family life. Because of their wealthy endowment, they could surely afford charity. To hint that the homosexual component in a man's nature plays a large part in helping him to understand and thus form a deep relationship with a woman, would have aroused discomfort: and to point out that the conduct of some of the philanderers in the House, compulsively chasing women, was determined by a ceaseless flight from their feelings for men, would have been disastrous. Some years later in 1971, during a Commons debate on a nullity Bill, I was able to introduce successfully, and in bolder terms, arguments which led to more financial protection being given to trans-sexuals who, after undergoing a surgical operation giving them an artificial vagina, had married. I said: 'Not all the human race can be neatly divided into two – and only two – separate compartments. Nature does not obey man-made laws and although this may be inconvenient to lawyers and legislators, we would be unjust and unfair if we persisted in continuing to believe that nature is not often shamelessly untidy.' But these were decidedly not the arguments to be used in 1966. Everything had to be done to contain not only the anxieties but the stifled fantasies of some of my colleagues. It was youth that my opponents were forever protecting from corruption: they felt the need to protect themselves from the yearnings, yielded to by the Greeks who were excited by the feminine qualities of boys, by their shy-ness and modesty and their need for protection and instruction. To disarm my opponents my Bill, therefore, had to contain heavy penalties against those seeking homosexual relations with those under twenty-one, a proposition which in turn aroused anger among supporters of the Homosexual Reform Society who considered twenty-one far too high an age: but I would not accommodate them, both because I was unconvinced they were right and because of tactical reasons.

The narcissistic element is so pronounced among some M.P.s that they are bound to fear its worst extravagance. The older men attracted to adolescents are those who, having passed through a phase of intense fixation to a woman, usually a mother, only leave this behind after they have identified themselves with a woman and taken themselves as a sexual object. They proceed in short from a narcissistic basis and look for a young man who resembles themselves and who they may love as their mothers loved them. Compulsive homosexuality of this kind, founded upon narcissism, could light up especially dangerously the self-loving M.P.s antagonistic to my Bill.

And besides, although not over-estimating the traumatic theories of homosexuality suggesting it can be precipitated by seduction, there is no doubt that many boys in their teens are able to work through a homo-sexual phase and attain heterosexuality. I doubt if the law could look with total indifference at the possibility that the wooing of such youngsters by older men could lead to some adolescents being permanently fixated and prematurely committed to live out their lives as homosexuals. Expediency and conviction, therefore, made me insist upon a twenty-one year age limit even though, on this clause, as on the clauses designed to prevent homosexual orgies and brothels, I was at loggerheads with the homo-sexual lobby who thought these clauses were so drawn as to be capable of much police abuse. But the legislator is inviting failure, or, worse, a disastrous piece of legislation if he becomes the puppet of any lobby, even one as sophisticated as the Homosexual Law Reform Society whose strength is dependent upon its blinkers: total vision would weaken the will of any organized lobby.

I was, however, not to eschew all psychological arguments in presenting my case, but the arguments were, perforce, highly selective and to that extent I acknowledge that my case was fraudulent; but one does one's best and hopes that in the process intellectual corruption can be avoided. I, for example, stressed that the absent or neglectful father could lead to little boys growing up lacking a father with whom to identify: and that instead of sending homosexuals to prison it would be wiser to mobilize social resources and have more male primary school masters and social workers assisting the children of the widowed and deserted. But in a

House where so many Tory M.P.s in particular had authoritarian fathers I was inhibited from stressing that another powerful motive urging towards homosexual objects could be the fear of the father: for fear of the stern father could exacerbate castration anxieties, and where there is a drive towards a narcissistic choice and a disinclination to tolerate the absence of a highly valued male organ in a love object, a clash of rivalries with a feared father can be avoided by renouncing all women. And the corollary that fathers should know how to love and be loving and not terrifying and remote would have fallen on much stony ground in the Commons.

In the event, after discriminating lobbying of M.P.s led by the persistent Anthony Grey of the Homosexual Law Reform Society, and a cautious plea by myself, the changed composition of the House enabled me to obtain leave to bring in the Bill. The vote, 244 to 100, was decisive, and Roy Jenkins obtained Cabinet approval to give me the time to have a second reading of the Bill, but I had no illusions that the battle was over. Andrew Roth, a discerning lobby correspondent, who regularly publishes a book of profiles of M.P.s, has recently commented in his introduction to his 1971 publication upon the extraordinary number of M.P.s whom he finds are mother's boys; and their presence in the House inevitably meant that at any moment a disastrous storm could break upon my head. There is a type of homosexuality that finds its psychical genesis in an intense attachment to a female person, mother or nanny, in the first period of childhood; and those who, while not practising homosexuals, remain, unconsciously, excessively fixated to the mnemic image of a mother or mother substitute, can react over-determinedly to a plea for a toleration to homosexuality, for they are ever fearful that they may yield to its attractions.

The excessive attachment to the mother can be evoked and encouraged by too much tenderness on the part of the mother herself and can be significantly reinforced by the small part played by the father during the boy's childhood. My conversations with some of my colleagues have often revealed to me how their fathers were pushed out of their proper place by mothers with masculine dispositions. Clearly a boy's passion for his mother dare not develop consciously beyond a certain point, and it must succumb to repression. But the repression is sometimes only achieved by putting himself in his mother's place, identifying with her, and taking his own person as a model in whose likeness he chooses the new objects of his love. M.P.s who, although not following this perilous course, have a life style which brought them dangerously near this path, had to be persuaded with much circumspection lest, otherwise, they protected themselves against my blandishments, and their repressed fears, by vigorous counter-attitudes.

As the important second reading debate approached, I felt increasing uneasiness. The opposition was inchoate, and inadequately organized; but its articulateness was no measure of its strength. The rumblings, dispersed, were too scattered, but real, and I did not know from which direction the storm might fall upon me. I wanted the opposition to focus its attack, to concentrate on a particular issue. Then, I could call upon my supporters, now over-confident, to mobilize, and either counter-attack or contain the objection. Providence came to my aid, and suddenly the National Maritime Board, representing the shipowners' and sea-farers' organizations, claimed to be alarmed by the effect the Bill would have on discipline in the Merchant Navy and made representations to Dick Taverne, then a junior Minister at the Home Office. Dick insisted the Bill was a private one over which he had no control and wisely directed them to me.

However prickly they may have found me, they little divined how warmly I welcomed their intervention. I realized it was an issue on which I could find a compromise: and in any event I could not take seriously their attempts to prevent buggery in the Merchant Navy. In practice, there were ships where it was tolerated and those where it was not, and men with homosexual dispositions rarely made the error of joining the wrong ship. No law would alter the prevailing practice, and even as they were making their representations, stressing that the safety of the ship would be endangered if seamen living in close communities could, with immunity, lapse into homosexual conduct and hence into violent dissent, I knew there were limits to which they could press me.

For they were embarrassed because the National Union of Seamen were in the course of negotiating a new Merchant Shipping Act free from some of the disciplinary codes that seamen had endured over long: and the Union certainly did not want to see their own efforts made ambiguous by demanding that severe penalties for homosexuality aboard must remain. I was more than conversant with the tensions caused by the existing disciplinary rules, for I had become much involved in them when I successfully defended during the Suez crisis a crew which had refused to sail out of Barry Docks with arms intended for troops on the Canal. I knew, therefore, that the unity of the seafaring organizations on the issue could be eroded. Nevertheless I played my negotiations with them long. I allowed the representations which were being made to leak to my oppon-ents who fell upon the fluent but extravagant case of the shipowners who were insisting that, if the prevailing legal sanctions against homosexual conduct were relaxed, the whole future recruitment of the British Merchant Navy was in danger.

The Press, learning of the battle, began with no discouragement from me, to speculate on the possible failure of my Bill on second reading. The temperature thus raised and my supporters thus rallied, when, at the second reading, I was able to hint at the possibility of a compromise formula being found, I could reassure the waverers and comfortably win the vote. With John Silkin's collusion, I was able to follow so speedily with a committee stage of the Bill, that my opponents were unprepared with the amendments that would otherwise have kept us debating for weeks. They made the error of assuming the seafaring issues would be prolonged and time would become available for them to debate their intended amendments later. But I had rapidly between the second reading and committee stage of the Bill reached an agreed compromise clause with the members of the National Maritime Board, and to the dismay of my opposition the agreed clause which, in limited circumstances and with limited penalties, retained homosexuality at sea as an offence was put through the committee in a matter of minutes: and since there were no other amendments to discuss the hazardous committee stage was over in an hour.

My tactics, and this particular ruse, enraged my frustrated opponents whose full fury was to be flung at me when the Bill reached its final report stage on the floor of the House. This attack came, unfortunately for me, at the moment of my maximum vulnerability. The Abortion Bill had been proceeding contemporaneously through the House and my onslaughts upon this bungling Bill had estranged many of those who had given support to my homosexual Bill. I was nearly impaled upon my own attempts to reshape the Abortion Bill: yielding to the political blackmail, I let it be known that I would lapse into silence on the abortion issue but the damage had been done. Lengthy and frequent speeches by my opponents meant that I had exhausted the time Silkin had secured for me by way of special morning sittings of the House. With the session drawing dangerously to its end, with now sadly depleted ranks behind me, and with an overgenerous Speaker permitting too many amendments to be debated, the final stage had to be taken right through the night.

Inevitably the opposition embarked upon a long filibuster. To close each debate on each amendment I had to obtain leave of the Speaker to move a closure, and then to have a minimum of a hundred M.P.s to join me in the Lobby to enforce the leave granted. Nine times during the long night, I went through the Lobbies, and on each occasion I had but a handful over the hundred required with me. It was not the arguments on each occasion which I had to counteract that caused me any difficulties: it was the knowledge that if one or two bored M.P.s went home I was totally undone and the Bill would be killed. When, after dawn had broken, the final vote was taken I had just 101 votes at my disposal. Then it only remained for Roy Jenkins as Home Secretary to congratulate me, saying the Bill I had put through was an important and civilizing measure. Quintin Hogg, then shadow Home Secretary, was more petulant. He was not going to join in any encomiums and grudgingly congratulated me on a Bill which he said was a small measure which would have very little effect on social life. His churlishness and devaluation were not surprising, not only because of his published eccentric views on homosexuality but perhaps because a skeleton was rattling in the family cupboard. Montgomery Hyde, the Conservative M.P. who was driven from his Belfast seat because of his support of reforming causes, has suggested that the rich philanthropist and founder of the Polytechnic, the Quintin Hogg who was Lord Hailsham's ancestor and namesake, became involved in a homosexual scandal which led to his early death, perhaps by suicide. But I was too emotionally drained to react to praise or blame. I took my car out of the Westminster Palace Yard where the gaslit lamps were still shining, and drove through the dawn up the Mall towards my St John's Wood home. My wife was in bed, still awake, anxiously awaiting me and my news: she took me into her arms. I needed her comfort. For nothing fails like success.

X

Early in April 1963 the Christian Churches of England and Wales issued
a statement, signed by their titular heads, which roundly condemned, as
an attack upon the basic understanding of marriage as a lifelong union, the
Divorce Bill I was then steering through Parliament. The *Times*, informing
me in advance of the contents of the statement, asked me whether I
appreciated that this was the first occasion in the ecclesiastical history of
Britain that, on a matter of doctrine, all the churches had combined: and
asked me for my comment. Intemperately, I replied that I was not surprised. It had taken a Jew to found the Christian churches and evidently
took another one to unite them. I indulged my anger: there are in
politics moments to accommodate but this was not one of them. This was
a time to stand up and fight.

I had, some months before, by good fortune, again drawn a place in the
annual ballot giving me the right to introduce a Private Member's Bill
and I had decided that the time was ripe for an attempt to reform the law
of divorce. As a lawyer I loathed the humbug and hypocrisy with which
the divorce law was replete. The insistence upon the doctrine of the
matrimonial offence, the reaffirmation and extension of which had been
the only method open to A. P. Herbert to reform, in 1938, the anachronistic law, was now bringing the courts into derision and the law into contempt. If a marriage had sadly broken down no release was possible unless
one at least of the parties had committed adultery, had been cruel, or had
deserted the other partner. Only incurable insanity suffered for five
continuous years enabled a marriage to be ended without an adjudication
of guilt and innocence. So, to end dead marriages, adultery had to be
committed or affected, the mutuality of partings had to be masked under
the pretence of desertion, and puffed-up allegations of sadistic conduct
had to be mounted to establish proof of cruelty. Divorce was granted as a
punishment for the vice of one spouse and a reward for the virtue of the
other.

Such an artificial law wrecked any hope of reconciliation between the
couple. The parties were uneasily forced into the conflict situation which
the law insisted on imposing upon them. Their chance of obtaining a

divorce depended upon their success in establishing one another's badness. Upon their extravagance and upon the skill of their advocates, condemned to act as scavengers first scraping together the worst obscenities of marital strife and then hurling them across the court room, depended their freedom. Accusations had to be made, and made in detail. Trivial incidents had to be inflated to their limit. And the doctrine of collusion made the situation still worse: so intent was the law upon maintaining a situation of conflict that it forbade the spouses to reach agreement on any aspect of their divorce proceedings. If the proceedings were begun or carried on by agreement between them, no divorce would be granted. So great was the risk of collusion that parties in dispute had often to be advised that they should neither see nor talk to one another. More, nothing should be said or done that could be interpreted as forgiveness: matrimonial offences were so heinous that the parties must never overlook the frailties of their spouses. To forgive might mean condonation of sin, and sin must attract unrelenting punishment. The law ensured that once the first step had been taken towards divorce everything conspired to inflame the feelings of the two spouses: inevitably the worst sufferers were the children.

Their parents were discouraged either from becoming reconciled, or from ending their marriages in a dignity that might help to mitigate the disruptive effects of the divorce upon the children. Meantime, too, husbands and wives, according to law guilty parties, who had parted from their original partners decades ago, and later set up permanent cohabiting unions into which some hundreds of thousands of children had been born, were left in a legal limbo. They could not regularize their later relationship if, out of spite, envy, neurosis, religious conviction, or pension preoccupations, the original partners refused to initiate a divorce. The original children of such marriages, in such an ambience, were made the estranged and vulnerable members of one-parent families, and the subsequent children of the illicit unions, possessed, like all children, of sensitive antennae, were too often brought up in an atmosphere of guilt, embarrassment and shame. It was not surprising that the churches, when I first introduced my Bill, decided to kill it by stealth not by an overt attack, for they well knew the existing divorce laws were indefensible and wished to avoid the opprobrium that their negative opposition was to attract.

In the long struggle to baulk my attempts at reform, they were, however, to find me a disconcerting opponent. They would like to have labelled me as a non-believer intent on easy divorce and lacking reverence for the family unit. But I proclaimed myself from the beginning an opponent of easy divorce, though a believer in rational divorce law: and the primary purpose of all the Divorce Bills with which I was associated was to seek, if it were possible, to buttress, for the sake of the family, any crumbling walls of a marriage and, if this were not possible, to create the conditions where a further stable family unit could be established.

I spring from a race commanded to multiply as the stars in the heaven and the sands by the sea. There was no ambivalence in my attitude to the institution of marriage: the advice given by that brilliant, noisy, neurotic Jew, Paul, however it was received by the Corinthians, was totally unacceptable to my ancestors. 'I say therefore to the unmarried and the widow, it is good for them if they abide even as I. But if they cannot contain, let them marry: for it is better to marry than to burn.' I did not grow up within a culture which proffered celibacy as an ideal. In Hebrew the word 'nefesh' means body and soul, and there is no fundamental cleavage between the two: the devaluation of and antagonism to the flesh was not part of my heritage, and the doctrine of original sin was not known to me in my childhood. Whatever the blemishes of the Jewish culture, it left me free from the sickly attitude of the Anglican, for ever conscience-stricken that the Church, in deference to State, had faltered and allowed doubt to enter the sacramental view of marriage. I did not have to justify sex by declaring God had entered into the marriage bed. In few cultures was divorce less restricted than among Jews: and in few cultures has family life been so essentially guarded. It was not only my rationalism that informed my attitude to the theologians who fell upon me: I had too the sustenance of a long tradition.

But the laws I wanted were those that would best sustain the modern family, the democratic family that is part of the larger achievement man has made in his move to the just society. It rests on a foundation of free personal choice by partners of equal status, and its basis is not legal constraint but personal affection; responsible and planned parenthood is expected of it and, within its comforting but not overprotective embrace, children enjoy a high status and parental concern and involvement. It is the family where decision-making is shared, and parental authoritarianism neither wanted nor enforced; where old repressive tyrannies have been replaced by open discussion and sensitivity to the needs of all its members; and where the greatest single need, to give a model for development of the child, is not shirked by the parent. It lacks rigidity but the purpose of its elasticity is not to respond to the demands of ever changing technology: it is, rather, part of its elan, the libidinal liberation from the obsessional chains of yesteryear. The making of the modern family has been part of the making of the new society; it is, as the sociologist Ronald

Fletcher has stressed, the institutional enactment of the achievement of a new, principled, democratic industrialized society. The legislature has the duty to provide laws which nurture not strangle such a proud creation. My Bill was a hesitant attempt at such fertilization. It included several provisions designed to mitigate the destructive effects of the old law and to foster reconciliation. One provision enabled the quarrelling husband and wife to come together and agree the terms relating to maintenance and to the custody and support for children without falling foul of the rule against collusion. I wanted the parties, instead of being encouraged to entomb themselves and refuse all communication, to come out of themselves, to have some incentive to meet and discuss their situation: it was not so much that I believed many would find discussion could lead to a renewed awareness of mutual need and affection, but rather because it could serve, for some, a therapeutic need, to assist in overcoming the trauma of a divorce. I proposed, too, that estranged parties one of whom had committed adultery or had been said to be cruel or to have deserted the other, could come together for a short trial period without prejudicing, if the attempt at reconciliation failed, the right to proceed with a divorce. Both these clauses were to reach the statute book: and both of them, as I was well aware, were eroding the doctrine of the matrimonial offence. They weakened the insistence of the existing law that divorce could issue only out of uninterrupted conflict between offended and offender. They obliquely recognized that divorces arose out of disharmony between two adult human beings, neither of whom was the personification of evil and both of whom would benefit from a rational discussion of the mutual problems which confronted them.

The Christians in the House were in difficulty in opposing the granting of such charity to unhappy couples: but their wrath against another proposition within my Bill, that in some circumstances, when spouses had been apart for at least seven years either party could obtain a divorce, knew no bounds. This abandonment of the innocent-guilty equation was sensed immediately as giving legal acknowledgement that the basic sentiments of an old social order were irrevocably disrupted.

Not all my opponents were perhaps aware of the basic assumption of Marx, Hobhouse, Durkheim and Weber that man was crucially distinguishable from other animal species by his purposive moral nature: and that man's establishment of values was seen to be the core of both the process of institutionalization and the ordering of the experience and behaviour of the individual which took the socio-psychological form of 'sentiments'. But what they did grasp was that morals, in the forms of sentiments and sanctions, lay at the heart of social institutions: that society was essentially a moral matter, and that I wanted the law to announce that the old decaying morality could no longer be reinforced and strengthened by the regular repetition of ritual practice and mythical doctrine. Parliament in 1697 had, by passing a Private Member's Bill giving the Earl of Macclesfield an absolute divorce from the Countess, established its authority in the matter of divorce and removed the jurisdiction from the prerogative of the Church: but, if it had diminished the Protestant Church authority, it retained its essential Christian sentiments. These sentiments my opponents correctly assessed were being challenged.

At first I was unaware that a secret all-Party cabal of church and chapel members had been formed to kill the Bill. On the Tory side it was led by van Straubenzee, later a Minister of State, who became the voice of the bishops; and from the Labour benches, Eric Fletcher, later an undistinguished deputy speaker, now in the Lords, a low churchman who co-ordinated opposition on the opposition benches. Both Straubenzee and Fletcher were highly intelligent men, the one incredibly pompous and the other infinitely dreary. Catholic members were also within the clandestine group but it was the Anglicans who took the initiative. The Catholic Church had a little more confidence in its position: since marriage was a sacrament, it was immutable and no man-made laws, however shaped, could end a marriage. But the Church of England had more dubious foundations, and the shadow of Henry VIII loomed over it. Divorce made the Church of England restless and over-nervous: it could not view any changes in the law with equanimity.

Fletcher manoeuvred himself to be the front bench spokesman on our opposition benches for the second reading of the Bill. The convention is that such an appointed Party spokesman, when a non-Party measure is to be debated, is there to watch, to protect the Party should any Party issue unexpectedly arise, and to intervene, if at all, with a short speech of determinedly benevolent neutrality towards the measure introduced by his Party colleague. But Fletcher overplayed his hand: there was an excess of condemnation and inadequate praise in his lengthy intervention. He illuminated the tactics my opponents were adopting and alerted me to the existence of the cabal. The Bill had attracted considerable and sympathetic press and public attention and to avoid an open confrontation, which could bring disrepute upon the churches, it had evidently been decided to let the Bill pass its second reading. Then when it was passing through its committee stages, less publicized, away from the floor of the House of Commons, when its details rather than its principles would be laboriously scrutinized, clause by clause, they would solicitously castrate my measure.

The appointment of members of the standing committee charged with the task of examining the Bill is carried out in theory by a small committee of selection: in practice it is usually arranged by the Party whips submitting names to the chairman of the selection committee who formalizes the appointments. It is customary that the opposition front bench observer in a Private Member's Bill is automatically selected to serve on the committee, but even before the committee had been appointed, Fletcher, anticipating his appointment, over-anxious, drafted and placed down on the order paper hostile amendments to the major clauses. His action exposed his intentions and fortunately angered among others the redoubtable Charles Pannell, an elderly tough trade unionist Member, saved only by lack of a formal education from the fate of becoming a brilliant lawyer or a disputatious historian. Like all trade unionists, Charles knew the rule books and Fletcher was not observing them: more he was avoiding them in order to penalize libertarian doctrines which, unusually for a traditional trade unionist, Pannell robustly, if somewhat indiscriminately, supports. At the weekly meeting of the Parliamentary Labour Party, with Pannell's friend and neighbouring constituency colleague Hugh Gaitskell in the chair, Pannell tore Fletcher apart. I naturally poured petrol on the fire, and Fletcher's apologia was ill-received. Bowden, the chief Whip, responding to the Party mood, vetoed Fletcher's membership of the committee and, leaning backwards to appease us, told me to submit to him the list of Labour Party Members I wished to have on the committee promising he would seek to have them appointed. The result of Fletcher's clumsiness was that I had a more favourable committee than I had dared to anticipate.

I had with care chosen a disproportionate number of Welsh colleagues to join me on the committee. If I was to face a cabal then no-one could cope better with them than a Welsh team: if the Welsh are not a nation, they are certainly a conspiracy. Confronted by a group dominated by High Church English ex-public schoolboys, by the hated 'crachach', they would meet the challenge with all the deftness of a Welsh three-quarter line fighting the English in the final game for the triple Crown. In the guerilla war that was to break out, the creatures of the prelates, whipped by van Straubenzee, found every stratagem was to be met by the cunning of a colonial people who had learned how to survive their conquerors. My allies were men like Ness Edwards, the Member for Caerphilly, a former Postmaster General, and Iorrie Thomas, the Member for Rhondda, who retained all their extravagant hatred of the chapel, against whose narrow restrictions they had rebelled in their adolescence. They were former miners who in their youth had been

chosen by their pit colleagues to be trained, along with others like Nye
Bevan, at the union-endowed Labour College where they were indoc-
trinated into a romantic amalgam of anti-religious syndicalism and neo-
Marxism. Iorrie Thomas, still acting out his last years against the repressions of the primitive Welsh non-conformity of the early part of the
century, squandered his rare eloquence mocking at the chapels' attitude
to drink, to gambling, to the Sunday opening of cinemas – all yesterday's
irrelevant battles. Only a battle with the chapels brought him to life: for
the rest indolence drowned his talent. But my committee was tailor-made
to his needs, the churchmen corroborating and feeding all his paranoia.
Welshmen who had endured the depression had no tolerance for the
unctuous pleas for the need at all costs to maintain the unity of family life.
The operation of the means test during the 1930s had played havoc in
Welsh working class families, compelling sons and daughters to live away
from parents if their unemployed father was to receive his dole pittance:
and lack of work had torn the families apart as the young and more
mobile were compelled to leave for Birmingham and Slough for employment. The silence and indifference of the established church is well
remembered by those of us who lived through those days.

Indeed the whole manner in which the politician churchmen advanced
their case on the committee was inflammatory: for they made explicit
what my allies already divined, that they were defending the bourgeois
ethic. They argued the fundamental sanctity of contract: and the marriage contract was equated with an important commercial agreement.
Calculated interest was put before a full humanity. The commitment of
the married parties lacked the deeper dimensions of emotional belonging:
it was limited solely to the terms of the contract. Association resting on
contractual definitions replaced the relationships of whole persons. The
parties to a marriage were traders and, having struck their bargains, the
law must be available to enforce ruthlessly the contractual obligations
into which they had entered. In all the circumstances, it was not surprising, with such arguments deployed over many committee sessions,
that towards the end of the committee stage my Bill remained almost as
pristine as my first draft.

Only the fag end of a committee meeting remained to be disposed of
before the Bill was to be sent back undented for the final report stage and
third reading by the full House of Commons. In despair the cabal plotted.
They correctly anticipated that only a handful of us would attend this
final committee meeting where there would be no votes and where the
chairman would just put the formal motion that the Bill now be reported
to the House of Commons, so that it could continue its progress. There

was, as far as I am aware, no precedent for an attempt to prevent a Bill being reported back to the House: but van Straubenzee had done his lawyer's homework and the plot was to allow only a few churchmen and Catholics to attend at the start of the committee, to lull us into a false security, and, then, when the chairman called for the Bill to be reported, the conspirators would at the last moment flood into the committee room and insist on dividing on the motion. If they carried the surprise vote, the Bill would irrevocably be buried alive, and with it the hopes of tens of thousands of men and women whose expectation of release from the bondage of dead marriages had been so raised. But almost every Welsh M.P. has an inbuilt seismograph recording the lightest of tremors at Westminster: and Iorrie Thomas could detect the smell of incense ten furlongs away. We learned of the stratagem at the last moment, rallied just enough of our troops, and with one vote in hand when Straubenzee, despite the plea of the chairman, challenged the further progress of the Bill, we scraped home. The cabal was baulked: any hope they had that the Churches, as such, could be kept out of the struggle, acquitted of direct responsibility for slaying the Bill, had gone. The cabal members ran to their cardinals and archbishops bringing them the grievous tidings that only open intervention could stop the Bill. Three days later came the historical condemnation signed jointly by the Archbishop of Canterbury, the Catholic Archbishop Heenan, the head of the Free Church Council, and in order to ensure the maximum degree of embarrassment for the Welsh members, by the Archbishop of Wales. The skirmishing was over and the open war commenced.

Soothsayers and astrologers may perchance be more realistic than many politicians and churchmen: the daemonic subterranean forces at work within our society can sweep aside with terrifying speed the frail architecture of legislators and political bishops, all so pretentiously affecting to construct our destiny. In April of 1963, with a Conservative government securely in power, the Churches mobilized the whole Establishment to obliterate my Bill. I had no party, no organization, no extant pressure group on my side: I had a hostile President of the Divorce Court, an unsympathetic Lord Chancellor, and, with a general election looming up in the following year, a shadow cabinet anxious to avoid any issue that would estrange the religious susceptibilities of the electorate, particularly those of the working class Catholic communities. Yet by July 1963 after three months, it was the Archbishop of Canterbury who was sounding the retreat, announcing in the House of Lords ambivalently and with evident reluctance, the formation under the chairmanship of the Bishop of Exeter of a Church of England Committee to review the law of England relating to divorce, a committee that was to recommend the abandonment of the position held by the Church for centuries. It would be arrogant to claim all this came about as a result of three further months' campaigning on my part. There were clearly powerful but less easily definable forces working on my side.

I suspect that a moment had come in Britain when the societal demand upon the family had become excessively oppressive. Familial withdrawal from society always constitutes a threat to the advantages held by collectivities which are highly organized and integrated. The American sociologist Talcott Parsons has long since pointed out that the actual prevention of incest is less important than the fact that it enforces 'marrying out': the tabu bars the nuclear family from becoming a completed autonomous collectivity and blocks the withdrawal of libidinal urges from those larger co-ordinated aggregates, the maintenance of which gives us the possibility of a civilized life. But man's libido is essentially finite: the libidinal diffusion, the social cement binding the wider community together, cannot be infinitely extended. At some point, the family or the dyadic (the couple) husband-wife union can tolerate no further its energic impoverishment. There is only one source of sustenance and the democratic family and the egalitarian dyad demands far more and will yield far less to society than did yesterday's authoritarian family. The arid structured demands of a traditional society could survive on a dry soil: but the more exotic emotionally released contemporary family unit needs instant recharging, and is resentful if too much libidinal energy is drained away by the community. Libidinal diffusion can, as the American sociologist Professor Slater points out, be directly equated 'with the de-eroticizing of the sexual life of the individual – the transformation of hedonistic activity into utilitarian activity'. It is impossible to minimize the strangulation of sex, as has been done within the modern family, without the balance between the intimate family and suprafamilial collectivities being seriously disturbed.

Slater has stressed that the real focal point of the conflict between dyadic intimacy and societal allegiances is the marital relationship: the marriage ceremony is, as he has elegantly shown, an intrusion ritual. There is a societal invasion of the free and exclusive intimacy of the couple: as the marriage approaches there is a rapid acceleration of the involvement of the families of the couple in their relationship, often even to the point where concern is shown about the social appropriateness of the wife for the organizational setting in which the husband must move. The marriage guests must be invited, attendants chosen and gifts for the attendants selected. 'The ceremony,' Slater has written, 'has the effect of concentrating the attention of both individuals on every other affectional tie either one has ever contracted.' The responsibility for the wedding rests with others: they are 'given' a marriage and the bride is 'given away'. The ceremony and all that surrounds it is designed to emphasize extra-dyadic personal obligations and societal dependence. It is true they are permitted a honeymoon, a socially sanctioned dyadic withdrawal free entirely from the obligations of a collective life: but it is not permitted for long. They must soon return to society, put away childish things, and 'the honeymoon is over'.

The social anxiety displayed over the marriage ceremonial to which Slater has drawn attention, is similarly apparent in restrictive divorce laws. Any suggestion that marriage partners should privately be able to conclude that their marriage has failed and, by mutual consent, without restriction, be permitted by themselves to agree the terms upon which the marriage should be ended, has been interpreted as a presumptuous and dangerous dyadic threat to the community. The community has insisted that a husband or wife can come as a supplicant, petitioning society for a divorce: but society will lay down the conditions upon which it can be granted, if at all; and certainly it is to be granted only if one party can be outlawed, stigmatized as guilty, and openly held up to contempt. As recently as the summer of 1971, after all the strides we have meantime made in our divorce laws, when I asked Lord Hailsham could not we now end the practice of permitting press publication of the fact of an individual's adultery or desertion when a marriage had been declared to be, by the courts, broken down, I received a dusty answer. The Lord Chancellor told me: 'The reading public is entitled to know the facts and form its own judgement. I am not prepared myself to argue whether such judgements as they do form are right or wrong. I personally believe that the general rule should be that proceedings in court should be public and published, and the inconvenience of the parties by being exposed to publicity must be secondary to the right of the public to know the facts.'

His hostility to any change, despite the clear benefits to children of marriages who now endure in the school playgrounds the taunts that inevitably follow when their mother's adultery or father's cruelty is emblazoned abroad, is not to be dismissed as sheer sadism: he is attempting on behalf of the old society to block a threatening dyadic withdrawal. The modern family and the old unjust society cannot live side by side: and those who overvalue the traditional society will idealize the roles of parents and children in the traditional family regime. Such idealizations mask the mutually destructive struggle for power within the traditional family and the result of the refusal to accord equal status to women, and respect to children. The modern British family, like all democratic institutions, has its own predicaments: but out of its soil real growth is possible. In 1963 it showed it possessed the vigour and courage to cut down the malevolent laws of a decaying society.

After the Churches' open condemnation, the communicators became aware of the importance of the issues raised by the Bill. On television and in articles I dramatized the problems: and above all else repeated and repeated the consequence of the existing divorce laws to the children of estranged and unmarried parents. Never in Britain have we had a wider section of the community taking with high seriousness and concern their obligation as parents: and to them I constantly appealed with calculation. Parliament is a stage and if you want to be heard you don't mumble or lecture. The electorate have a right to histrionics, panache and style: the bugles must blow and the flags and bunting fly. The grey politicians are not worth their money: they are paid to act, to give the great audience a tumultuous catharsis, and if the players lack the principle which alone vitalizes the performance, then they should be compelled to quit the stage. They have failed if, at the end of the show, democracy is given only two cheers, not four.

The Churches felt the need to bring in their allies. Jocelyn Simon, then President of the Divorce Court, usually so engaging but now evidently rattled, having failed in a private lunch at the Law Courts to dissuade me, quit his position of judicial impartiality and made a ferocious and highly publicized attack. Only a divorce lawyer overestimating the importance of his work could attribute such magic to the divorce decree. I mocked at the President's view that divorces wrecked marriages: by the time the public exchanges were complete the community had fully grasped that divorce as such should cause no lost sleep to anyone. Our social concern should be focused not upon the divorce but upon the marriage breakdown. Just as a death certificate records the death of the individual, so does a divorce only record the death of a marriage. Journalists and editorials were soon kindly quoting my comment that the President would believe death certificates caused death.

When John Heenan, later Cardinal Heenan, then Archbishop of Liverpool, joined in the fray, I was even more brutal: but my indiscretions were not impromptu. I knew that after the Churches had acted I could not, under a Tory government, put my Bill through Parliament: the Church of England was still the Conservative Party at prayer. It was to the country not to Parliament I was speaking; and although I knew it would take some years before the walls finally fell, this assault had to be fierce if the foundations were to be irrevocably weakened.

Heenan condemned the Bill in strange concupiscent language. The Bill was an attack on women: it would impose on them 'a new era of slavery'. Dr Heenan maintained: 'The unscrupulous man would use a whole series of young women to satisfy his pleasure, and when he tired of them would take a few years' rest before starting another adventure.' I hit back, even lower beneath the belt, making clear that however vivid such fantasies might be to the Archbishop, they told us more about the emotional problems of the professional celibate and his morality than they did about reality. Since at this stage I was to be sunk, I was determined to go down with guns blazing. Any fool can reap the harvest of victory: the art, as Dunkirk and de Gaulle in Algiers reveal, is to wrest triumph from defeat.

By the time the final report stage and third reading was due to be debated in the House, some of the more sensitive churchmen M.P.s were becoming concerned at the adverse criticism now heaping upon the Churches. On the eve of the debate Jeremy Bray, then Member for Middlesbrough, approached me with a compromise: if the seven year clause was dropped, I could have the rest of the Bill. I could do a deal with Jeremy Bray: some of his colleagues spoke to me as if they had a private line to God but he clearly limited his claim to a line to the Archbishop of Canterbury, and that was a far more important telephone number for me. I agreed to his suggestion: the truncated Bill would, as final legislation, still severely dent the doctrine of the matrimonial offence, my main target. But in my agreement with him I made it clear that I would publicly explain in the debate the reasons for the withdrawal of the seven year clause and I carefully refrained from giving any undertaking as to my attitude to the passage of the Bill when it left for the Lords. I had too many friends in the other chamber to let the curtain drop once the Bill had left the Commons.

In the event, in the Commons debate, I so indicted those who were compelling me under duress to wrench the main clause from my Bill, that, infuriated by my taunts and accusations, it was only by a hair's breadth that even the remains of my Bill obtained a final reading. But although my opponents had their pyrrhic victory on their day, I had the press on the next: and with a sympathetic Press picking up the outraged mood of much of the community, I rallied my forces in the Lords.

Eddie Shackleton willingly agreed to my request to take over the Bill in the upper Chamber: and, as he very professionally proceeded on his way, with no less relish Lord Silkin agreed to put down amendments seeking to place back the clause taken out in the Commons. The whole battle re-opened: but this time the Lord Bishops had no covering troops. They had to face the attack personally and, under withering fire, they retreated. When the time came for the Archbishop of Canterbury to ward off Silkin's amendment, to ensure its defeat and continuing controversy, he announced the formation of the Church of England Committee charged with reconsidering the attitude of the Church to the State divorce laws.

To everything there is a season . . . a time to plant and a time to pluck up that which is planted. There was now a need for a hiatus. I had played my part as a catalyst. Soon the historical forces would erupt and the enemy would be overwhelmed.

XI

Nearly three years later in July 1966 the Archbishop's Committee issued their report *Putting Asunder*. As Balak raged when Balaam, called in to curse the children of Israel, blessed them fulsomely, so did my opponents fulminate as, to their discomfort, they found the Church committee astonishingly declaring marriage breakdown to be the truest justification for divorce.

Never has there been published a more effective condemnation of the divorce doctrine of absolute matrimonial offences. But the committee's insistence that there should in future be no accusatory procedure, no guilty party and no innocent party, and that the breakdown of marriage should wholly replace the doctrine of the matrimonial offence, was not the usual zeal of the newly converted. In return for giving up the community's right to control marriages by condemnatory pronouncements of offences, in future candidates for divorce would be compelled to submit to a prolonged inquisition. A court hearing into a divorce would become an inquest: and only after a lengthy hearing, if the court was satisfied that the marriage was truly at an end, that no reconciliation was possible, that adequate financial provisions had been made for the dependent spouse and children, and that there was nothing in the conduct of the petitioner that would make it contrary to public interest, would a divorce be granted.

I did not mock this report. The candour with which the matrimonial offence was condemned meant that the theological apologia which for centuries had buttressed the doctrine was ended. The alternative solution proffered was so ramshackle that it would collapse under its own weight. It was demanding a revolution in the whole modus operandi of judges and lawyers, and the legal establishment is not given to such flightiness; it required an army of social workers to assist the tribunal in its probing enquiries and society would not pay for investigators when in any event it had wiser priorities; it meant above all the end of the existing uncontested undefended divorces and the community was in no mood to regard as tolerable the involuntary exposure of their personal intimacies, before a searching inquisition, as a precondition to divorce.

At this time, too, I was no longer involved in a lonely battle between the Churches and myself. A Labour government was in power supported by back benchers many of whom were young, intellectually able, and committed to social reform. The new Lord Chancellor, Gerald Gardiner, wanted the divorce laws radically altered, and the Law Commission, the instrument he had forged, was equipped to supply the researched reply to any conservative on either side of the House using technical or legal sophistries to block change.

Harold Wilson, in his account of the years of his premiership, apart from a reference to capital punishment, gives no account whatsoever of the major social reforms which took place while he happened to be Prime Minister; and to the Law Commission he devotes but a few lines. Yet the creation of the Law Commission, a new institution within the British Constitution to advise the Lord Chancellor on law reform will, when the dust has settled, probably be regarded as the most important lasting contribution made by the Labour governments of 1964–70. The Commission is an independent body of lawyers whose programme of work is agreed upon with the Lord Chancellor. Its reports may become the subject of government legislation or they may be adopted by back benchers and reach the statute book through the ballot procedure. Its creation was looked upon, initially, with suspicion by more conservative lawyers: and with jealousy by many parliamentarians, fearful that the body would usurp their functions by making social judgments. Fortunately Gerald Gardiner made an inspired choice by appointing one of our most distinguished judges, Leslie Scarman, as the first chairman. He is not only a great and courageous lawyer: he possesses wit, an exquisite tact and is the most formidable non-political politician in the land. His most extraordinary achievement is that he almost succeeded in concealing his talents, and those of the men surrounding him like Jim Gower, now Vice Chancellor of Southampton University, so that conceited, weak politicians and temporary Lord Chancellors can now deceive themselves into believing that the Law Commission is an anonymous body composed of servile civil servants.

It was to this body that, upon the publication of *Putting Asunder*, the Lord Chancellor referred the document for advice. Scarman's team within four months had produced a wide ranging commentary *The Field of Choice* which gently but irrebuttably made manifest all the weaknesses of the inquisitorial proposal urged by the Bishop of Exeter's committee: instead the Law Commission, willingly accepting the demolition of the doctrine of the matrimonial offence, put forward their alternative patterns for the legislature to consider, divorce by a period of separation, divorce by consent, and the breakdown of marriage, without inquest, linked by a period of separation.

Before the Law Commission had reported I had already started awakening the Commons to the need for renewed involvement in the issue: by obtaining the leave of the House to introduce a ten-minute rule Bill, albeit one not intended to reach the statute book, approving of divorce by either party after five years' separation, I made the Church and its committee aware of its weakness in the new liberal Parliament, gave encouragement to the Law Commission to proceed boldly and made publicly clear the issue was not necessarily going to be decided by bishops and lawyers. A debate in the Lords initiated by agreement between Dr Mortimer, the Lord Bishop of Exeter, and the Lord Chancellor exposed further the Church's impossible proposition: and with the Archbishop of Canterbury's approval the Law Commissioners and the Church committee began a series of meetings to seek a compromise solution: it was reached and finalized in July 1967. I was not without my lines of communication, and for my part, the neat and ingenious consensus reached was an acceptable one.

Breakdown of marriage should be the grounds on which a divorce is granted, and the old standard matrimonial offences remained not as offences, but as evidence of the breakdown. Divorce after separation of two years became available by mutual consent, and after five years' separation, subject to financial safeguards, divorce would be possible even against the wishes of one of the parties. With the established Church and secular reformers thus agreed, with the Law Commissioners engaged on the sophisticated task of drafting the Bill, with the Labour Cabinet via the Lord Chancellor at least silenced if not tacitly in support; with my friend John Silkin chief Whip in the Commons and my old ally Lord Shackleton now Leader of the Lords, the work of turning the consensus into legislation seemed a simple political task. All that appeared to be needed was that a sympathetic Member of Parliament should draw a place in the autumn annual ballot for Private Members' Bills and the work should be completed during 1968. When William Wilson, M.P. for Coventry, drew a place and agreed to act as sponsor of the Bill, the Divorce Law Reform Union was in high glee and this propagandist body which had been reactivated by the publisher Alistair Service, a charming political voyeur with considerable lobbying skill, arranged a celebration reception.

But I was in no mood to celebrate before the event, and I gave a chilling warning. I was intuitively aware that there were other restless forces at work. Attempting social legislation in a society in transition is a more complex and bewildering task than altering laws of a more stable community: the politician today is legislating on a moving staircase, and society had moved a long distance since 1963. The theological objections and anxieties had been overcome: but new anxieties were abroad. The relative status of male and female within the family has lost its old definitions: husband and wife no longer had their confident roles and women, having cut adrift from their old intolerable moorings, had a quest but no certain destination. All the floating suspended anxiety of women suffering a crisis of identity was, for two arduous parliamentary sessions, to rest, suffocatingly, upon the Divorce Bill.

So often, prominent women active in public life, in and out of the House, are at odds with their own womanhood. Their character disorders are of a special kind, distinguishable from those of their male colleagues, and frequently their drive, imperfectly sublimated, is extraordinarily vigorous and destructive. They are continuously in a state of protest: and although their protests, often directed against real evils, result in needed changes, the shrill persistence of some women politicians, their ceaseless and humourless challenges and their exaggerated impatient demands are absurdly disproportionate to the wrong they seek to command the House to remedy. They lambast the House; they demand of the House; they complain and sometimes whine; but surprisingly, they rarely woo the House. Their behaviour, it has been suggested, is the over-determined reaction of the culturally deprived: that the extra battle a woman has to reach the top politically leaves an ineradicable impress upon her. The argument is persuasive: but I doubt it. Whatever political Party they belong to, so many remain in rebellion although society has given them limitless esteem and acknowledgement: still they clamour, still one senses they remain sulking and unassuaged. Are they really rebelling against their destiny? And since anatomy is destiny, is Freud correct in his didactic assertion that the discovery that she is 'castrated' is a turning point in a girl's growth? Are many of our women politicians the little girls who refused to recognize the unwelcome fact that they lacked a penis and, defiantly rebellious, exaggerated their masculinity and remain clinging to their earlier masturbatory clitorial activity, albeit displaced into faintly disguised political forms?

There are those who protest that such an assessment arises out of the study of a special type of career woman who, in marked conflict and suffering from dysfunction, turned to psychoanalysts in a state of partial breakdown, and that although the clinician can best study human nature in conflict – because the very conflict delineates borderlines and clarifies the forces colliding on those borders – the study reveals the problems only of particular and not of all women. Erikson has reproved Freud for remarking that we see a crystal structure only when it cracks, demurring that an organism or personality is not an inanimate crystal but an organic whole which cannot be broken up without a withering of parts. There may be some validity in these and other qualifications, and some will find these reservations of sufficient strength to doubt the universality among women of the envy of the penis. But I believe essentially many of our women politicians are aberrant women, doubtless not dissimilar from the women upon whose disorders Freud made his construct of femininity. They are endowed with high intelligence but are fated by constitution or upbringing never to attain a full creative femininity: that requires the full travail of working through the developmental stages that follow the little girl's genital trauma when suddenly she comprehends that she has not and never will have a penis. Many of our women politicians have not reconciled themselves to that loss and move in perpetual unworked-through bereavement. The women who turned to Freud for relief did so on the couch in the privacy of the consulting room: but the typical woman politician seeks to work out her problems seen, observed, and most certainly heard.

If Freud is right, most women have emotionally moved on beyond the point reached by the typical women politician. Freud asserts three lines of possible developments start from the little girl's discovery of her 'castration'. The first leads to neurosis, and he has a surfeit of case material to relate the sexual inhibitions of the grown woman to her loss of enjoyment as an infant of her phallic activity, of her excitation of her clitoris. Mortified by her comparison with the boys' superior equipment, she renounces her masturbatory satisfaction, repudiates her mother who has both failed to have and to give her a penis, and at the same time may, at the cost of later neurosis, frequently repress a good part of her general sexual trends. But there is another possible reaction of the infant girl: there is a refusal to acknowledge the inferiority of the clitoris; she disavows her lack of a penis and, in spite of everything, asserts her masculinity, and behaves as a boy. If the child does not overcome this reaction soon enough it puts great difficulties in the way of her later regular development towards femininity: and all these difficulties are painfully apparent in many assertive women politicians. Sometimes of course, these difficulties express themselves overtly in homosexuality, and certainly there exists among women in public life more lesbianism than a naïve community appreciates: but the only relevance to society of the masculine protest of women politicians is the distortion of some of their judgements on public affairs.

Transport House is currently much concerned lest the refusal of constituencies to adopt women candidates leads to the situation where Labour has even fewer female M.P.s than the Conservatives: and perplexed political officers of all parties persistently claim that neither women Members of the constituency Parties nor women members of the electorate will support women candidates for Parliament. It does not occur to the Party officials that the women may be displaying more wisdom than the officials give them credit. The woman in the street recognizes in fact that these women do not give voice to what the mass of women are groping to say: that these political women are atypical members of the species.

Erikson has said that 'a major problem exists in the relationship of leading women to each other and to their followers.' The more sensitive political practitioner would surely confirm the psychoanalyst's speculation: among women active in constituency Parties I have found, combined with some admiration for leading Labour women politicians, not only a measure of scepticism, but, more significantly, compassion and indulgence for their freakishness. Most women have dealt with their masculine sexuality, making room for their own femininity more successfully, and they are aware of it. The more usual little girl recognizes the anatomical distinction between the sexes, and this forces her away from masculine masturbation on to new lines which lead to the development of femininity. She takes the point that in masturbation she cannot compete with boys, and it would therefore be best for her to give up the idea of doing so. The girl's libido, as Freud has explained 'slips into a new position along the line of the equation penis-child'. She gives up her wish for a penis and puts in place of it a wish for a child. She is on her way to womanhood. And because she has found her route, she looks quizzically at the campaigning women, so often lost, who stridently insist they know all the signposts.

But, nevertheless, our modern woman lacks high confidence, and can be disturbed by the agitators. The tyranny of the authoritarian family has ended in the middle class home and abated in the working class: the woman no longer knows her place and no longer has the certainty of her serfdom. She does not wish to be estranged from the family, and so suspects those women who, depreciating woman's place in the home, explicitly or by their zeal for public life, idealize typically masculine professional and public roles. Yet she cannot go back: she works, earns, decides, and has all the bewilderment choice and the pill bring. She is urged to be liberated, but she is irresolute, uncertain, fearing the new freedom is a trap. Her anxieties can be fanned and exploited: and since divorce, at an unconscious level, is a threat of loss of the penis of her husband, demagogy can only too easily pick painfully at the original wound to her narcissism, and raise alarm at any suggestion of changes in divorce law.

It is, of course, the middle-aged women who feels most threatened: she fears her physical charms are fading and, wrongly interpreting her middle-aged husband's failing libido as the consequence of her decay, she suddenly loses the protection of her physical vanity which, Freud says, was her late compensation for her original feeling of sexual inferiority. To feel she is losing her looks is sufficient humiliation; to have it confirmed by her husband's diminishing sexual prowess is a double agony; and then to be told legislators are making laws to snatch away what is left of her husband is quite insupportable: and, if the telling is told with tales of how their middle-aged husbands will be able to recover elixirs in the arms of waiting young beautiful secretaries, the anger of such women against the divorce legislators is limitless.

Professor Peter Richards of Southampton University in his careful study of recent Bills of conscience found himself compelled to ask why the parliamentary campaign was so protracted when all the general pressures of opinion and organization tended to favour the Divorce Bill. He found the answer in the wider ramifications of the Bill and suggested a galaxy of argument was bound to be provoked by consequential issues in the social security, child welfare, pension and property fields when a divorce takes place. At one level his diagnosis is correct: but the avalanche of protest, anxiety and vituperation, mainly coming from middle-aged, middle class deserted wives, that I endured with each post taught me that all the compromises, additions and alterations we could make in the Bill could not give to these sad women the emotional security they sought. The irrational demands that, through the medium of a Divorce Bill, the whole field of property law between all married couples should be altered, that all the pension schemes in the private and public service field should be overhauled, and that the whole field of national insurance radicalized to deal with all the problems of one-parent families, were the pleas of displaced women, refugees from the new order where women in a society of near full employment are expected to marry young, dispose speedily of their offspring, and then resume work again, standing on their own two feet even if sometimes it means treading hard on their children's toes. My correspondents, mainly, did not belong to today; they had contracted to be housewives supervising the running of the home and the upbringing of their children, often with the aid of maids and nannies, and their husband's duty was to provide all the money. His infidelity had left them uncomprehending and shattered and often destroying themselves with hatred, their remaining interest now was in their husband's death, not life, in the pension which would fall to them: and meantime they sought to regain their lost idyll by a frantic demand for more maintenance and money, insisting all the time that they would keep their husband in financial and legal chains, never divorcing him.

But their anxieties during the Divorce Bill debates infected many other women in our transitional society. We have a right to boast of the merits of the modern family, of its tolerance and egalitarianism; and to affirm that it has been created as a necessary part of the larger process of approximating to the central ideals of social justice in the entire reconstitution of society. But a democratic way of life in a family brings burdens of responsibility and tolerance: and for many such rationality is hard to bear. The emancipation of the women and children of a family from former oppressiveness and exploitation does not automatically mean an increase in the psychological well-being of the household. The external familial changes may be more apparent than real, involving conscious but not unconscious experience. An excess of equality may deny a woman her right to her much needed masochism; it may reduce a husband, already feeling sterilized by the pill, to the ambiguous and unsatisfactory paternal role of a mother's help. The repression of fundamental needs, consciously regarded as incompatible with the image of the family the spouses wish to maintain, leads to an insecurity, with the partners desperately anxious to have reassurance from the community that their house is in order to an idealized extent. Frank discussion of divorce within the community, of the reality of the breakdown and of destructive conduct between partners is alarming: it raises to the surface too many resentments and frustrations that are being concealed, and the insecure woman responds willingly to the idea that the divorce law reformer, not the reality of the tensions within her modern family, is responsible. It did not require excessive skill on the part of some turbulent public women, waging their ceaseless private battle of the sexes, to cast me in the role of scapegoat.

More, there is real cause for grievance within our laws which do not, in property matters, accord to women the regard which their new status demands: nor can the State be excused from its responsibility in failing to devise, and subsidize, a rational system of collecting and enforcing maintenance payments for deserted wives. And the failure of the State to intervene in the field of private pensions, to ensure that a divorced wife need not lose all financial aid in her old age, as its hesitancy to reconstruct national insurance schemes to insure marriage against breakdown, are genuine and serious grievances felt keenly by feminists. So it came about that on the Divorce Bill were unloaded all the fears and resentments, rational and irrational, of the insecure wives of modern Britain. The question has been put by Professor Richards – why was the Divorce Bill campaign so long and difficult? The real wonder is that the Divorce Bill ever reached the statute book.

No one was more successful in delaying its passage, and in arousing hostility to its objectives, than Edith Samuel. She is better known under her maiden name as Edith Summerskill. A late middle-aged woman, once beautiful, very tall, of more than average masculine height, her temperament and background enabled her to be singularly equipped to tune in to the latent apprehensions of fading middle-class, middle-aged women. She appended, with great elan, the label of the 'Casanova Charter' to the Bill and relentlessly pursued me, harrying me in press, radio and television and from her place in the Lords. Her odd brand of feminism has on the conscious level, little in common with the women's liberation movement: women, she implies, need constant protection from marauding aggressive philandering men, and indeed her concern to protect the female from the bad man has led to her association with at least one useful and constructive piece of legislation; but simultaneously she makes a loud assertion of the independence value and equality of woman. It is difficult in the face of such contradictory attitudes not to ask whether her strident affirmations spring less from a genuine belief in the equality of women than a pressing need to deny and overcome her own doubts. Her emphasis upon the weakness and defencelessness of women seems to betray a resentment, if not envy, of male aggressiveness and sexuality: and certainly her lurid accounts of the potency and potential promiscuity of the Casanova-type man I was about to release on the community were the products of a rich fantasy life. In all her many courageous battles the same leit motif reappears: even her campaign on the dangers of taking the contraceptive pill has, surely, been given an impetus by her fear of male sexuality. And her notorious campaign against professional boxing openly revealed her fear of, if not attraction to, male aggressiveness. It may well be indeed that the operation of the psychological mechanism of identification with the aggressor may have led her to deal with this fear by adopting a particularly aggressive social role: if such be the case, certainly in the divorce reform battle I was her victim. Her influence in the Lords, too sophisticated an institution to be moved by obvious emotive argument, is minimal: but in the country where her views are less fiercely scrutinized she can still find some response to her alarmist clarion calls. It is to her credit, or discredit, that she succeeded in delaying the coming into effect of the Divorce Act by some two years.

I was fortunate in having women allies, some of them friends, some journalists and others in both Houses of Parliament, ready to challenge her views. One yearns perhaps for the impossible, that one could find in public life many women who could as legislators bring to our social inventions the same mood as women so frequently supply privately: to nurse and nourish, to care and tolerate, to include and to preserve – all these capacities have never been more desperately needed in political leadership than today. Driven men, yielding to self aggrandisement, and for ever conquering new worlds and now insanely conquering outer space in phallic spaceships, have no time for the interior life, the inner space which is the creative centre of woman. Even to hint at woman's procreative task, even to suggest that from the womb wiser government can be created than can be fertilized by the penis, is to arouse the ire of feminists protesting that we wish to 'condemn' them to the doom of perpetual motherhood. But there are fortunately women, although few in number, who, at least fitfully, bring into public life some fullness, warmth and generosity, the psychic analogues to the woman's pregnancy, childbirth, lactation, and to the richly convex parts of her anatomy. And there are, too, some public women who have wisely not repudiated or attempted to repress their original trauma. Such a woman is reconciled to the loss, and does not in a mocking or frantic denial refute Freud's description of the infant girl's reaction to her newly discovered differentiation. She makes her judgement and her decision in a flash. She has seen it and knows she is without it and wants to have it. Such a woman has grown up: and the pain of her loss, of her inner periodicities, and sometimes of childbirth make her a true dolorosa. She uses her singular understanding of deprivation and pain to relieve with insight the suffering of others. Public women like public men can deploy their private conflict and deep grief destructively or constructively: it was fortunate for me that there were some public women able to transcend trauma and denial and so help to ward off Summerskill's onslaughts.

We commenced William Wilson's Bill with a blunder. He could have claimed an earlier Friday, the day allocated for Private Members' Bills, than the one chosen. But we wished to prepare with care, and the Law Commissioners were engaged on the draft of the Bill, and Wilson had committed himself to a parliamentary trip to India. Although it was arranged that the Bill should be published and that I should launch it at a press conference before Wilson's return, we still should not have yielded to our convenience, and should have been more aware that opposition would be so prolonged that we could run out of parliamentary time in the current session. The large press conference was tough, went well and the Bill was sympathetically received in the notices the following day: but already the more persistent questioners at the press conference anticipated the reservations or hostile attacks that were soon to be made by the National Council of Women, the Council of Married Women, the Medical Women's Federation, the Mother's Union and the National Board of Catholic Women. More, to my astonishment and dismay, the Archbishop of Canterbury issued a statement regretting the Bill's proposals 'to retain and enlarge existing grounds for divorce' and deploring the provision which would allow what he called 'divorce by consent'.

After all the painstaking work to reach a consensus, I regarded his statement as outrageous. I publicly accused him of a breach of faith, for so it seemed to me. The proposals in the Church Committee's report *Putting Asunder* had the express approval of the Convocation: and the subsequent meetings between Law Commissioners and the Church Committee, which hammered out the consensus document, took place with the Archbishop's approval. The consensus document, too, I was aware, had been submitted to him: and I had seen, at the risk of offending some of my more liberal supporters, that the published Bill had slavishly followed the consensus document, so that the Church, now on the hook, could not slip away.

What I did not know at the time was that although indeed the consensus had been presented to him, he had expressly declined to approve or disapprove it. The wily prelate evidently decided to keep his options open, and to retain complete freedom of manoeuvre. If I had known this at the time of my attack upon him, I doubt if I would have been less generous to an archbishop following the principles of Machiavelli.

The Bishop of Exeter, however, kept his agreement with me absolutely: he maintained staunch support for the Bill and met the Church caucus in the Commons; and after his meeting the caucus, if not enthusiastic in its approval, was at least muted in its dissent. The renewed row with the Church that I feared after the Archbishop's initial comment ended with my attack upon him. Lambeth appeared to have second thoughts: the danger of internal Church tumult and the fact, soon to be shown by the opinion polls, that the nation was in support of the Bill, no doubt weighed heavily in the Archbishop's decision to desist.

The second reading of the Bill gave us a most comfortable majority: I was fortunate in having by my side as an indefatigable and intelligent whip, Peter Jackson, then M.P. for High Peak. His lack of guile, his deep innocence, gave him a charm enabling him to woo and coax the most refractory and indolent of members into our Lobby. With such a decisive vote we were able to claim and obtain an equally decisive majority on the standing committee appointed to examine the Bill in detail. But then our trouble began.

The Bill, totally revolutionizing our divorce laws, was, by its very nature, long and complicated: any responsible opposition politician would want to probe such a Bill phrase by phrase, and all the anxieties of the women's organizations were to be tardily and nicely weighed. As every lawyer knows, no matter how keen the scrutiny of a Bill by the legislature, each Act creates new ambiguities that ultimately can be resolved only by the judges adjudicating upon litigation brought before them. Legislators are poor prophets and their capacity to anticipate and guard against future contingencies is limited. It would therefore be irresponsible to do less than one's best in seeking to avoid uncertainties and hardships in a Bill dealing with poignant and personal problems. And Richard Wood, now Minister of Overseas Development, and Sir Lionel Heald, a former Attorney General, both fairly and scrupulously probed the Bill. Wood is the younger son of Lord Halifax, a former Foreign Secretary associated with the appeasement policies of the thirties, a man who had a prominent place within my adolescent demonology. Halifax was a self-righteous man armoured against any shafts of insight by his certainty that he was an agent of the divine will: his belief in immortality enabled him to bear, with Christian fortitude, the sufferings of the Jews under Hitler. And his rigid adherence to religious principles made him a heartless bigot who condemned divorce followed by marriage, whatever the circumstances, as indistinguishable from bigamy. Richard Wood has not, inevitably, totally emancipated himself from his father's prejudices but he is a courageous and sympathetic man who has overcome his serious war wounds with fortitude: he has philosophy and the capacity to elevate an issue, unlike so many grubby politicians: and Heald, bearing the personal scars of his own divorce, brought delicacy and courtesy to the debates. It was no filibuster, but, with all the misgivings of the middle class women's lobby being ventilated, the whole proceedings took longer than I had anticipated and when at the end of May after thirteen sessions the Bill emerged out of committee, it was being reported to a House that was in legislative shambles.

Dick Crossman, the Leader of the House, in his enthusiasm, had permitted a flood of governmental legislation to erode beyond repair the parliamentary time for that session. Even if I had been able to build up enough steam to compel the government to give time for the Bill to complete its journey through the Commons, it was abundantly clear to me that it could never pass through the Lords within the parliamentary session. In retrospect I sometimes wonder at the talent of Harold Wilson's seven years' administration to be ever possessed by a constant flurry and yet, probably, in the light of history, barely to qualify for more than a footnote. Outside the legal and social reforms for which the collective Cabinet can claim little of the credit, only the placing of the steel industry under public control will be regarded as worthy of mention and that would never have come about without the insistence and persistence of a back bencher, Michael Foot. Most of the other schemes, however well intentioned, came to naught, or were so precariously based that the Tory administration could demolish them with ease within twelve months of coming to power: the Prices and Incomes Board crashed; the needed but clumsy public intervention into weak and inefficient industries was to be speedily dismantled; and such overambitious projects as the Land Commission demolished without regrets. It is difficult not to feel a sense of humiliation when contrasting the achievements of Attlee's administration which, working within much more severe financial constraints, brought about the welfare state, meantime taking a large sector of industry under public control, with the slight work of Wilson's government: other times, other men. It was painful to find my session's work running into the sands largely through the incompetence of others, but I had to accept their timetable and the Bill was bound to fail.

All I could do, was to insure for the next session and I, therefore, spent time in the current session publicizing my failure. Professor Richards has in his researched recording of events accurately written:

Faced with non-cooperation from Ministers, the divorce reformers led by Leo Abse organized an effective campaign of protest within Parliament, especially within the Parliamentary Labour Party. It was intolerable, they argued, that a measure which had been extensively debated and which enjoyed not merely majority support but almost overwhelming support, should be delayed by the technicalities of the parliamentary timetable. Why should all the time and work invested in the Bill be wasted? Why should the Bill not be allowed to carry over from one session to another so that proceedings on a Bill in a new session could continue from where they had reached at the end of the previous session? Why should the Upper House not have a rather shorter summer recess in order to pass a measure desired by Parliament and which could bring comfort and relief to thousands of people? Quite substantial publicity was obtained for these views in the mass media. Inevitably they appealed to all those who felt that Parliament should where necessary amend its traditions to become a more effective vehicle for social change. There can be no doubt that this campaign, as Abse intended, had an effect on the decision of the government to assist the Divorce Bill in the following parliamentary session.

I did in fact in July 1968 drag out a government assurance that if the Bill was reintroduced in the next session, time could be found for its completion.

My ability, however, to have the Bill reintroduced in the next session was once more dependent on the ballot for Private Members' Bills. This time, anxious to go into instant action to persuade a highly placed member to sponsor the Bill, I attended the ballot personally. Only the first eight names drawn can be certain of a full debate on second reading for whatever Bill they choose to introduce. The ballot was a near-disaster: not one of the first eight members was approachable. For the first time since I had commenced the campaign I was gripped by despair. But then came the ninth name, Alec Jones, the Rhondda Member who on Iorrie Thomas's death in 1967 had come into the House on a by-election. I realized that, if I could persuade him to sponsor the Bill, by careful selection of one of the days to be used by a Member having priority who was introducing a less controversial Bill, we could have a little time left of that Member's day at least to start a second reading debate. And if I could start a debate, albeit one fated to be incomplete, I could then dig my teeth into the government and compel them to give the promised time to enable us to go on.

I dashed down to find Alec Jones; and found him working in the room of the Minister to whom he was parliamentary private secretary. It was indeed an evocative room to conceive a Divorce Bill: this had been Parnell's room and from the window, when the House rose, he would see Kitty O'Shea leaving with her unspeakable husband. Alec Jones yielded to my plea, and we began together the final assault to release many from scandal and bondage. Parnell would have approved.

With Richard Wood undertaking new shadow Cabinet duties, the opposition fell into the hands of the Philistines. Professional blinkered divorce lawyers, politically unsophisticated, in love with their tired procedures and practices, subjected us to filibustering arguments, intellectually febrile and, worse, aesthetically repugnant. It was disagreeable but it was endurable because we had both the majority and the full co-operation of John Silkin constantly manoeuvring to give us the parliamentary time we required.

Unfortunately, I had been pressing myself too hard and, on my refusing to yield to an ear infection, the body hit back. I was laid low: meningitis was feared and I was pumped with antibiotics; the infection was mastered, but the ever present crackling in the eustachian tube to my ear remains with me as my divorce war wound. Worse, reluctant to release me for my duties, as the infection diminished, the body probed other weaknesses: my appendix flared up and I was rushed to hospital. The operation proved to be more than minor, the appendix in my body being eccentrically behind my liver. By the time I was able to crawl back, poor Alec Jones had endured many a committee stage balancing on a knife's edge, since there were other casualties on our side, barely enabling our supporters, on their own, to maintain the needed quorum for business to proceed. Indeed on one occasion the squalid opposition taking advantage of our sickness withdrew from the committee leaving us without a quorum and compelling the Bill to be brought to a temporary halt. But Alec clung on by his finger nails until I returned. It was no easy task for a new Member and non-lawyer to carry the Bill alone: but this conscientious and determined schoolmaster had mastered his brief and he had the guts to use the unanticipated experience as a political maturation process which has since stood him in good stead.

I returned with the inevitable character modifications that come after a flirtation with death. I have observed how, after a coronary, clients of mine, unselfconscious business men, despite the warnings of their physicians, far from curbing their commercial adventures, plunge into more and often wilder schemes. It is their response to the threat of death and they fight back, and yet more avidly they assert their hold on life, and too often life, for them, only finds a meaning in the attempt to acquire more wealth. Their frantic reaction frequently leads to financial disasters and the provocation of their own doom.

There are, however, happier responses to the threat of extinction. Parliament and the nation have certainly been considerable beneficiaries of the serious motor car accident that removed Michael Foot from the House for twelve months. His contributions to the House before the collision were worthy but unremarkable. It was after his return, all diffidence gone and his blocked aggression cleared from obstruction, that he attacked with an elan that soon established him as our most commanding Parliamentarian, and the fury he unleashed, no longer choked back, substantially diminished his asthma. Nor, I notice, does he complain as he was wont to do as he walked through the lobby, of his piles. From Luther, who received the command to challenge the Pope while suffering from haemorrhoids on the privy at Wurttenburg Cathedral, to the suffering Marx whose piles, when writing chapter one of *Das Kapital*, Engels has told us, the bourgeoisie would come to curse, haemorrhoids have been the classical psychosomatic symptom of suppressed aggression.

The nationalization of steel, as Michael's relief from piles, owes more to Jill Foot's bad driving than any other single cause.

Illness, however, compels us to acknowledge the body's inevitable decay: and with our new awareness come sad ironies. At the very time when we feel we have attained some intellectual certainty and gained our most certain wisdom, that is the moment when, physically, we know it is a case of downhill all the way. Tomorrow is the second day of the rest of our lives: and we are chasteningly aware how much of our allocated 840 months has already passed. I came back to the House less patient with the hollow political conventions of Westminster, the insincere congratulations offered by M.P.s to one another on their speeches, the absurd over-valuation of the importance of the size of majority in every division on every piddling issue, and all the other cloying circumlocutions clinging to the institution. Life is too short and death too final for time to be wasted on such fripperies.

Bob Mellish was the first recipient of my new mood. One day I left the unsuspecting John Silkin at his chief Whip's room before lunch, having arranged with him a continuation of the morning sessions of the House at last to complete the Commons report and third reading of the Bill. A few hours later when I was returning to the House I read on the placards of Silkin's dismissal and the appointment of Mellish in his place. Bob Mellish is a Roman Catholic who had been privy to the cabal that had sabotaged my 1963 Act: and my suspicions grew as I found I was not to have my morning sessions, when it was comparatively easy to whip in my troops, but that I was to be given an all night session to complete – if I could – the Bill. Worse, the night allocated was a Thursday night, and Members all wish if possible to leave late Thursday or early on Friday morning to return to their constituencies.

But my anger knew no bounds when I found that Mellish, unnecessarily responding to a motion placed on the order paper by Sir Lionel Heald and opponents of the Bill, condemning the government for giving us more time, had also agreed to a debate on their motion: and that this debate would take place on the Thursday night, before we could commence on the further stages of the Bill. In practical terms this meant that we would have to keep our forces, never allowing them to drop beneath a hundred, in or about the Chamber from 10 p.m. on Thursday night until Friday afternoon. The burdens upon Alec Jones and myself were the least of the difficulties: keeping a cool head and answering all the intricate amendments of a prolonged report stage on the floor of the House requires stamina, but one is curiously buoyed up by the challenge. To demand the same response from our supporters, who are expected not to prolong proceedings by speaking and are to act only as Lobby fodder, at a time when morale was low and disaffection rife because of Wilson's inept attempts to impose an Industrial Relations Bill upon the Labour Party, was asking the near impossible. I expressed my resentment against Mellish both privately and publicly when, during the debate on Heald's motion, I poured withering scorn on him in a manner to which chief Whips are unaccustomed. Maybe I over-reacted and his maladroit arrangements were due to naïvety and not malice: but at that time I was not prepared to err on the side of generosity although certainly, from this incident onwards, I never had cause in any further activities in which I was involved to receive anything but generous help from him.

Despite the time arrangements, however, we scrambled through. Politics is not the art of the possible: that is its most menial function. Politics is the art of the impossible, and real achievement comes to those who do not submit to the obvious. By the lucky afternoon of Friday the thirteenth of June 1969 we had, with more than a hundred stoical Labour M.P.s present, completed our third reading and the Bill was ready at last to quit the Commons to be passed on to good Frank Soskice to steer through the Lords. But I left the chamber in sombre mood: the eruption of anxiety from women had taken on a new and threatening form. We had won the votes in the Commons but my domestic life, like that of most men, had taught me there is no victory in winning an argument with a woman.

The clause in the Bill permitting divorce against the wishes of an unforgiving party had focused attention on the law's failure to acknowledge the partnership created by marriage. The debates had illuminated the precariousness of the legal rights of the married woman in the matrimonial home, in the furnishings and in a deceased husband's estate. She had some protection against eviction but none whatsoever against a disposition by the husband of the home and not a shred of right in the proceeds of the sale. She was only entitled to one half of such savings as she had made out of the household money given by her husband and as for the money he saved because she was a thrifty housewife, or because she bore part of the household expenses out of her own earnings, the law is ominously silent. All these and many other financial disadvantages suffered by the married woman were well known to many lawyers who had for a while taken their eyes off their conveyancing deeds and observed the revolutionary changes around them in an increasingly property owning democracy where married women often did at least part-time work outside the home, and where motherhood was regarded as professional, not casual, work.

Gerald Gardiner was keenly aware of the especial problems that arise in England and Wales because people marry without giving any thought to their respective property rights, since the marriage does not affect those rights. This may be very romantic, but it certainly leads to many women paying dearly for the romance. Our approach is in contrast to the position under the civil law in continental Europe and some States of America. Under those systems there is usually some form of community of property, under which certain property is held in common during the marriage or is divided between the spouses at the end of the marriage: but since spouses are free to enter into a formal marriage contract, in which they may vary the community system, it is more common in such countries for engaged couples to consider property rights before marriage.

To change our anachronistic laws so that the wife is no longer treated as a mere dependent of the husband, but is regarded as an equal partner, is a formidable task. To insist that the law recognizes the importance of the wife's function in the home by giving her a share in the family assets will require legislation both complex and delicate: and to have laws for the wife who is working, or has at some stage of the marriage worked, which clearly define her interest in family assets, even if they are in her husband's name, presents a host of difficulties, not all of them by any means mere legal technicalities. Not least such laws must not be tension-making within a family: and they must take cognisance of the brutal fact that amongst large sections of the working class, as amongst a large class of top directors, husbands would resent their wives even knowing how much they earn. Because the problems required a sophisticated and prolonged enquiry, long before we had introduced the Divorce Bill, Gerald Gardiner had requested the Law Commission to commence a study of the family property laws of England. Those of us who, together with distinguished professors of family and international law, have participated in some of the private weekend conferences of the Law Commissioners on these issues, know how tough a job is before them.

But fools step in where angels fear to tread. The simple may receive their blessings in heaven but on this earth, as legislators, they cause infinite mischief and misunderstanding. To my dismay whilst the Divorce Bill was proceeding, one of those who had gained a high place in the Private Members' Ballot, with the full legal equipment of an enthusiastic lay magistrate of a provincial court, decided, by the proverbial stroke, to resolve all the problems surrounding the effect of marriage on the property of spouses. His aim, although certainly not translated into effect in the hideous drafting of the Bill by some supporting shameless academics, was to ensure that on marriage the husband and wife would retain separately anything they brought into the union, and anything they individually were given or inherited during it: but all other resources and property accumulated during the marriage would belong to them equally. More, although property which a spouse acquired during the marriage by gift or inheritance, as any property owned by the spouse at the marriage, would continue to belong solely to that spouse, any increase in the value of such separate property during marriage was to be treated as belonging to the spouses equally. The sponsor of this concoction, Ted Bishop, was undoubtedly well intended. But 'qui fait l'ange fait la bête'. It was not only accountants, valuers and inland revenue officers who recoiled with dismay from such a scheme: the sociological implications had in no way been thought through or the contribution it could make to increasing rather than diminishing marital stress. There are few admonitions I have found less persuasive than 'Si vis pacem para bellum': preparations soon become provocations, and the Bill was a prescription for the exacerbation of marital irritations. The law officers dismissed the Bill as near lunatic and the government logically, but mistakenly, decided to place a whip on to ensure its defeat. Edith Summerskill predictably, however, although it only incidentally raised questions relating to the property rights of divorced women as distinct from married women, became quite rhapsodical about the Bill. She was so impressed by this potential battleground for warring partners that she announced that if Bishop's Bill was passed she might even drop her objections to the Divorce Bill. Logically I could have opposed this ridiculous panacea, treating it as yet one further obstacle thrown across the Divorce Bill's passage to the statute book: that I did not so respond was not only because I had no intention of providing ammunition to Summerskill to accuse me of denying women's rights.

I have, professionally, encountered too frequently the despair of the woman, penurious or wealthy, who has lost her man, by death or desertion, to proffer icy logic as the balm for her wounds. A man sometimes protects himself from this empathic horror, as he senses the depth of her anguish, by a refusal to understand or by an overdetermined dismissal of her irrationality. Erikson has told us that clinical observation suggests that in female experience an 'inner space' is the centre of her despair, even as it is the very centre of her fulfilment: the arrogance of the penis-man, and perhaps his fear of the loss of his manhood, turns him away from acknowledging that for a woman to be left is to be left empty, and emptiness is indeed the female perdition. It is not enough to dismiss impatiently the hurts which in a woman can, by small slights, be so easily aroused, as a manifestation of penis envy. The narcissistic mortification of the little girl has been reinforced by her despair as she became poignantly aware of the other deprivations to which she must submit. Not for her the urethral eroticism accompanied by fantasies of omnipotence enjoyed by the boy as he throws into the air his triumphant jet of urine: her genital organs are hidden, and she must renounce the fulfilment of her scoptophilic impulses, so easily enjoyed by the boy, even as she despairingly renounces her onanistic wishes, enviously believing that boys only are permitted to masturbate as they alone are encouraged to take hold of their genitals when urinating. These more primary feelings of loss can be provoked throughout the whole feminine life cycle: as the moon changes, with each menstruation, she re-experiences it; each miscarriage emphasizes the initial agony; each child grown up, leaving the home re-opens her terrible wound; and the menopause is a final cruel mockery. Her fear of loss, of emptiness, must be understood, and all the reassurances given: and the available psychological equivalents of loving reassurance, of which money and property is one, should be delicately entwined within our family law. When people vote they bestow a kiss on the ballot paper for their chosen candidate. The least we who are chosen can do is to return that love through our legislation: but we should remember that it was a celibate son of God who declared that the laws must be made for men. They must be made for women too: and that means the legislature must not view the world through the narrow aperture of male consciousness, that sometimes it must throw away the props of logic, and stride boldly towards the super-reality which can be the vision of the most ordinary woman.

On at least two occasions my insistence upon building the illogical into the law has brought me into conflict with formidable lawyers and legislators, and on each occasion, perhaps because I had the forces of the irrational on my side and they had mere logic as their shield, I have won. The first occurred when I was assisting in putting through a Bill prepared by the Law Commission abolishing the action for breach of promise to marry. It was of course sensible that such an action should be ended, for there can be no wisdom in permitting the law to be used as a means of dragging reluctant grooms to the altar: we suffer enough subsequent marriage breakdowns from enthusiastic grooms, without adding predictable casualties to the total. But one of the side effects of the Bill was that, whatever the circumstances of the ending of the betrothal, the man would have the legal right to recover the engagement ring. I felt unease and tested this intended provision upon my wife. She exploded with all the force of a volcanic eruption overwhelming any seemingly rational arguments that I advanced in favour of the intended rule; I tried the proposition on some of the Labour Party women's sections in South Wales and had an equally unequivocal response. The highly charged symbolism of the engagement ring makes it no bauble.

I went along to see the Lord Chancellor, Gerald Gardiner, who treated me, as ever, kindly, but not wanting to be troubled with such nonsense which he clearly thought ill became me, suggested I talked this over with the Law Commissioners where he doubtless believed I would be talked out of my whimsy. My friends there were indulgent but adamant: they thought this was one extravagance too many even for me. I observed that my wife, when at private functions she met Leslie Scarman, wooed him in vain: and although she beat a suffering Gerald Gardiner over the head on the matter at more than one party, she made no progress.

There was nothing left to do but fight it out openly. Soon the House was being told:

... although some men may regard an engagement ring as a bauble, for most women it is still endowed with the romance and magic of an ancient betrothal ceremony. An engagement ring is, I believe, the external symbol of an inner dedication and in these days, when it is overfashionable, perhaps, to take marriage lightly, we need to be careful that we do not erode the well tried betrothal rituals that, in one form or another, belong in the histories of all civilizations.

In early medieval Britain, betrothals were marked by an interchange of rings, a kiss, and the joining of hands. Not all of course could afford a ring and for the peasantry of oppressed Wales, the place of rings was often taken by a coin, which was broken between the pair, each taking a part. In some parts of Britain a bride-elect received a bent or crooked sixpence but for the most part a ring was the time honoured symbol of troth, and so it remains, as we all know and as the jewellers' shops proclaim throughout the High Streets of the land.

Whatever certain metropolitan circles may think, however much engagements and engagement rings may be for them something outmoded, fortunately, in my opinion, for the family life of Britain the young women of this country expect their boy friends still, when a decision to marry has been taken, to put a ring on the third finger of the left hand. By this sign the girls receive, as all of us know, from their fellow workers in offices or factories, considerable acclamation ...

It is, too, I think, a sign to other men to 'keep off the grass' ...

In my view we should not scoff at such ceremony within life. It is not only part of the wooing by a man of a woman; it is, too, an important stage in the advance of a young man and a young woman to greater responsibility, one for each other.

It is part of the maturation process and one not to be dismissed frivolously.

An engagement ring has a very special and very deep emotional significance for a woman. No over-logical lawyer in my judgment, has the right to pass laws that trample quite unnecessarily on a woman's feelings. A man, like a woman, must be left free to change his mind but . . . why should a heel who has misused his girl friend have the right to have his engagement ring back as a right? The average woman, perhaps, if a man lets her down, would throw the ring in his face. But if her release of emotions requires it, if it helps her to overcome her humiliation of the rejection, then surely she should have, if she wishes, the right to throw the ring in the river.

The public reaction was immediate, extensive and unanimous: the issue, seemingly trivial, tapped subterranean resentments among women, and responding to the mood, the media gave the issue widespread coverage: I stirred the pot in articles in the popular press, on radio and television and, sensing the danger of a flood engulfing the whole Bill, my exasperated friends conceded defeat, and permitted me to move an amendment to the Bill, ensuring that an engagement ring should be presumed to be an absolute, not conditional, gift. My wife, and womankind, had their way: and jilted girls in Britain can now keep their rings, sell them, throw them in the river or at their faithless lovers. My legal friends wondered that my eccentricity should be shared by so many: and despaired that a Bill drafted so neatly should only by becoming so untidy be acceptable to the absurd women of England and Wales.

My other battle was a more weighty one. In the 1970–1 parliamentary session, Arthur Probert, a South Wales Member, drew a high place in the ballot and was kind enough to ask my advice. He was a sponsored Transport and General Workers' Union M.P. and I was aware of the concern of the legal department of his Union for a considerable number of widows of men who had died from bladder cancer which, it was discovered after their death, had been contracted in their work as a consequence of their employers, years before, negligently using a particular chemical process. The existing limitation laws preventing the commencement of actions after certain periods of time, had barred these widows from making a claim for damages. There was also a substantial number of miners and their widows who were similarly placed: the discovery of the negligence which had resulted in their contracting the deadly disease of pneumoconiosis came too late for claims to be made, and the National Union of Mineworkers was smarting under the grievance and Gerald Gardiner, to whose attention the problem had been drawn, appreciating not only the grievance but the complications of the limitation laws, had during his term of office referred the issue to the Law Commissioners, and, since I had encouraged at least one union to give evidence to them, I was in touch with the situation and knew they had completed their labours: and the incoming Tory government were now to have put to them some varying remedial suggestions, one or none of which they could accept. I suggested to Arthur Probert that he should use his Bill to implement the most generous of these proposals: as chairman of the Transport and General Workers' parliamentary group, and having many miners in his constituency, he willingly agreed if I in turn would, in view of the legal technicalities of the Bill, assist him by co-sponsoring it.

We had clearing talks with some of the unions concerned, and Arthur Probert told his constituency party of his intentions. I then made an appointment to see the Lord Chancellor with a view to enlisting government assistance for the passage of the Bill. However, I made the mistake of informing Quintin Hogg's private secretary in advance of the purpose of our visit. We arrived a few days later to find Quintin in one of his most truculent moods: the government had accepted in principle the recommendations of the Commissioners, but he informed us we were not to have the Bill. He had decided that he would give the Bill to young Winston Churchill who had also drawn a place in the ballot. With characteristic refreshing frankness he made it quite clear that he was doing this solely for political reasons: Churchill had arrived recently in the House for a marginal constituency, and an immediate publicized display of concern for stricken workers in his constituency would doubtless be a splendid way of consolidating himself.

I gently demurred, pointing out Arthur's union connection, and that it was also a problem linked with the Welsh mining constituencies in particular, and that the considerable legal technicalities made it desirable that it should be partially steered by a lawyer. Hogg would have none of it.

Arthur remained silent but I sensed his anger, for he believed that, if I had not alerted Quintin Hogg of the potential existence of the Bill, the Lord Chancellor would never have had the chance to so pre-empt the Bill. The Lord Chancellor mistook Arthur's taciturnity for lack of fight: and mistook the deference given by Arthur, although merely a display of Welsh courtesy to the office not the man, as timidity. The Lord Chancellor went too far: he patronizingly and almost flippantly told Probert that he could give support to Churchill from the Labour benches when Churchill introduced the Bill. I could hear the knife turning, but Arthur, a controlled man, simply said he would think matters over.

The distribution of largesse by a Tory Lord Chancellor to a scion of the Churchill family may make good sense to a former national chairman of the Conservative Party: it is highly provocative to a South Walian of Arthur Probert's vintage. The older Welsh have long and unforgiving memories and, despite the war, the name Churchill for them evokes the Tonypandy riots and the belligerent class enmity of the General Strike. In my constituency local councillors refused to give a single penny to Churchill's commemorative fund and I, at that time, sensing the depth of their emotion, kept a still tongue. When we went to see Churchill in an attempt to persuade him to take on another Bill this charming young political ruffian refused, and, with bravado, tapped his breast pocket declaring he already had the draft Bill. I knew this to be impossible, for the Bill inevitably was to be a highly complicated one, and I had a shrewder assessment of the time needed by parliamentary draftsmen to set this on its feet than did this inexperienced young man. But I now had had enough of this nonsense: I have lost the habit and inclination for playing Party games but if they are to be played then I learned the rules in a hard school.

I told Churchill that if we were to have no government assistance then, although it would mean work and time, I would draft the Bill for Probert myself and that, since the Bill would embrace all the Law Commissioners' recommendations, he would be at a serious disadvantage: Probert had drawn fourth place in the ballot and he had drawn fifth. If two Bills of similar content were presented to the House, we would have priority and the Speaker would direct the subsequent one to fall. I told Churchill he was throwing away the rare opportunity to put through a Private Members' Bill: and suggested he should discuss the matter with his whips.

In order to make it equally clear to the Lord Chancellor that I was not bluffing, I decided to extend the scope of the Bill and to call an immediate press conference: if we were not to be bound to the wishes of the government, then I decided to use the occasion to draw attention to other grievances of widows. There was one grievance in particular which I wished to end and which I had repeatedly raised in the House: it was the legal rule which insisted that, when an award of damages was to be made to the widow of a man killed in an accident, a deduction should be made for her marriage prospects. This meant that a judge was compelled to assess the attractiveness and charm of the woman before him, to measure her capacity as housewife, her age and, no doubt, her bedworthiness, in order to come to a conclusion as to what deduction should be made from the sum he would otherwise have awarded her. Beauty is in the eye of the beholder: and not a few judges had demurred about the speculative and irksome duty imposed upon them. But all women of course resented the humiliation of the inspections, and solicitors found it repugnant to hint to their clients they should go to court, in itself already sufficient an ordeal, looking their worst. I had once declared that these women were being treated as slaves in a Persian market: this brought an indignant letter to me from the Iranian Ambassador informing me he was instructing his public relations officer to notify the press that I was misinformed, and that there were no slaves in Persia. But my remark made its point elsewhere, and the issue, from that time, received continuous attention from women's organizations and the media.

After my press conference, with the Bill now 'glamorized' by this easily understood issue, there was ample and sympathetic coverage of our Bill and its aims: and I waited for the thunderbolts to descend upon me from the Lord Chancellor's office. After a few days silence the summons came. Hogg was in a surly, misogynist mood: what did I mean by bringing in this extraneous issue into this Bill? There were enough complexities in the issue of a limitations Bill without adding a controversial marriageability clause to which so many logical objections could be raised. I told him that none of this would have arisen if he had given, as he should have done, the Bill to Probert in the first instance. I allowed the storm to blow out: and then we did our deal. The government would give us full assistance in the drafting of the limitations part of the Bill and encourage support for its passage: but after the second reading, at the committee stage, on the undertaking by the government that they would refer the marriageability question to be considered in depth by the Law Commissioners, I would withdraw that section so that it did not pass into law in the manner I wished. We exchanged correspondence confirming our treaty: but with the winds blowing as they were – and I did not discourage them to continue blowing – I privately hoped I would not be called upon to fulfil my undertaking.

The second reading was a great success: I kept to my bargain and scrupulously dealt at length with the weightier and more complex alterations we were making to the law relating to limitations, but almost everyone else preferred to speak about the well-publicized deduction made in widows' damages awards. And, of course, everyone was on the side of the angels battling against a cruel law. Quintin Hogg, too shrewd a politician to allow himself to be nailed as a persecutor of widows, informed me that I was released from my undertaking and he was content to leave the matter to a free vote in the committee and third reading so that the House of Commons could decide the issue without further delay. This was promptly done without a division, and the intact Bill proceeded merrily to the

Lords, where a curious and unprecedented storm broke out.

The Law Lords responding to the outraged cries from the Temple at such legislation, sternly intervened. Three of them, Lord Diplock, Viscount Dilhorne and Lord Donovan gave notice of their intention to strike out the offending clause. Truth to tell, all logic was on their side: the whole basis of the English law of damages rested upon the principle that the amount a widow is awarded must be based on the pecuniary loss she actually suffered. The law looked at her financial dependence upon her late husband, saw how much her husband contributed to her and on that basis quantified her loss. It would be absurd according to their logic that a young widow who had been married to a low earning husband killed in an accident should receive an award without an adjudication for marriage prospects, and then marry a wealthy man twelve months later. It would mean widows could gain rather than lose from losing a husband. The Law Lords, some of the most upright men in the kingdom, wanted justice to be done: but I wanted love, not justice, to be bestowed by the law, and of course my demand was most unreasonable and most necessary.

The Law Lords properly carry great weight: they are in the Lords to counsel and advise. But their position is a delicate one: as judges they must administer the laws made by the legislature. In a country that uses the strength of long established convention and eschews a written constitution, there is not, as in the U.S.A., a separation of powers between judiciary and legislature. But the participation of the Law Lords in the legislative process requires men subtly sensitive to their role, able to contribute and advise, but not challenge or thwart. They are primarily judges, men who constitute the ultimate court in the land, and they must suppress their prejudices and carry out scrupulously the will of the legislature. They blunder if they advertise over-extensively their private views or prejudices: if as judges they are to preserve their role of impartial arbiters, above the battle, then they should not themselves raise the dust. In their legislative role they must tread warily if they are not to be compromised.

I decided a firm warning shot was necessary before the Law Lords became over-involved. There was, I was aware, no woman M.P. who would regard as tolerable the inevitable intrusions into the private life of a widow that the existing legal rule required: insurance companies wishing to diminish the claim made against them were employing agents to snoop upon widows to see if they could present evidence to the court of an association which could lead to a marriage. And, more, every woman lives with too fundamental a sense of loss not to feel an empathy with a stricken woman, cursed with the fate of the sudden emptiness of widowhood: after such devastation, who could care to assess nicely her loss, and what man-made law could presume to convert that infinite loss into the small change of any currency? I drafted a letter to the Lord Chancellor calling on him to resist the Law Lords' demand, and obtained the signature on that letter of every woman M.P. The Lord Chancellor was displeased to receive it, but the press were delighted. The Law Lords were well aware at their breakfast tables that they had stirred up a hornets' nest.

Their political sense, alas, is as slight as their legal knowledge is profound. Nothing daunted, and overprotected in their courtroom from the buffetings which teach politicians when to run for cover, the Law Lords, believing themselves to be reasonable men, decided to compromise: they placed on the order paper, in substitution for the outright rejection of my clause, a series of infinitely elaborate amendments designed to maintain the principle but soften the blow. They had no appreciation of how provocatively they were behaving: the women were not interested in their logic chopping, and were totally impervious to the arguments contained within their long winded amendment. The Law Lords were meeting passion, a force with which they are unfamiliar, which is fortunately excluded from the courts and which must blow with gusto in every real legislature.

I arranged with Lord Stow Hill, who had undertaken to steer the Bill through the Lords, to call a meeting of the women peeresses. They responded bravely, and battle was prepared. The debates began: on four occasions for hours the Lords Derwent, Donovan, Diplock and Pearson and Viscount Dilhorne, to the accompaniment of hostile outside opinion, doggedly pursued their over rational view: but with the peeresses on both sides of the house lashing them hard, with Frank Soskice in superb form and Gerald Gardiner as our ally, the flagellations became too much for them. Somehow or other before the debates were concluded these men who possess the greatest forensic skills in Britain had not only lost the debate but had lost the argument too; and they were aware that there were murmurs abroad complaining of the constitutional impropriety of such active intervention by judges. Rather than face the final humiliation of a crushing vote, they threw their hand in: and privately must have consoled themselves in the belief that they were beaten by feminine hysteria. The judges, when the Act was passed, still furious at the defeat, were to prise open a small crack in the legislation: they managed to decide that although Parliament had decided a widow could not have any deduction made from her damages, the widow's mite could still have a small deduction made from her damages if the court thought the child, because of the mother's marriageability, could one day gain a stepfather. It was a mean attempt to hit back at what the sulky judge who gave the ruling described as a 'bizarre Act'.

Bizarre it may have been, but for my part, none of my law-making has given me greater delight. It is rare in our legislature that wisdom and insight triumph over justice.

I was certainly not, therefore, prepared to participate in the folly of a headlong collision with the supporters of Bishop's Property Bill even though the wretched concoction now straddled the Divorce Bill's path to the statute book. I hit on an evasive stratagem that could give us a clear way. I was aware that the Law Commissioners had in their study of the problems of matrimonial property substantially reached certain conclusions on a number of peripheral matters: and I therefore sought the help of those able to influence a decision that an announcement could be made undertaking to implement these conclusions. These conclusions, if implemented, would mean that in future a divorced woman's maintenance order would not necessarily cease on her former husband's death, but could be made for their joint lives with a sum deposited to secure the maintenance should the husband die: it meant, too, courts would have new powers to order the settlement of property by the husband for the wife and the children; and the new proposals would also include the end of many of the inhibitions preventing judges from awarding lump sums or the giving of financial relief for the benefit of illegitimate or adopted children who had become part of the family.

When the second reading of Bishop's Bill came, as it would, to a thin House on a Friday afternoon, my plan was that I would mildly reprove the sponsors of the Bill for its weakness, praise extravagantly its good intentions, and demand that the government meet the well-founded concern of its sponsors by undertaking to implement these minor but not unimportant proposals which, in advance of any other suggestions, had been thoroughly explored by the Law Commission; although in any event these matters would have been ultimately implemented, the sponsors of Bishop's Bill could withdraw their Bill believing they had wrested out of the government real concessions, and the women's organizations could believe Bishop and his sponsors had been gallant fighters. And meantime the way to the conclusion of the Divorce Bill would be clear. I laid on the scheme with the connivance of those in authority.

Perhaps such a Machiavellian scheme did not deserve to succeed: in the event, thanks to human frailty, it went awry. When the debate proceeded the Speaker called me, as I wished, midstream in the discussion. I went through my prepared charade with rhodomantade and verve, demanding the front bench to give victory to Bishop and his innocent do-gooders by making a firm announcement which could enable the current Bill to be withdrawn. I sat down to the applause of the supporters of the Bill which I guiltily received: but I did not have to reassure myself for long that the means justified the end.

By a chance absence, the front bench spokesman was not as I had hoped, Sir Elwyn Jones, the Attorney General, but Sir Arthur Irvine, the ponderous Solicitor General. Elwyn Jones, possessed of more public charm and persuasiveness than anyone in the House, would have been able to collaborate with an ease and assurance that would have deceived the flattered innocents into a belief they had won a great triumph even as they withdrew their Bill. But the well intentioned Irvine lacked the political sophistication to participate convincingly in the prepared pantomime: even before he had completed his proesy I knew we were to pay the price for the absence of a subtle son of Llanelli who knows how to play the game in the House as his fellow townsmen play on the rugby field.

Irvine was disastrous: he has all the defects conventionally attributed to lawyers. He loathes economy and, if asked, would carefully qualify his view on his own legitimacy. What was needed was a short sharp speech where the vigour of presentation masked the febrile content: and the promises given, though intrinsically of little weight, should have been given almost dramatically and certainly unconditionally. His speech was windy, too long and replete with reservations and conditions. It was as flat-footed a performance as I have ever witnessed in the Chamber: he lost the ear of the House, and the dogged proponents of the muddled Bill, far from being wooed, now full of suspicion, refused to withdraw the Bill and took it to a division. The Party whips, rarely able to adjust speedily to a fluid situation, finding their expectations of a withdrawal dashed, went into a panic. They dragged out of their Whitehall offices as many Ministers as they could find late on a Friday afternoon in a vain attempt to vote the Bill down. Inevitably the whole incident led to a row in the Parliamentary Labour Party, and only by the Lord Chancellor giving assurances that a government Matrimonial Property Bill would be introduced in the next session if the Bishop Bill was withdrawn could the storm be allayed.

Worse, Frank Soskice, Lord Stow Hill, who had stoically taken over the steering of our Divorce Bill in the Lords was to find himself dogged by the Commons shambles, as an opinion was deliberately created by my opponents that no Divorce Bill should be passed until a Matrimonial

Property Bill had been fully seen and enacted by Parliament. I was fortunate in having Frank Soskice as my ally: he is one of my comrades in disbelief and his rationalism, which leaves him unencumbered with the suspicions and sentimentalities of those who are excessively reverent, enables him to grasp and present the basic elements of even the most complicated of issues with a disarming directness and simplicity. He is a great reader of classical novels, and the near literary language in which he speaks in the Lords, though sometimes quaint to the modern ear, is in an idiom that reassures an elderly, well read membership. His courtesy never fails: and the more aggressive his opponent, the more courteous he becomes, though his courtesy, then, will be leavened with a pretty wit.

His critics, when he was at the Home Office, bitterly complained about his indecisiveness: and indeed his vacillations over the tactics to be adopted to put through the Divorce Bill often drove the divorce law reform lobby to despairing telephone calls to me begging me to rush to the Lords to pursue the harassed Frank until he came to a firm and strategically wise decision. But for my part I found his habit of mind congenial. If he is under-decisive, my sin can be over-decisiveness, and certainly when I was younger I always found it hard not to resist the temptation to do something when the wise decision was to do nothing at all. More obsessional characters, like Frank Soskice, are often indecisive because they are inhibited by always seeing two sides of the question: the more hypomanic character, ebullient, dynamic, making rapport easily, dares not stop making, and acting on, decisions for if he did he fears depression would seize him. So our temperaments contained each other and, once Frank Soskice was on his feet in the Lords, he pursued the agreed formula with an authority that did not in any way reveal his hesitations. I realized the importance of being the last person with him before he rose to speak: then, confidently, he fought singlemindedly with the skill of a great advocate.

In the event, to gain the Lords' approval we had no choice but to agree the Divorce Bill should not come into effect for a year to enable meantime a Matrimonial Property Bill to be enacted by the Lord Chancellor which would come into operation at the same date. This sufficiently appeased the critics to let the Divorce Bill go through but it inevitably meant that the proposed Matrimonial Property Bill was to prove puny and inadequate for it was a hasty product of political expediency. It helped to establish the principle that on a divorce a wife, in her capacity as a wife and mother, could claim a share of the matrimonial home, even though she had not contributed financially to its purchase: but it was not the fully thought through Bill on matrimonial property that one day I hope to assist to the statute book. Lady Summerskill with some justification called it a 'miserable Bill' and claimed that 'a confidence trick has been played on the women of the country'. We certainly need a Bill that will give, at the least, to every woman upon marriage a firm stake in the matrimonial home and a fixed and indefeasible minimum share in the estate of her husband if she is left a widow. And we need such a measure not only to remedy the injustices that flow from the present law, but for the sake of mankind. Woman's sense of deprivation is so profound that man must, in property terms, make her more equal than equal: only then will she feel that she does not degrade herself by being a woman.

When the day eventually came for the Divorce Law Reform Bill to receive the royal assent, I was too weary and exhausted to feel any elation: the battle had been too protracted. My wife and I did not celebrate but, to mark the victory, we gave a name carved into a piece of Welsh slate to our London home. We called our house by a Hebrew word, *Beulah*, found only once in the Bible but adapted by scores of chapels in Wales. It means the site of a happy marriage: there are no more blessed plots in the whole world.

XII

One of the outstanding debts that, up to 1966, I had not discharged to my mother, was a Family Planning Act. Jewish mothers have justifiably gained a certain notoriety: their love for their children is powerful but adulterated. Too often, they love their sons' achievements, not their sons. It is not only in the novels of New York intellectuals that Jewish sons are burdened with a neurotic sense of guilt because they have failed to live up to the expectations of their mothers: 'nachas', the glow of pleasure-pride in a child so often spoken about by Jewish mothers, has maimed many of my Jewish contemporaries. It is the heavy price Jewish males pay for perpetuating in a modern culture the ghetto-relegation of women: idealized in theory but relegated in practice behind the segregated grilles of the orthodox synagogue, the diaspora Jewish woman, left behind in the current race for equality between the sexes, seeks her compensations and lives dangerously vicariously through her sons. So it is wise for a Jewish son to err on the right side when calculating his account, lest he overpays.

But to try to give my mother and, incidentally, the next generation a Family Planning Bill was irresistible, for the great heroine of my mother was the redoubtable Annie Besant. As a child, her praises were ever sung to me by my mother. Indeed, it was only when I was grown up, and knew my mother's age precluded the possibility, that I really understood her regular recital of the details of the remarkable trial of Besant and Charles Bradlaugh in 1876 for defying the law and publishing a pamphlet on contraception was not an eyewitness account. Marie Stopes and Annie Besant were clamorous women from whom I would have fled: but at least my mother's odd choice of mentors had helped to blow some of the cob-webs out of the mind of a callow provincial youth. Whatever the deeper motivation of those campaigning feminist birth controllers, or indeed those of my own mother, I had been the beneficiary. The legacy needed acknowledgment. As a fortunate result of an adjournment debate that I initiated in 1966 I was, by happy fortune, able to discharge the obligation in full.

I had over the years frequently probed in the House the inadequacies of family planning services in Britain and its dependencies. I had used a number of stratagems to focus public attention on existing needs, not least in a series of attacks on the abuses and prices of the monopolistic rubber contraceptive industry, which ultimately in 1972 I was to have referred to the Monopolies Commission: and my commentaries on the situation in some overseas territories had led to not a little turbulence. The Earl of Oxford and Asquith, grandson of a former Premier, dominated by his attractive, opinionated Catholic wife had indeed threatened to resign his Governorship of the Seychelles when the courageous Nigel Fisher, then at the Colonial Office, was willingly yielding to my demands that the Governor should cease to obstruct the establishment of family planning clinics in the island. All these and other involvements of mine in the issue had, I thought, clarified for me the nature of the resistances against State involvement in family planning services.

I had sensed, in almost all those hostile to my encouragement of contraceptive services, a keen personal resentment: I was taking away from them the enjoyment experienced by the pure and chaste which springs from their greater virtue. It was the same resentment that I experienced in my attempts to remove legal disabilities from the illegitimate. The birth of children, and especially of illegitimate children, was seen as the rightful punishment for sexual indulgence, exposing the shame of the participants and imposing pain, responsibility and anxiety as the price of the illicit sensual pleasures that had been enjoyed. If the wicked can with the aid of contraceptives sin without fear, what reward is left for the chaste? The notion that punishment is the justifiable consequence of sin is deeply rooted: to outwit God's laws is the crime of hubris and the wrath of the Lord will shortly be brought down upon humanity for daring such cunning. Such primitive apprehensions, albeit expressed in a more sophisticated and theological vocabulary, had ensured that political parties and individual M.P.s, conscious of the Catholic vote, firmly left the spread of family planning to voluntary agencies and barber shops. Our courageous crusading press was no less pusillanimous, almost all of them until recent months still banning advertisements for contraceptives; and the Independent Television Authority ensured for years that our screens were similarly left unsullied.

Many politicians in the past have possessed the temperament that collaborated rather than challenged the consequences of this guilt ridden theology: it would otherwise be difficult to understand how it took almost a century from the time of Bradlaugh's campaign to my precipitation of the first Family Planning Act in Britain. There is, of course, a curious ambivalence in man's attitude to his sexual impulses and organs. They are regarded, as in traditional Christian morality, as the source of impurity and sin, treated with contempt and attempted to be sternly controlled: yet they can also be a source of pride intimately connected with our self-esteem, dignity and power. And few are more prestigious, more concerned about power, than the politician. Potency and virility are at least unconsciously equated with that self same power and indeed, ability in general. In virtue of this equation, not only the specific sexual capacity but the whole individuality may be felt to suffer an affront, a threat or an emasculation, at the idea of a curtailment of fertility. The preoccupation of Hitler, Mussolini, and Petain with the necessity of a high birth rate reflects their feelings of personal insecurity at the prospect of even a reduction in the rate of increase of population: men more confident of their potency would not have screamed for the re-assurance of more and more births. There can be sinister repercussions in the political sphere when some of the anxieties of the castration comp-lex produce distortions of this order. In Britain we were spared some of these excesses but even here, in 1947, the present Lord Chancellor was putting forward in his influential book *The Case for Conservatism* the argument, now proved absurd, that this country was going to be so short of manpower that there was urgent need in the long run to increase the birth rate.

With the intake of a new House in 1966, I felt it likely that there were more balanced opinions available to be mobilized against the prissy, traditional State attitudes. When the Ministry of Health granted doctors employed within the service a new right to charge patients for contra-ceptive prescriptions, I was able to seize my opportunity and initiated an adjournment debate criticizing the decision, which, unusually, was well attended. It was harsh that my criticism had to fall upon Kenneth Robinson, the Health Minister for, to his credit, he had issued earlier in that year a circular giving some encouragement to local authorities to give help to family planning services: that circular ended a period of over thirty years which had passed without a single word of advice on family planning coming from any government. The Minister, however, acknowledged to me in the debate that it was a source of disappointment to him that he had discovered that there were statutory limitations on local authorities which compelled them to confine severely their activities to those who because of strict medical requirements may be in need of contraceptive advice. The surprise Kenneth Robinson felt in finding himself, by law, so hamstrung was not shared by me: my previous in-volvement had made it clear to me that my goal must be to remove these very restrictions.

The debate revealed to me that there were now new responses abroad. A listening new Member, a young geographer, Edwin Brooks, who was unknown to me, introduced himself after the debate. He had drawn a place in the Private Members' ballot and generously offered to co-operate with me in any Bill I might have in mind to increase family planning facilities. Although I was overstretched, I willingly accepted the offer. We worked well together: he is an earnest and conscientious man, and his defeat in the general election of 1970 was an unfortunate loss to the House where he had worked with an unusual sense of duty.

We put together a Bill which gave local authorities for the first time a right to set up or support family planning clinics where contraceptive advice and contraceptives could be given to all, married and unmarried, and for which some or no payment need be charged: and the Bill also gave the local authority power to undertake domiciliary visits which would enable the doctors and social workers to reach homes where advice was much needed. I carefully avoided making the duties mandatory, and by allowing the local authorities to choose to what extent they wished, if at all, to exercise these powers, we sought to avoid any provocation to Members of Parliament in any areas where prejudice may be too strong. With the Bill in this form we obtained the willing approval and active help of Kenneth Robinson and his department.

I commenced then on my familiar task of mobilizing the lobbies that would be likely to assist, wooing the journalists, discussing issues with those active in the family planning field, sounding out influential Members in all Parties who would help us to put the Bill through the House, and not forgetting to tackle those who I anticipated would oppose. To my astonishment I found we had no opposition whatsoever. Unknown to me, or indeed apparently to anyone else, the rapid change of public opinion and private conduct had already totally undermined the walls of former prejudice. Bradlaugh's battle had been won years ago; and politicians and reformers had in fact been afraid of joining forces against an enemy who had long since fled. The religious opposition that in earlier days I had encountered had shamefacedly evaporated: it was not surprising to me a few years later that the Pope threw his followers into rebellion when he sought to insist that all but rhythm methods of contraception must cease. The old traditional Church attitudes were no longer meaningful and the caution and pussyfooting of those engaged in family planning propaganda came from an appraisal of yesterday's public opinion, not of today's. Yet in many ways I found it more disturbing that I was putting through a Bill without opposition than when I hacked my way inch by inch towards my goal: for on this issue the enemies were in fact in the ranks of my allies, and I recoiled from the essential morbidity of their enthusiasm for my cause.

I spoke of planned parenthood and personal choice: they spoke of birth control, with the emphasis on control. They described the unplanned children as 'mistakes', with no appreciation of the unconscious need and demand of a woman for a child that often will mock at all contraceptives. They labelled the women using no regular contraceptive technique as being at risk, as if pregnancy was a disease. I wanted to aid parents to have planned, well spaced and happier families: they unconsciously grudged the establishment of a family at all. And, of course, they were zealous population planners, as apocalyptic in their prophesies of the consequences of overpopulation in Britain, as in the 1930s and '40s the population fanatics had been of the consequences of underpopulation. All their extravagant unfounded population prophesies, I observed, went to the year 2,000. That was their doomsday, even as mediaeval man believed the year 1,000 was to bring the end of his world. It is perhaps a sociological riddle why earlier in this century castration anxieties of many politicians were warded off by urging more and more conceptions; and yet later in the century, using the well-worn psychological mechanism of projection proceeded by denial, so many politicians and publicists refused to acknowledge their own fear of the threat of castration and then dealt with their still acute anxieties by demanding the symbolic castration of all others through state population control policies.

I sought as we moved to the second reading of the Bill to keep a firm distance between these determined Malthusians and myself, and the publicity which I gave out, acting as a curtain raiser to the Bill, did not adopt their arguments. Malthus, indeed, had been part of my adolescent demonology since his notorious essay on population was initially based on a polemic against the anarchist egalitarian Godwin and the early Welsh Co-operator, Robert Owen, who were among my boyhood heroes. I saw no reason to be less suspect of him in my middle age. Indeed, some of those in and out of the House supporting our Bill, by their attitudes, illuminated the passions of Malthus.

I divined Malthus felt keenly the overcrowded family life in which he was brought up. His place, as one of eight children in the family constellation, as a second son, was evidently keenly felt and resented. He was not the first, and his short period as a second son soon ended as six potentially fecund sisters arrived on the scene. He was avid for sole attention and love and he later fiercely attacked those who said all should be shared, and all should be treated as equals. He had been displaced, and others, who could create still more, deprived him of the continued suckling for which he evidently still yearned: the other children should not have been born taking away his food. His elevation of his personal predicament to a powerful philosophical argument, warning that there would not be enough food in the world if the population increased, is an arresting example of how philosophy can be rooted in a psychological prejudice. The pessimistic man, who so early felt the hostility of life as he was brushed aside, all his days revealed his early oral disturbance not only in a neurotic anxiety over food but also in a marked speech defect: and we are not surprised to learn that the world-shaking essay arose directly out of a tumultuous argument over Godwin that he had with his own father who, by siring so many children, had betrayed young Thomas and overpopulated his young world.

Predictably, in his essay, Malthus, advocating sexual restraint, put the desire for food as more powerful than the desire for sex: but although he lived up to his precept that marriage should be postponed when, at forty, he yielded to marriage, having discovered 'the most exquisite gratifications', he incessantly copulated. He preferred to demonstrate against his own parents and, perchance, his own children than to face posterity with his logic intact: he triumphantly bred 11 children, three more than even his father. I saw no less a display of paradoxes and irrationality in some of the uncongenial neo-Malthusians who came to our aid to put through the Family Planning Bill.

But one cannot, in politics, choose one's allies: at the most one can strive to contain them, and, avoiding discussion of population policies, we managed without any vote being taken at any stage of the proceedings to put through the Bill. It was to prove a more important measure than even I had anticipated, for the zealous use of its powers by many local authorities demonstrated its widespread need. When, in 1973, as part of the reorganization of the health services in Britain, the government decided to integrate the local authorities' health services into the National Health Service, it found, in Lords and Commons, an overwhelming demand that the services in use in some local authority areas should now become nationally available. The government yielded to our pressure and accepted that, as from 1974, within the National Health Service, there should be provided a full family planning service with contraceptive advice freely given to all and with contraceptives available on payment only of the usual prescription charge. I take some particular pride, therefore, in having shaped the seminal Family Planning Act which was in no way debased by neo-Malthusian doctrine and yet has helped to provide to many families some of the exquisite gratifications so enjoyed by old Malthus himself.

Five years after the passage of the 1967 Family Planning Act there was no further prospect of restraining the determined life haters from raising their lamentations against man's fertility. The overspill from the U.S.A. doomsday scientists had reached Britain: and a wave of pessimism moved across the Atlantic. With rare hyperbole, the green revolution was scorned, the benefits of technology scoffed and children treated as pollution. Every conclusion or projection that queried the gloom was angrily rejected and the better informed the doubters, like John Maddox, the editor of *Nature*, the authoritative scientific journal, the greater the indignation expressed against them by those insisting that they alone could save man from the end of the world. It was familiar evangelical prophesying, and the self-disgust of these latter day Jeremiahs was often reflected in their distaste for life itself.

Population growth became the fashionable scapegoat, and blamed for every pressure of industry on environment that sacrificed amenity. When Maddox who, it must be conceded, as I have observed, is guilty of enjoying his personal life and family, after a careful evaluation, concluded in an editorial that it was 'at least as good a bet that the population of the U.K. will be the same at the end of the century as it is at present', the jejune and unrealistic riposte was that Britain should, nevertheless, set an example by reducing its birthrate as a contribution to dealing with the problem of the mounting overpopulation in the under-developed countries of the world. It was quite inevitable that with Prince Phillip, whose children are so well financially cushioned by the nation, expressing his antagonism to family allowances, and distinguished doctors calling upon the government to 'combat the British disease of over-population', some response would come from the House of Commons. The stage was set: and Parliament, being what it is, is never short of eager players. With a part of the Establishment panting to give approval, a grand opportunity was available for the full acting-out, unashamedly, of a sado-masochistic Genet-like fantasy. A Private Members' Bill was introduced to amend my Family Planning Act: recklessly disregarding the imperative need for safeguards or checks, it sought to give an almost untrammelled right to our local councils to sterilize the males of the kingdom and to charge the cost to the rates.

This Vasectomy Bill gave me the occasion, in a form which but a few years previously would have been impossible to attempt, to bring home the hazards of yielding to the masochism now infecting our society. The nation has been well and repetitiously alerted against those who excite, or pander to, the sadistic impulses in the community. There are so many who protest against the results of violent films and television plays: some in the House of Commons protest on rational grounds and some out of envy of the cruel actors so uninhibitedly releasing the violence which the protestors have imperfectly repressed in themselves. The apprehensive lobby, fearful lest viewers stimulated by these violent fantasies will live them out in real life, leans heavily against the Home Secretary and the censors. But although concern is founded on the danger that some, seeing these spectacles, may identify with the savage heroes, little concern is expressed for those who morbidly enjoy identifying with the victims.

It is not surprising that the significance of the masochism presently abroad has eluded the attention of our publicists who, often for doubtful motives, so eagerly explore the more obvious aberrant moods of the human condition. The genesis of this strange compulsion in man to seek pleasure in pain and self abasement has been bitterly contested: and the disputes its alleged aetiology has occasioned, not least among the psycho-analysts who have dared to follow clinically its convoluted manifestations, give ample opportunity to those, fearful of its strength, who wish to over-look its importance in determining the nature of our society and of our institutions. Yet, if Freud is right, and if masochism is indeed older than sadism, then man's history of wars and of violent class struggles are part of the frantic attempts of man to ward off his yearning for the ultimate delight of self destruction. By resisting the temptation of a still and lifeless Nirvana, and directing his erotically loaded aggressiveness outwards, away from the interior life, for a little while man postpones the joy of his submission to death. The challenge Freud gave this century, illuminating the importance of sex in our lives, has been only superficially met: gripped with panic, we dodge the awful implications of an hypothesis that a biologically determined instinct, bathed in an exciting sensuality, draws us to our nemesis, and that we can only advance a little the date of our masturbatory death by deflecting some of the force of this terrible instinct into sexually inspired cruelty against our fellow men.

It is easier to avoid than accept these fearful implications, easier to regard the vast sale of punitive Soho pornography as a minor titillation for the ageing than a corroboration of a fundamental need of man for humiliation and ill treatment as a pre-condition to the little death of tumescence: easier to view the self-mutilators in our prison as freaks than as only slightly distorted mirror images of Everyman; and it is certainly more comfortable to find solace in myths than to acknowledge that the wide-spread practice of circumcision among African tribes, Jews and Moslems and public school parents, is a symbolic castration reluctantly accepted as compensation for being denied the full consolation of self-immolation.

Freud's assertions anger the facile optimists, conventional liberals and socialists who, believing man to be naturally good, prefer to sponsor evil illusions by which mankind can expect their lives to be beautified: it is wiser to face and thus learn to temper the Dionysian self-hate which possesses us.

There is no novelty at this stage of the century in doctors telling us that a crippling neurosis which has defied every therapeutic effort may vanish if the patient becomes involved in the misery of an unhappy marriage, or loses all his money, or is stricken by a dangerous organic disease; men must suffer, and often only by gaining the satisfaction of another choice of suffering will he give up his existing painful pleasures. But there is, surely, a novelty in the way there hovers over contemporary Britain an erotogenic despair. There are occasions when, at a cinema with audiences largely of young people, one senses their relief as they find their empathy with a negative, depressive, feckless non-hero or non-heroine drifting into ultimate defeat. The sententious condemnation of violence and sex rarely extends to the vogue of the theatre and literature of despair: yet, as is corroborated by the witness of so many young people becoming alcoholics, drinking themselves to death, or of young drug addicts yielding sensuously to their oral masochism which will destroy them, far more dangers lurk in the luring of the young into the slough of despondency. The force of this ebbing tide pulling us towards hopelessness away from life is not to be underestimated.

I felt its full tug after I had, for the first time in the history of Parliament, raised the issue of vasectomy during the second reading of the abortion debate in 1966. I had, on that occasion, scoffed at those colleagues of mine who were using their zeal for what they believed to be a law reform to wage the class struggle: the wealthy had abortions so why should the workers be denied them? I insisted there was no need to incite the workers to commit the folly of the hated bourgeois, and that it was droll to proffer abortion, as a solution of our difficulties, to the pregnant poverty-stricken wife who had already had half-a-dozen children and was living in squalid overcrowded conditions. If she was aborted, the indifferent husband would, within months undoubtedly impregnate her again: it would be more rational to sterilize the man, and I suggested that the law relating to the performance of vasectomies, then as now ambiguous, should be clarified and facilities made available. My suggestion was received coolly in 1966, although, for sick, not rational reasons, the House initially was to view the matter differently in 1972. The male members of the 1966 Parliament were however tolerant only towards an assault being made on women's essential femininity. They had other views on what could be interpreted as an attack on maleness. I was certainly conscious as I spoke on the unfamiliar subject of vasectomy how many Members were wriggling in their seats.

But my reported comments provoked a different response outside the House. The latent masochism embodied within the community became manifest and I felt its ensnaring pseudo podia slimily reach out to me. I was astonished to find myself deluged with approving letters from men in all parts of the country. I recalled the anathematization by Justinian of the second century martyr Origen: all the synods' condemnation of the early heretic had not influenced twentieth century semi-Christian England. My correspondents, judging by their fervour, had been gripped by Origen's heresy and wanted a vasectomy as a penultimate step towards the self-inflicted sacrificium phalli followed by the great scholar. My postbag taught me the need to be wary. Certainly in the years that followed I did not change my opinion that there were especial social circumstances where it would be wise to encourage a vasectomy: and that after skilled counselling the State in proper surgical conditions should give assistance to mature couples, with completed families, living in a stable union, who wished to adopt this fateful and probably irreversible operation as a contraceptive of last resort. But now I had learned of the need for sophisticated screening if we were to distinguish between those who seek sterilization as part of a voluntary programme of planned parenthood and those who neurotically desire self-abasement.

The pervasiveness of this prevailing masochism is, no doubt, contributed to by our failure to find satisfaction by directing our self-destructiveness outwards: it is hard to endure peace, and our young people can only wear regimental uniforms and Vietnam camouflage suits for sick fun as they make their cool deliberately non-related passeggiata through Chelsea. Impeded aggression, if left to its own devices, can cause grave injury. And meantime, too, we have lost some of the classical methods which have served us well in overcoming some of our masochism: our society is not engineered to encourage the life instinct to overcome its eternal adversary, and the search for pleasure in infertility or death is insufficiently obstructed. The purpose of Eros, Freud has taught us, is to combine single human individuals and after that families, then races, peoples and nations into one great unity, the unity of mankind. But our technology can thwart this purpose: in the large factories men and women work essentially alone not libidinally bound to their fellow workers but chained to a machine. We are becoming a society, not a community: and it is in the condition of loneliness that masochism flourishes. Indeed, the most clamorous of those many correspondents demanding of me that the State at no expense to themselves should end their fertility were lonely unmarried men: in these secular days they cannot gain, through religion, the release of their boundless masochistic desires, by contemplating the agony of the Cross. Nothing short of themselves becoming sacrificial lambs would be satisfying.

The dangers of a society corroborating rather than reassuring us in our loneliness were insightfully understood by the Marxist psychoanalyst Wilhelm Reich when, before he went mad, he published his work on the masochistic character. Angered by Reich's emphasis on the disastrous consequences of certain social conditions, that could tease out our masochism, Freud extravagantly condemned the contribution as written in the service of the German Communist party: but Reich has richly added to our understanding of the dynamics of masochism, and helped us to see the origins of the awkward atatic behaviour that nowadays is so infuriatingly and provocatively displayed by so many young people in their manners and intercourse with their elders. Indirect and disguised as is the demand, the meaning of the provocations is an imperious request for love. This is the way of all masochistic characters, needing never ending proofs of love which will reduce their anxiety and inner tensions. Behind the provocations is the deep disappointment in love that has to be felt by every child: but for the more flawed, aware, in fact or fantasy, of the total failure of the loved one to gratify his excessive demands, there arises the terrible fear of being left alone, the fear of losing contact. Afraid of being alone in the universe, he inadequately seeks to establish his contact through spite and provocations: or, less deviously, re-establishes his lost contact with the skin of the early beloved, by wishing to be pinched, punched, fettered or whipped. Our sullen youth, like the current huge sale of flagellation pornography and the large demand for the Miss Flags of Soho, reveal that our society fails to act as an emollient helping to soothe the hurts of the rejected. Our lonely society is the well fertilized base upon which masochism flourishes.

The reaction to my almost casual references to the merits of vasectomy in 1966 had made me circumspect. Extroverted personalities, emptying out their masochism in aggressive attacks on society's wrongs, can, with a high measure of success, convert the menacing self-punishing elements of their nature into sadistic attacks upon evil institutions. This leaves them with little deposit of masochism in their interior life and so, unacquainted with its dangers, they singularly fail to recognize the masochism in others. But I had now been alerted and my subsequent explorations into the practice of vasectomy both in the private sector of medicine and in some of the voluntary associations providing facilities for male sterilization did not reassure me. The population control lobby was growing vociferous and, assessing the dangers, I gave a number of reported speeches outside the House seeking to explain in simple terms the danger of leaving the sterilization of men to mere technicians. Each speech brought me to more evidence of the wreckage caused by camouflaged enthusiasms of the sterilizers. But when in the House in 1970 I urged on Dick Crossman, then the Minister responsible, the need to insist that strengthened counselling and psychiatric services were available to men seeking sterilization operations, he brushed aside my misgivings as unfounded. Crossman, notorious for his intellectual bullying, would be almost the last man in the Commons to peer behind sadistic conduct into the aetiology of masochism: and, worse, it was clear to me that he had the support of the heads of his department who were even then engaged in discussions on extending the birth control facilities so as to increase the availability of vasectomies.

When, therefore, a Member successful in the 1972 Private Members' Bill ballot announced he was introducing a Vasectomy Bill, I was not surprised he was to receive more than benevolent neutrality from the Ministry. Philip Whitehead, the sponsor, had come into the House as recently as 1970 and it was soon clear to me that he was in danger of falling into the hands of the experienced population control and abortionist lobbies. Initially he resented my interventions and warnings but, as the Bill proceeded, he had the wit to see the dangers created by his enthusiastic allies and was to collaborate with me. However, this only came about after he, seemingly irrelevantly, had in the early debates emphasized that he was an adopted child. This prompted me, in public and in private, to advise him to guard against his possible motivations. An adopted child can usually have little love for his father: the mother, so sinned against, may be forgiven but the abandoning father must forever remain hated. It would be likely that an unrecognized son would have buried resentments towards a natural father, but it would be an ironic twist of events if such a son worked through his deep grievance by precipitating the symbolic castration of thousands of natural fathers throughout the realm. My hints, presented I hope with sufficient delicacy, were not unkindly received by Whitehead, and after our early clashes we were to work together. As so often happens with a Member who has a high potential, the steering of a Private Member's Bill helps him in his political maturation: the only difficulty I was to have with Whitehead was his incapacity to modify his responses to the provocations of opponents.

I understood well at the start of the Bill's progress that I would be a maverick in these proceedings. Some would support it because they coveted another weapon in the armoury of population control; others, like some Catholic M.P.s, would oppose the Bill as part of their orthodox disapproval of any form of birth control. I, almost alone, however, wanted the Bill passed as an aid to family planning, but also wanted strong in-built controls that would check the psychologically sick gaining social approval for their morbid indulgences. I decided, therefore, at the second reading to steal the Bill and capture the headlines. The problems had to be levered to the surface and, if I was to leave my impress on the Bill, the thoughtful public had to understand the issue in depth. I gave the longest speech I have ever made in the House, speaking, not for the first time, at different levels and in dramatic language with macabre illustrations, and yet with a weight of evidence which mocked at the simplicity of the views of the absolutists supporting and opposing the Bill.

The strategy succeeded: my contribution was an arrogant one but it dominated the debate, and the subsequent committee and press comment. I gained the centre ground, Whitehead's co-operation, and then the collusive support of Michael Allison, the intelligent and sensitive junior Minister looking after the government's interest in the Bill. By the time the committee stages were completed, the British Medical Association, and the Medical Defence Union, the body protecting doctors from actions for professional negligence, had both turned to me for aid. They were entirely sympathetic to my approach and defined for me still further the needed safeguards. Any residual opposition within the Ministry bureaucracy crumbled and on the eve of the report stage at a meeting between Allison, the senior officials and myself, I received the undertakings for which I had fought. On the Bill becoming law both administrative and medical circulars were to be sent out to local authorities making it clear that no approval or grant should be afforded to them to enable them to become involved in vasectomy unless they conformed to strictly defined criteria: and those criteria, including a proper standard of pre- and post-vasectomy counselling, would be sufficiently and expansively drawn to make it most improbable that any but older husbands of completed family units would be made sterile. More, to ensure that the counselling which would be given would be of a proper quality, the Ministry agreed to set up a special advisory committee of those who had the required expertise, to advise the Ministry in laying down the criteria for the local authorities.

All then seemed set fair for the final stages of the Bill: but, in fact, the population lobby had overplayed their hand. Their intemperate propaganda had been taken seriously by the anti-immigrant lobby in the

House who now suddenly and belatedly joined in the show. The population controllers may, in their propaganda exercise, have felt relief at throwing off their castration anxieties by denying them in themselves and recommending their symbolic equivalent to others: but the very anxieties they were unloading were falling heavily upon those who were so burdened themselves that the extra load broke them. None are more uncertain of their virility than the anti-immigrant M.P.s. Indeed, it is their faltering and fissured sexual attitudes that prompts their fear of the black man. Sin is black and sex is black and dirty: and their fears of the dark passions are the precursors to their fear of and antagonism to the dark man. The black man to them, becomes the symbol of potency: and, anxiously, lacking confidence in their own capacity, they exaggerate the sexual prowess and fertility of the newcomers and puff up their own. The Vasectomy Bill was interpreted by some of those in the anti-immigration lobby as a direct attack on their own virility. I once told the House that a society with fewer eunuchs would create fewer Enochs. Powell's prurient and excessive preoccupation with the births of immigrants barely masks his fear of their ability for copulation. He has publicly in a television study declared his wish to be a monk: men, more comfortable and confident in their sexuality do not yearn to escape to celibacy. The population controllers in their vasectomy propaganda lit up the fears of the anti-immigrant lobby who became haunted by the fantasy that the white men would be sterilized and the field left clear to the lascivious blacks. The disputes that smouldered in the House between the anti-life and the anti-black brigades, both suffering from the same soul sickness, although selecting different symptoms, will be case studies for the future psychologically-informed historians: but in the present, some of the racialist views expressed both publicly and privately were the worst obscenities I had encountered in Westminster. In the midst of this degrading clamour, it was not easy to manoeuvre the report stages and third reading through the House. But with the deployment of some intricate procedural stratagems, and the assistance of Allison, by a hair's-breadth, we evaded the filibusters and put the Bill on the Statute Book. This Act, and its parent Act, together, may perchance have added a little to family happiness in the land.

XIII

My intervention in the vasectomy controversy was a success. Thanks largely to the Abortion Law Reform Association, my intervention in the Abortion Bill debates was a total failure. The Association was begotten and indeed initially financed by some of the officials of the Eugenic Society, a body for whose follies the nation still pays a heavy price. Each generation produces sham reforming bodies offering their false solutions. Manned by the disarrayed, preferring the escape of activity rather than the anguish of insight, they peddle their spurious panaceas. Their aims are often dressed up in an unfeeling rationality justifying, in the name of the collective good, unspeakable cruelty.

The propaganda of the Eugenic Society was largely responsible for the segregation into huge isolated colonies of the mentally sub-normal. Britain accepted the view of the avant-garde intellectuals of the period that, without segregation, the mentally retarded, endowed with greater sexuality and fertility than the civilized, would ere long drag down the intelligence of the nation. To contain this threat many of the mentally retarded were removed into isolated asylums where not only were they prevented from spreading their seed among the more intelligent but, under strict supervision, in enforced celibacy, the women cut off from the men, lived out their miserable lives leaving no polluting progeny. This 'rational' solution to mental subnormality was founded on superstition: the mentally retarded have a low fertility rate and intelligence we now know swings to the median. Today we are engaged upon the tasks of emptying out these grim asylums which have become a national scandal and of educating the community to receive the banished harmless simple ones back into its midst. Real reforms are indeed not necessarily brought about by those who pretentiously describe themselves as reformers.

The Abortion Law Reform Association, founded by the stockbroker treasurer of the Eugenic Society, came into existence in 1936. It carried forward the fallacies of the earlier eugenicists, claiming that, without abortion, as the professional classes and more intelligent mastered the art of birth control, the feckless and unfit would breed the next generation of Britons. The Association was originally dominated by a cluster of intelligent shrill viragos, Janet Chance, Stella Browne and Alice Jenkins. This trio would have fully approved of their successors who, thirty years later, were to bring to fulfilment the misshapen dreams of the founding reluctant mothers. The three women all resented their feminine identity, and their writing and speeches reveal their keen sense of deprivation. Janet Chance was choked with envy for the sexual revelling which she colourfully imagined in the pre-war years was the sole prerogative of the males: in one book she revealingly called upon women to demand the same rights of sexual enjoyment for themselves that men had, she claimed, always taken for granted. Stella Browne, a loudmouthed, filthy story telling ragbag, repudiated all signs of her womanliness by dressing herself in aggressively unfashionable clothes that effectively covered such little feminine charms as she may have possessed. As for Alice Jenkins, the fierce administrator of the organization, one suspects that although the mother of three she lived her adult life still unconsciously clinging to the cloacal theory of birth, a fantasy entertained by so many infants: filth and children become curiously interconnected, and the differentiation between the two ambiguous. She acted out her pathetic and dangerous dilemmas by becoming the driving force of an organization wishing to cleanse women of children, and by founding the equivalent Anti-litter League.

The pathological disorders of these women were projected into the Abortion Association. It began and ended as a sick organization. Long before I entered the House I was aware of the odour of this sick-bed; this was one self-styled reforming organization to which I gave a wide berth. Indeed, the early sponsors of abortion law reform Bills in Parliament had the wit to refuse to be manipulated by such intemperate people. Lord Amulree, the Liberal doctor peer who introduced a reforming Bill in 1953, found the irrational clamour of Alice Jenkins and her followers, who really wanted abortions available on request, so intolerable that he peremptorily refused to proceed further with his Bill. And in 1961 when Kenneth Robinson unsuccessfully introduced another Bill seeking to modify the abortion laws he too evidently felt the necessity of shielding himself from this feverish lobby. He wisely insisted, as a condition of introducing his Bill, that for once these noisy women stilled their tongues and desisted from organized pressure. When Lord Silkin steered an abortion Bill to a third reading in the House of Lords, he kept the abortionist lobby so determinedly at bay, that the officials of the abortion law reform association openly declared that they only comforted themselves with the thought that his Bill could not become law because of the interruption of the 1966 election. Later in 1966 however, David Steel, a young man possessed of greater political conceit than sophistication, fell completely to their blandishments: and, despite subsequent protestations to the contrary, during the passage of his Abortion Act not even his wilfulness enabled him to escape effectively from the Association's tentacles.

It was tragic that a cowardly Tory government and an intolerant House, forever looking over its shoulder, did not use Kenneth Robinson's Bill in 1961 as a basis for discussion: that Bill was, with little protest, talked out. It was precisely because much needed, though minor reforms, in the abortion law were then thwarted that eventually the consequent dammed-up indignation was available to be stirred up, with such disastrous results, by the abortionist lobby. It was indisputably clear long before 1961 that changes in the law were needed. A bold judge, Mr Justice Macnaghten, and a courageous obstetrician, Alec Bourne, had together in 1938 put the laggard legislature to shame. Alec Bourne, who later was to recoil from Steel's Bill, and was to be one of its most severe critics, had aborted a child who had been subjected to multiple rape, had informed the police of his action, had been charged and then acquitted. In his judgment Macnaghten claimed that if a pregnancy was likely to make a woman a physical and mental wreck, a doctor was justified in aborting her. That was good sense but doubtful law. If the legislature had been ready to corroborate the judge-made law and extend it to include the case of women to whom there was a genuine threat to mental or physical health if a pregnancy was left to full term, then there could have without difficulty been sufficient safeguards to be sure such provisions were not abused. Such an Act would have totally taken the steam out of the abortionist campaigners. Instead the Tory-dominated House of 1961 yielded to the religious lobbies, then still believed to be powerful, and so gave the guarantee that ultimately the abortion lobby would be able to claim total victory.

For my part I could never regard any abortion Bill, narrowly or widely drawn, as a triumph. Every failure we make to plan so that every life, within its puny transient span, can live out its full potentiality is a defeat, just as every hanging of a murderer, every imprisonment of a rapist or a traitor is a defeat for the community: these are the signs that the community does not know how to gain loyalty, and an admittance by the nation of its failure to know how to deal with its failures. An abortion can result from a defeat because of a failure of medical science as yet unable to rescue a malformed unborn child from its fate; it can be precipitated by the selfishness of a society too indifferent to save women and children from intolerable housing conditions; it can come from a vengeful society, now sophisticating its hostility to the illicit love of the unmarried by proffering abortion rather than providing the financial and social support desperately needed. Worst of all it is a defeat for women. It is illusory to claim abortion on demand is an extension of women's freedom: on the contrary, it is an enslavement. It enslaves her to the selfishness of the narcissistic lover fearful of taking the step towards parenthood and maturation, even as it enslaves her to the husband who treats her as a convenience to be periodically flushed out. Abortion on demand is a triumph not for women but for the men who fear to love, to give themselves in love, the thwarted men who, evoking their initial feelings of rejection as babes, release their hate upon all womankind, working off their old scores against mothers by slaying motherhood. Legislation can sing with love and concern: but it can also be replete with envy and revenge. The politics of the abortionist lobby were the politics of hate.

For the unmarried mothers, the aid the abortionists wished to bring was as vicious and of the same quality as that extended by the Victorian moralists saving them from sin. From my earliest days in the House I had fought with not a little success to change the discriminatory laws working against the illegitimate, and my involvement had taught me there was no more naïve error than to suppose most unmarried mothers had their children as a result of 'mistakes'. Neither increased birth-control facilities nor easier abortion had any appreciable effect on the illegitimate birth-rate. So often illegitimate births arise out of the profound unconscious need of the mother. Often feeling deprived of love from her own parents, she yearns to have a child from whom she can receive and to whom she can give the love she lacks: sometimes indeed she wants the child to demonstrate to her unfeeling mother how she will treat a child and give it the love her mother has been incapable of giving. To offer abortion to the unmarried mother whose deepest need is to have a child is a terrible cruelty even although it may meet with the approval of the prim grandmother, and the extended family, protecting themselves from their neighbours by pressurizing the girl to accept the abortion. The hospitals were to find that aborting such a girl and so denying her real need, was to mean she often proceeded to make another bid for a child, and so succeeded, or, worse, came back to exercise again her new sad 'right' for another abortion. The woman in child in difficulties demands our compelling concern; but her problems although incommoding society far more if dealt with by insight and in depth, are not ended by the cutting scalpel of a surgeon.

No less lacking in delicacy was the abortionists' insistence that the law should spell out in detail the right of the woman to abort a child who may be born handicapped. That some pregnant women, even with support, cannot tolerate such a possibility, is indisputable, but such women could be protected by an all-embracing clause acknowledging the need to safeguard the mental health of the potential mother. To declare, by legislation, that a potentially handicapped child can be thrown into the dustbin is a sickening thought to all those parents, teachers, nurses and social workers who live out their lives gaining infinite rewards from their dedication to the less well endowed. Parents do not love their children for their perfection: we do not shop around for our children with a copy of the consumer guide in our hands. The children with blemishes, and those who assist them, oft times have a style of life which inspires our society. Once we draw boundaries to our compassion we begin to shrivel. The heart cannot be compartmentalized: if we attempt it the whole heart hardens. Any diminution in our reverence for life, faulty or blemished as it may seem to be, brings infinite dangers. And for those of us who are comrades in disbelief, those who are humanists valuing this life because we believe in no other, the humiliation, when we must sometimes concede that in this far from ideal world a life must be ended, is all the greater: for we know of no eternity except that to be found in our children, and in our works in society.

Such thoughts would have been unlikely to have troubled David Steel when, having drawn a high place in the annual ballot for Private Members' Bills in 1966, to the delight of the Abortion Law Reform Association officials, after a delay he agreed to their request that he should sponsor an abortion Bill. The younger pace setters in the Association were no less clinically interesting than their early predecessors. The vice-chairman was a woman ever in anguish over motherhood: her friends in their published partisan account of the history of the Abortion Act tell how each one of her three pregnancies was 'a nightmare'; how each childbirth was followed by depressive illness. Only an abortion had saved her, we are told, from the desperation of a fourth pregnancy. It is fortunate that such reactions to the blessings of motherhood are atypical. But it is from such stuff that abortion reformers are evidently made. Her committee colleagues included the geneticist lecturer Martin Cole, who was later to attain national notoriety as a maker of a sex education films for children whilst marrying, for the fourth time, a lesbian pupil who, with his approval, explained at length their personal relationship to the Sunday papers; and no less persistent as a campaigning colleague was Dr Peter Darby, a rabid right-winger whose desire for change seemed to be so narrowly confined to the abortion law that, as part of his outright opposition to the welfare State and the national health service, he even strongly disapproved of government participation in birth-control facilities. Presiding over these committee members was Professor Glanville Williams, an academic lawyer of some distinction. His aggressive approach to abortion reform endeared him to the younger zealots but the objects of his aggression have been highly selective. During the war against Hitlerism, his convictions made him an absolute pacifist but he is a great fighter for legalizing euthanasia for, among others, the aged and the handicapped. Once I had a very lengthy television debate with him in which he supported and I opposed euthanasia. We enacted a trial before a jury of young lawyers and students calling, examining and cross-examining witnesses: he was severely trounced, as the verdict of the jury and the television critics revealed, and we ended the occasion with the same quality of mutual regard and esteem for each other as we began. It is mortifying that such a group of people, backed by funds from a cranky American endowment in an unsuspecting Britain, became for a while the most successful political lobby of the post war years.

This lobby did not, however, immediately succeed in latching on to Steel when the ballot result was announced. He wished to claim the support of his constituents by putting forward a Bill which he believed would aid tenant farmers but when he found the government was not prepared to assist him in such a project he gave up that Bill without a fight, and turned to other possibilities. Lord Arran, as one member of the Liberal Party to another, urged him to take up homosexual reform, since this had been approved by the Liberal Council, but the circumspect reformer, on discovering the Church of Scotland had opposed the Wolfenden proposals and on taking the temperature among his own Scots constituents, refused to accept Arran's minimization of the political risks involved, and brushed aside Arran's assessment of Commons opinion on the rival issues of homosexuality and abortion. The abortion law reform historians who have written that Steel only understood the subject of abortion reform, and what he wanted in the Bill, six months after he announced his sponsorship of the Bill, are no doubt right in indicating how little prior thought he gave to the content of the Bill before its publication. But no-one could fault the sums of this calculating young man in his assessment of Commons opinion. Arran understands the Lords well but, not surprisingly, has no understanding of the temperament of the Commons. His judgment was faulty in concluding that the Commons would be more sympathetic to homosexual rather than abortion reform: and, if change can be brought about by the taking of soft options, then Steel was right in choosing by a process of elimination the Abortion Bill. In fact few division Lobby decisions illuminate the characterology of many members of Parliament better than the overwhelming supporting vote they gave to the second reading of the Abortion Bill. The only compensation I wrested from my whole participation in the abortion controversy was the additional understanding it yielded to me of the dynamics of political motivation.

It should never be forgotten that amongst politicians there is a surfeit of rejected lovers, and the House of Commons is no exception to the general rule. All our sexual lives are diphasic, occurring in two phases, and the rebuffs we receive in the first five years of our lives can leave far greater scars than those we romanticize in our second phase. All my political experience compels me to acknowledge that the events that have occurred in the lives of my fellow M.P.s and, of course, in my own, when two or three years of age play a much larger part in our collective decision-making than any other single factor. It is true that we are, inevitably, a disparate and diverse crew, but there nevertheless is no imprint stamped more generally and clearly upon contemporary politicians than the spurning they endured when within their phallic phase.

Freud has told us that among the principle findings of psychoanalysis is that sexual life starts with clear manifestations soon after birth and that it comprises the function of obtaining pleasure from zones of the body, a function which is subsequently, although sometimes imperfectly, brought into the service of the function of reproduction. The first organ to make its appearance as an erotogenic zone and to make libidinal demands upon the mind is, from birth onwards, the mouth; then we attain the sadistic-anal phase when satisfaction is sought in aggression and the excretory function; the third phase is the phallic one when a boy, from about the age of two or three, feels pleasurable sensations in his sexual organ and learns to procure these at will by manual stimulation. This is the time, Freud has demonstrated, that he becomes 'the mother's lover'. 'He desires to possess her physically in ways which he has divined from his observations and intuitive surmises of sexual life and tries to seduce her her by showing her the male organ of which he is the proud owner.' It is the rebuff that so many politicians received at that time that ever reverberates around the House of Commons.

For the mother well understands that the infant's sexual excitement refers to her; and she begins the prohibitions which contain the explicit or implicit threat of castration, soon to be underlined by the spectacle of the woman's lack of a penis. The threat and the spectacle constitute, Freud insists, the greatest trauma in a man's life: to save himself the child must make the renunciation which outlaws his sexuality, dissolves his Oedipus complex, permits him to live more serenely through a latent phase, until with puberty, the boy in the new resurgence of sexuality reaches his fourth phase, the genital phase where the earlier oral, anal and phallic phases are subordinated to the primacy of the genitals. But this process is certainly not always carried out perfectly: and for some, the frustration of the phallic and exhibitionist activities at the height of their development at two or three years of age, by the very person towards whom the activity is directed, shapes their whole future character. The change from the approving mother, encouraging and praising the child as he ejected his excreta, to the disapproval given when he shows his later capacity of an erect phallus to the mother is too abrupt, and the hurt to his pride can sometimes never be forgiven. In some combinations of particular circumstances, when the mother was the stronger of the parents, when she was a martinet, a 'masculine' personality, when the father had died early or was otherwise out of the picture, when, in short, the main frustration the child is enduring seems to him to emanate directly and almost solely from the mother, then the sadism he displays in his adult life towards all women is his way of belatedly exacting vengeance on his strict mother.

The faulted child, never having come to terms with the rebuff he received at his phallic phase, is the adult whom Reich has described as a phallic-narcissistic character, and the traits Reich enumerates as belonging to this character type chasteningly abound among successful politicians.

The typical phallic-narcissistic character is self-confident, often arrogant, vigorous and often impressive . . . Everyday behaviour is never crawling but usually haughty or derisively aggressive. In the behaviour towards the object, the love object included, the narcissistic element always dominates over the object – libidinal, and there is always an admixture of more or less disguised sadistic traits . . . In relatively unneurotic representatives of this type, social achievements, thanks to the free aggression, is strong, impulsive, energetic and usually productive . . . Relationships with women are however disturbed by the contempt which is rarely lacking for the female sex.

The mother may have refused his erect penis but he will not accept her depreciatory verdict; it is his special pride and it is not surprising that the analysts find that such men are characterized by a proud self-confident concentration on their own genitals. Typically, we are told, analysis reveals the identification of the total ego with the phallus.

To the unconscious of the man of this type, the penis is not in the service of love but is an instrument of aggression and vengeance . . . In such a man the sexual act has the unconscious meaning of proving to the woman again and again how potent they are; at the same time it means piercing or destroying the woman, in a more superficial sense degrading her.

Always the pride in the real or fantasized phallus goes hand in hand with strong phallic aggression.

The community has its gains from the persistent exhibitionism of these politicians who displace their phallic erective potency into their displays of political wares: the stamina, the compulsiveness which they show as they draw attention to themselves, ever inviting approval, means the community is treated to a constant stream of ideas, projects and programmes. More diffident, less clamorous and perhaps more mature men, would not find such conduct endurable: but for the phallic-narcis-cist, as Nye Bevan once commented, speaking for a whole range of politicians, the only bad publicity is no publicity. The more they are in the news, the more they bloom. Inevitably, however, the genesis of their dynamism is not wholly concealed: it is revealed often in the shallowness of the proffered ideational content, and the narcissism obtrudes in their insensitivity or in the spurious tone of their expressed concern for others.

Similarly the ever accompanying phallic aggression means that the community has at its service men ready to attack wrongs, stale insti-tutions and established tired thinking: or indeed, belligerently and courageously to defend the nation as Churchill did, ever wearing his phallic hats, waving his huge phallic cigars, and giving his sign of erect fingers which everyone understood contained a double entendre extend-ing its meaning beyond the V-for-Victory. But there are of course dangers to the community from such men who can never be at peace: for these are the men who are frightened to move forward, for more selflessness based upon love not hate for women, founded upon a genitally organized character, is not for them, and equally they dare not move back. Writing of those who have failed in the more conventional manner to dissolve their Oedipus complex, Freud has explained that clinical experience has shown that a degradation of the libido takes place – a regression of the libidinal organization to an earlier stage. The phallic character fears however to regress to the passivity of his earlier anal phase; he fears his passive homosexuality and therefore exaggerates the manifestations of the phallic stage. The nation consequently has 'big characters' as they are popularly called, at its disposal, the men larger than life. But their exaggerated manifestations, although frequently beneficial, are too compulsively neurotic to be constantly benign. The aggression must be ceaseless and is often misdirected. Turbulent men may have their place but they bring war not peace, and they cannot leave society to enjoy calm and harmony.

The Abortion Bill proved to be a bespoke piece of tailoring well fitted to suit the temperamental needs of a phallic-narcissistic character type. No greater assault upon a mother can be devised than to savage her creation in the uterus: and here not in private fantasy but in public debate, without reproach, in the guise of reform, was the grand opportunity to pay off the old grievances. The temptation was so irresistible that the House of Commons, uncharacteristically throwing all precaution to the wind, allowed the sponsors of the Bill to deceive themselves and the majority of the House that the Bill they were passing was not giving abortion on request to the nation. Within a mere four years an ashamed Parliament seeing the havoc, all of which was foreseeable, the Act was causing was compelled to set up a full-scale enquiry into its workings. Such extraordinary events can only be fully explained in terms of the psychopathology of the abortion lobby and of many politicians.

My contribution inevitably, at the beginning of the Bill, on second reading, was sulkily received. The House wanted approbation; it resented being made to feel guilty, as was my intention. I was insistent that turning life into death could never be a reform: that it was politically, as biologically, reactionary. The House did not wish to be told that the comfortably-off married man who sent his wife to Harley Street to have his unborn child killed was in need of a marriage guidance counsellor, not an abortionist; that the working class wife with six children perhaps needed her husband vasectomized and certainly not a series of abortions; and it disliked being told of its ambivalence to the plight of the unmarried mother. The House was irritated, as all people are, by bewilderment: it understood stereotypes better than human beings and, since I had been the champion of divorce, homosexual and family planning reforms, I was expected to display the usual liberal syndrome, irrespective of the merits of the particular issue. Their feelings were not calmed by my insistence that some legal changes were needed; for I stressed that almost all the changes that were needed arose out of the selfishness of a society unwilling to sacrifice sufficient of its resources to ensure equality of opportunity to all the newly born. The supporters of the Bill wanted to feel good men, noble social reformers, blowing the trumpets to bring down the walls of prejudice. They were being told they were advertising their defeatism, stressing their disbelief in their capacity to bring about the needed changes in our society. I concluded my speech by insisting the Bill needed more reshaping but, even if well shaped in its committee stage, as legislators when the Act was passed, we 'should apologize and with dismay and with no great enthusiasm pass it on to the country'. A majority of the House wanted clear clarion calls, and I indeed was striking a discordant note.

Any hopes that I had that in the committee stages the Bill could be improved were to be dashed. For two-and-a-half months over twelve bitter sittings, the thirty of us selected to serve were embroiled in the most disagreeable of committee proceedings in my experience. A holy war was waged between the proselytizing abortionists and their outright opponents, mostly Catholics; their taunts and jibes, increasingly emotive as time went on, inflamed each other to an unyielding dogmatism and the *ad hoc* amendments recklessly being put before the committee by Steel, often without any consultations with his vexed supporters, added to the tensions. In vain did Bernard Braine, the late Sir John Hobson, William Deedes, Angus Maude and myself, try to create a rational consensus: the Bill remorselessly went on becoming increasingly, line by line, an invitation to every psychopathic and mercenary doctor in the land to exploit women hesitating in their pregnancy. But although, amidst the ideological clamour in the committee room, our contributions went unheeded, our analyses and prognostications were reaching outside. Half-way through our proceedings the Royal College of Obstetricians and Gynaecologists became increasingly alarmed and successfully pressurized the British Medical Association to join in an attempt to arrest the further degeneration of the Bill. The officials of the Ministry of Health were about to lose their nerve too. When it was clear I was about to frame amendments which would have married the views of the five independent members on the committee with the British Medical Association and the Royal College of Obstetricians, Julian Snow, the Parliamentary Secretary to the Ministry of Health who sat on the committee to watch over the department's interests, invited me to a private meeting. We agreed together an amendment which was acceptable to the Royal College and to the B.M.A., and Snow, after some further consultations with his department and with the Minister, Kenneth Robinson, came back to me with the assurance that by speech and vote he would support me if I placed down this complicated but crucial amendment. If the amendment had been accepted it would have meant, in fact, that only a consultant, usually a gynaecologist, who was or had been within the Health Service could carry out the operation. It was designed to ensure that those who carried out the operation were skilled and would be unlikely frivolously to carry it out, and to prevent private racketeering outside the Service.

The amendment was painstakingly and fiercely debated over three sessions and, honouring his promise, Snow spoke in support making it clear that it was Kenneth Robinson's wish that the amendment be passed. When the vote was taken, in probably an unprecedented open display of government divisions in a committee, the other government Ministers on the committee, the spinster Alice Bacon representing the Home Office and Bruce McMillan representing the Scottish Office, neither of whom had made any contribution to the debate, both failed to support their colleague. Grim-faced when the division was called they refused to register a vote and narrowly, by two votes, the amendment was lost. The open dispute between the Home Office and the Ministry of Health became a matter of immediate comment in the House and I was plied by non-committee Members wanting to understand the issue that had caused this almost unprecedented breach between the Minister and his officials in one department and the Minister and officials of another department. I used the occasion to do my own proselytization. The abortion lobby in the weeks that followed became, justifiably, alarmed that when the Bill was returned to the full House for its report stage I would succeed in persuading the House to reverse the committee's decision: and thus came their counterblow which was to silence me for the rest of the Bill.

I was politically blackmailed. It is the only time in my life that I have ever yielded to blackmail and it will be the last. My Homosexual Reform Bill was going through the House contemporaneously with the Abortion Bill and it was made clear to me by many Members, not a few of whom have since repented, that if I pursued my course on the Abortion Bill they would withdraw their support from me on the Homosexual Bill. The threat came to me from too many quarters, and was being hinted at by too many pro-abortion newspaper columnists for me not to realize that the pressure on me was deliberate and organized. The abortionist lobby fully understood the significance of my amendment and the consequence to them if on the report stage I succeeded in my effort. Their historians writing of 'the Abse amendment which had been so narrowly beaten off in committee' have recounted: 'Both the Abortion Law Reform Association and Steel recognized they must resist the introduction of this clause or risk emasculation of the Bill. Had it been added it might well have created a physical and psychological bottleneck which would greatly have reduced the number of abortions actually carried out under the new law.' What it certainly would have done was to have prevented abortion on request, and the subsequent commercial exploitation. At first, I held out against the pressure upon me but as I saw my support for the Homosexual Bill melting away, rightly or wrongly, I yielded: and thereafter to my shame I remained during all the further stages of the Bill completely silent.

The Lords, however, when the Bill came to them took up the issue and a slightly modified form of my amendment was passed by them. Once again however the relentless abortion lobby adopted similar tactics. By speeches made by their prominent M.P. supporters, and by the manipulation of sympathetic journalists, the threat came that if the Lords insisted on retaining this amendment against the wishes of the Commons then the pro-abortionist M.P.s would invoke the Parliament Act. Under this Act a Bill defeated in the Lords automatically becomes law after twelve months if it is approved in its original form by the Commons in the next session of Parliament. The Lords, aware of the hostility of many of the left wing Members who were supporters of the Abortion Bill and who were antagonistic towards their institution, over-estimated the dangers of a constitutional crisis, and they, as I had done, yielded to the intimidation. There was then but one further blow to fall, in the shape of the Lord Chief Justice's last minute crass legalistic intervention when he put forward a new solution, which was accepted, to the definition of the element of risk which would justify an abortion. His proposal was intended to assist the courts when adjudicating upon a charge of an illegal abortion: it declared that if the risk to life or the risk of injury to health is greater than by terminating a pregnancy then an abortion should be legal. The only help this amendment gave the courts, although that was not Lord Parker's intention, was to make it highly improbable that anyone ever appeared before them: it was a profound change in the law, making it almost impossible for a prosecution ever to challenge in a criminal court a doctor's abortion decision. Judges who stumble into political decision-making frequently appear quite daft. The abortion lobby greeted the unexpected bonus with glee and I suffered in my self ordained silence. The curtain came down, the Bill became an Act and abortion became available on demand in Britain.

The Act was no sooner in operation than the scandals began. Britain became Europe's abortion centre; property speculators had a new field in developing abortion clinics; an irresponsible minority of doctors set up abortion factories earning large sums in cash payments upon which tax was not paid; touting of free pregnancy advisory services proliferated, and taxi drivers found a new source of income in commissions for steering the victims to the slaughter houses. The number of abortions mounted – legal abortions were soon to reach figures which even the abortionist lobby had never formerly claimed to have taken place illegally. Their propaganda had almost made some women believe that abortion was a duty not a right: and the medical profession as a whole deeply resented the pressures which the Act had placed upon them and felt themselves the scapegoats for the legislators. An alarmed Parliament, which had so

confidently passed the Act in October 1967, by July 1969 by only eleven
votes turned down Norman St John Stevas's request for permission to
introduce a Bill which would have made my original amendment part
of the law.

Even after the passing of the Homosexual Act my hands remained tied,
for now I was pressing on with divorce reform, and the same inhibitions
if I was to obtain sufficient support in the Commons for that reform,
remained. However I counselled St John Stevas to frame a motion calling
for a government enquiry into the working of the Act: gradually, I felt
certain, as the predictable abuses mounted, he would obtain sufficient
Members' signatures to his motion to compel the government to set up
the enquiry that could be the preliminary to the needed changes. During
the early committee stages of the Bill St John Stevas had acted provocatively, and dogmatically: but as the controversy developed his liberalism
had informed his especial brand of Catholicism and the views he was later
to present acknowledged fully the rights that in a democratic plural society
must be respected. For more than two years, following upon my suggestion to him, he led the campaign for an enquiry with extraordinary
stamina and courage, braving the derision and distortions of the abortion
lobby with dignity.

When at last, with my reforming Bills passed I was free to join in the
fray, I did so with no pleasure. It is one matter to give oneself to healing
tasks: it is another to squander the spirit unravelling ugly distorted knots.
But although it attracted the same hate towards me, as had been patiently
borne by St John Stevas, it was an irksome duty that had to be done.
It meant investing time I would have wished to husband for more creative
causes and which I now had to spend in the usual round of meetings,
marches and newspaper articles continuously demanding amendments
of the law.

There was no limit to the vituperation these activities could precipitate. The chairman of the Parliamentary Labour Party, Douglas
Houghton, a man for whom I have much affection and regard, threw his
considerable wisdom over his head and, doubtless on the prompting of his
wife who was chairman of the Abortion Law Reform Association, wrote
to me wildly after a daily paper had published an article in which I had
made the passing comment: 'Our legislators should not be stampeded by
shrill atypical feminist abortionists, often childless, who in their demands
for women's rights trample upon women's needs.' Douglas demanded
to know: 'Why ever did you write such a hateful article? . . . You are now
counted among the section of this House which has always opposed you
and to whom you are doubtless a prized renegade . . . To see you in the

same lobby as Stevas and other Papists I found quite revolting.' The copy letter he enclosed from his wife to the newspaper containing the article explained the outburst. She wrote to the editor 'The assumption that abortion law reformers are also "often childless" is ridiculous . . . Mr Abse knows that I am childless: ipso facto the rest of us must be childless.'

I had, of course, when I had written the article in no way had the Houghtons in mind. I had never met Mrs Houghton, of whom I knew nothing, and until Douglas wrote to me I was quite unaware that he was childless: but although I certainly would not have wished to have given him such evident personal hurt, his letter revealed, as did many of the other reactions of the abortion lobby, that my now unrestrained attacks were exposing quivering nerves.

When I was about to lead an anti-abortion march of some 9,000 supporters through the streets of Birmingham, the abortion lobby tastelessly reacted. They timed for the same weekend a press interview with a woman doctor engaged upon full-time private abortionist work and a mother who bitterly complained that the National Health Service, unlike the 'kind' private abortionist, had refused to abort a twelve-year-old child who was pregnant by a boy of thirteen. The object of this exercise was to deflect attention from the anti-abortion lobby and concentrate public opinion on the alleged restrictiveness of the regional health service towards abortion: and to pillory the doctor who refused the abortion to the hapless four-months pregnant child out of fear that the child would become permanently sterile. For good measure the abortionist doctor announced she had now protected the child by giving her a twelve months' supply of contraceptive pills.

It was repugnant to me that a child should have become a pawn in the battle but I had no alternative but to counterattack. The real question was what was the quality of care the twelve-year-old child had received which had caused her to become pregnant and remain so for four months, unknown to her parents: and if at eleven to obtain affection she was seeking precocious sex, was it out of lack of concern from those nearest to her? Press interviews may have helped the mother to reject her own feelings of guilt, but publicity itself would be of little use to the child and giving pills to her was a cruel way of avoiding the giving of love and affection. I was not prepared to acquiesce in the private abortion sector unilaterally deciding a new legal age of consent to sexual intercourse. It was only after a hard fight by reformers that in 1929 the age of marriage was raised to sixteen from twelve for a girl and fourteen for a boy. That ended the scandal of older men marrying children to avoid charges of unlawful sexual intercourse: and ended, too, the traffic in married little girls which had primarily prompted the reformers to urge the change in the age of consent. The change had saved many children from premature sexual experience that would have severely maimed their emotional development. It was not surprising that when as late as 1967 the lively, government-appointed Latey Committee reviewed the age of consent to marriage and sexual intercourse they had unanimously agreed on the necessity of maintaining the age at sixteen. I regarded inadequate parents and aborting doctors in the private sector as the worst judges of the desirability of lowering the age confirmed as desirable by the Latey Committee.

Through a series of questions in the House to the Secretary of State for Social Services and the Attorney General, ranging from the calling of an enquiry as to whether there was a need for the child to be brought under the care of the children's officer of the area to a demand that the full circumstances should be enquired into by the Director of Public Prosecutions to see if any offence of encouraging unlawful sexual intercourse with a girl under sixteen had been committed, I drew public attention to the issues which were really involved. A frenetic week followed as the whole issue blew up into a national debate in the press and on television: not all the interviewers to whom I submitted myself could keep their detachment. At least one woman correspondent of a national newspaper, still working out her difficulties over her own abortion, became hysterical as she found my replies to a hostile question too personal and disturbing. But after some days in which, in many television programmes, I was given the full opportunity to put my point of view, it was clear to me that the callous ploy of the abortionist lobby had boomeranged back upon them.

Parents who give love can also lay down acceptable boundaries for their children: a youngster needs to have a boundary wall both to contain his anxieties and to lean against. The mail that came to me showed how relieved so many parents were that, as a parent not regarded as a reactionary, I was challenging those who use over-permissiveness as a means of abandoning responsibility. But although the public were not to know, it was the sad aborted child who was to prove my point. Having received, alas as a result of the controversy, such a surfeit of attention, she refused to take any of the pills and with pleasure gave up her joyless sex. It was a tortuous and grim path for a child to have to follow as a means of feeling that others cared about her.

It was against the background of such disagreeable brawls that in the end Sir Keith Joseph, despite his reluctant officials, first announced the setting up of a government enquiry under Justice Lane and then, after I had led a deputation of Members of Parliament to him, in an exchange of correspondence with me, placed an interpretation upon the over-restricted terms of reference of the enquiry that could give the committee, if they are bold, just sufficient elbow room to give a report which could lead to a less sick law. But I remained sceptical: the committee appointed may be well intentioned but it is politically unsophisticated and, when it reports, may not know how to find the road back from the legislation of hate to the legislation of love.

The problem of undoing the damage will be made so much more difficult because too many of those who will determine events – the male women who feel motherhood as a humiliation and the politicians – cannot give the love they have never received: they suffered too much as neonates. Perhaps the fate of these women and of the phallic narcissistic politicians was presaged even before their second or third year. For many of them the very foundations of their earliest ego-identity were faultily laid. The strict ungentle mother, who insensitively rejected her two-year-old's advances, was the same woman when the child was born. Busy, bustling, organizing, dominating, determined, feeding the child at the time her time-table dictates, for ever 'doing things' to him, the fundamentally unmaternal mother shapes her child's destiny: and judging by the number of prominent politicians who had such mothers or nurses, can shape too the destiny of a nation. For pushing the frontiers of psychodynamic research back to the absolute beginnings, the very start of the human personality, the English psychoanalysts Fairburn, Winnicott and Guntrip, have all illuminated that these are the women who do not have the children who develop a confident, secure ego able to give love without fear, so certain of the bliss of their primary dependence that they have the capacity as adults to yield to a woman without feeling threatened by loss of identity or collapse of independence. The maternal mother tuned in to her baby's emotional needs, letting him feed at his own pace, willingly allowing him, within her embrace, to sleep peacefully and restfully, gives him the most complete experience of security possible in human life: this is where the foundation of identity rests. I am because I *feel* secure, and, therefore, real, and feeling only serenity and not hostility to the woman's gentle embrace the baby encapsulates within himself a caring female element; and since the feeling 'I am' leads to the question 'What am I?' it means the experience of 'being' and leads on to the growth of self-consciousness, self-knowledge and self-realization.

But such 'being' created by the safe warm reliable contact, bestowing relationship, love, interest, attention, everything that enables the infant to feel securely 'in being', does not fall to everyone. No-one can regain the paradise lost linking us to the cosmos within the womb. As the ancient Jewish saying recounts: 'In the mother's body man knows the universe, in birth he forgets it.' But as far as the initial pre-natal stillness can be recaptured, it comes from the mother knowing her babe by feeling and identification; and those unblessed with such mothers are the casualties that have presented the clinical material to the psychoanalysts enabling them to reach out to the source of the core of our being.

Amongst the busybodies in public life, men and women, in and out of the House, there are not enough endowed with a secure experience of 'being', the being at one with the maternal source of life: and lacking such endowment, their activites, their 'doing' are not an easy natural self expression. Their doing sometimes takes on the tone described by Guntrip:

Activity is forced, tense, strained, an attempt to compel an insecure personality to carry on as a 'going concern'. This may become a manic or obsessive compulsive activity for the 'mind' cannot stop, relax or rest because of the secret fear of collapsing into non-existence. It is the individual's incapacity for experiencing a sense of 'being' that is primarily dissociated, left unrealized at the start of development. He cannot get at his capacity to feel real, because at the start of his life no-one evoked it. His mother gave him so little genuine relationship that he actually came to feel unreal.

On the public stage he must continue to act in a never ending play without intermissions for, if the lights went on, the man as well as the actor, would disappear. But his script must enable him, if he is to survive even as an actor, to rail however subtly against the female elements, which out of fear he has projected out of himself and against which he can then unleash his frightening destructive impulses. A more integrated man, as a babe, has absorbed into himself the loving mother and from his bisexual make-up has the capacity for sensitivity towards what others are feeling and does not, as a lover of a woman, or as a doer, shield these elements as weakness to be resisted, resented, and hidden behind a sham tough exterior: but the man with a discordant mother has imperfectly absorbed femininity which he senses as a violation of his ego, as smothering and threatening. He casts it out of himself and then savages it, as does a murderer like Brady killing little girls, or as does the professional abortionist doctor returning back his own sense of violation by violating mothers. And public men and women too, can, in issues like abortion law reform, exquisitely rationalize their resentments against their mothers who failed to infuse them with the fundamental experience of 'being'.

Those who believe that they have some understanding of the causes of this basic ego weakness must not in compassion allow such men and women to wreak their havoc. Politics to be worth while must strive for a society which can improve, not debase, the quality of human relationships. If, sadly, there are many who from the start are faulted, it is not for us to relieve them of their individual neuroses by insisting that by law it becomes the collective neurosis of the nation.

XIV

The worth of a society is to be judged by the concern of one generation for the next; and fortunately I have on occasions been able to mobilize sufficient parental tenderness to support my legislative efforts. The modern democratic family releases the energy which was formerly repressively engaged within the tyrannical structure of the authoritarian family; the overspill, politically channelled, can bathe society in a warm caring concern. But the old family dies hard, and the over-controlled child brought up under the old regime becomes the controlling parent: the hated child becomes the hating parent. The antagonism to children endemic to English culture is a formidable force, and, once again, now expressed as indifference, I found that force working against me in my prolonged efforts to overhaul the adoption laws of Britain.

Initially I was innocent and arrogant enough to believe that my propagandist talents revealing the consequences each year to tens of thousands of children of our casual adoption laws would ensure a speedy response. I was not only, however, overestimating the rate of growth of the just and egalitarian family structure: I was making wrong assumptions about England based upon the warmer and more affectionate family units of the Welsh valleys and upon the passionate Jewish family life with which I was so familiar. The English are possessed with resentments towards children quite alien to my personal experience: and I consequently misled myself. The chastening truth is yet again revealed in the recent cross-cultural studies on child-rearing in six countries in the West and Eastern Europe conducted by Une Brunfenbrenner and his team of social scientists. These Americans concluded 'England is . . . the only country in our sample which shows a level of parental involvement lower than our own with both parents – and especially fathers – showing less affection, offering less companionship and intervening less frequently in the lives of their children.' If so many English parents are so cool towards their own children, it is not surprising that I found it so tough a task to engage public sympathy for the fate of other children abandoned by their parents.

The curious pattern in England of the dislike of so many for their young has a long and dishonourable history. That peculiarly English institution, the Royal Society for the Prevention of Cruelty to Animals was founded in 1824: but it was not until sixty-five years later that the National Society for the Prevention of Cruelty to Children came into existence. When in Liverpool the first local society for protecting abused children took action to establish a Home for Children instead of a Home for Dogs the president was compelled to explain apologetically to the unsympathetic citizens: 'I am here for the prevention of cruelty and I cannot draw the line at children.' The various Royal Commissions on the employment of children during the nineteenth century indeed reveal as much about the disturbed consciences of a section of the ruling class as about the exploitation of little children. It is hard not to suspect the prurient preoccupation of some of the Royal Commissions, like the societies for the prevention of cruelty, with the horrid thought of cruelty inflicted on the helpless: there is too eager a desire to harrow feelings, as a glance at the vivid literature describing the misdeeds wrought upon children show. These sick preoccupations continued into the twentieth century: a survey in the early fifties of the popular Sunday papers showed that almost half the published material was devoted to cruelty to children and animals, and to the punishment inflicted upon the perpetrators. The findings of the anthropologist Geoffrey Gorer in his extensive studies in 1955 of English character illuminated how the controlled, stiff-upper-lip Englishman gained his renowned poise by directing much of his aggression towards his own children.

There is a basic historical continuity in the English character, and Gorer's assumption of twenty years ago that fundamentally it had changed little in the previous fifty years, is probably unchallengeable. The more permissive upbringing within the modern family is now, however, undoubtedly bringing about widespread changes and the greater spontaneity and the decline of obsessionalism in contemporary Britain are some of the resulting benefits, but these gains are slowly achieved; and traditional attitudes were contributing to a continued resistance to my demands during the six years from 1964 onwards when I was urging an overhaul of our adoption practices and laws. Although adoption is final and irrevocable, unlike marriage which can be dissolved, I could not bring home the importance of choosing, with care and sensitivity, parents for some 25,000 children annually. All my questions to Ministers and my private importuning of them, as the blemishes and abuses of the present system became increasingly apparent to me, were of no avail: nor for a long time could I seriously interest my allies in the press or the television companies who no doubt considered the subject as of little public interest.

The lack of attention which, despite all my wiles, I could not initially overcome, is psychologically even more significant when one considers how large a section of the community have in fact become involved in the adoption process: since the Adoption Act of 1926, thousands of mothers have given up some 800,000 children to be adopted by more than a million-and-a-half men and women.

The sources of this indifference to the fate of so many children are not, however, to be found exclusively within the vestigial traces of the traditional character structure still embedded in the Englishman of the seventies. There are, too, contemporary evil forces at work; our late capitalist system manipulatively, and with intent, encourages young men and women to marry and breed on condition that they lack the capacity to take on the parental role of assuming responsibility, becoming self-sufficient adults, knowing how to love as well as fuck. The advance to the more just egalitarian family system must enfeeble parental authority but, although we may welcome the increasing absence of tyranny in the home, we cannot welcome the increasing absence of parents. With both parents out working, seduced by commercial advertising into the illusion that only by surrounding themselves with yet more material objects can happiness be achieved, the houses become stuffed with consumer goods and empty of love. The parents, as real persons, are missing: there are no targets open to the children against whom they can rebel, no authority because it cannot be pinned down to any person. The child never learns how to resist: his family unit is a sham and a totally unsatisfactory training ground. The advance from puberty to adulthood cannot be taken: the love-hate relationships, the identification with the parents, all of which, if manhood and womanhood is to be achieved, must be worked through, become arrested. We have too many growing up with the bodies of men and the feelings of pubescents. We cannot expect to evoke in such people an adult concern for children and, in political terms, a grave concern for the next generation.

Some of the German new left socialists, unlike their English counterparts, show an understanding of the threat the latest excrescences of modern capitalism are to growth in human personality. Reimut Reiche has eloquently drawn attention to the commercial forces that keep young people in bondage, condemned to perpetual puberty. Contemporary capitalism is in fact striving to create a fetishistic society: its technique, by way of manipulative advertising and by the sexualization of films, magazines and fashions, is to stimulate an insatiable appetite for objects which, to use Rudi Deutsche's term, have been 'falsely sexualized': the objects are all claimed to be absolutely necessary, promise eternal gratification and pleasure and yet leave the purchasers unsatisfied, immediately yearning for more. They develop what Reiche has described as 'an attitude of striving towards ever greater satisfaction which dooms the individual to a state identical in its essentials to that of the sexual pervert who is forever stuck at a preparatory stage of the sex act, and remains perpetually frustrated'.

When vague or absent parents, object and status seeking, fail as models for their children, the pubescent become easy prey for the hired ad-men, the mercenaries of modern capitalism, out to capture the young and ensure that they become for life the avid unassuaged consumers. Marx and Engels underestimated the capacity of the capitalist system to safeguard its processes of production and reproduction: they believed that a destructive polarization would occur and, as riches grew and fewer people would be allowed to enjoy them, making a revolution by a dispossessed class would be a push-over. But capitalism, to safeguard itself, has found sophisticated techniques to exploit the instinctual urges of the masses and turn them into frenetic consumers whose unceasing demands will ensure that production goes on. The object-pushers must begin by hooking the vulnerable adolescent: on every television screen, film, and hoarding, the addiction is cultivated through sexual excitation and titillation. The cigarette, the bath soap, the branded drinks, the motor cars, the perfumes, the package tours, all by overt salacity or innuendo are eroticized, all are transformed into fetishes. In soothing, seductive tones, all are held out as fore-pleasures which are the true ultimate delights.

If the adolescent submits to these distorted emphases on fore-pleasures, his later capacity for parental concern is arrested. Capacity for concern is a maturational node, and if the environment is damaging, not facilitating, such capacity may never be obtained. Freud has warned us:

The attainment of the normal sexual aim can clearly be endangered by the mechanism in which fore-pleasure is involved. The danger arises if at any time in the preparatory sexual processes the fore-pleasure turns out to be too great and the element of tension too small. The motive for proceeding further with the sexual process then disappears, the whole path is cut short, and the preparatory act in question takes the place of the normal sexual aim.

The advertiser uses the commercial artist to clothe the offered product in symbols, often oral or phallic, hoping the response coming from the viewer's stimulated erotogenic zone will take the form of a sale. But if the over-stimulated viewer lingers too long over his purchase he may become corrupted. In the end he may find that he is stunted: the component instincts ensconced in his more primitive erotogenic zones may have been adequately subordinated under the primacy of the genitals, in the service of reproduction. Even if he is able to copulate, he is unable to make love. He fucks, but lacks concern, unable in intercourse – beyond the pleasure – to take responsibility for the result. He can acquire objects, but cannot relate to a subject. He lacks a truly genital character: he possesses only what some of the German new left writers, blaming the manipulative nature of late capitalism, describe as the genital façade.

The new iconoclastic forces of capitalism are not, however, invincible, and morbid traditional English attitudes to children are not inevitable. History is man-made, and I have never had much patience with the politicians who use historicism as an excuse for inaction. I have always admired Trotsky's scorn of 'the pusillanimity of an historic fatalism which in all questions, whether concrete or private, passively seeks a solution in general laws, and leaves out of account the mainspring of all human decisions – the living and acting individual'.

The difficulties I met in my attempts to overhaul our adoption laws, were not, however, due only to obstructive historical forces. I found it unusually difficult to present the defects in our existing adoption practices in sufficiently simple, dramatic, yet conciliatory terms, to ensure an understanding and a response from the wider public. Adoption is an ambitious technical method of resolving sterility, illegitimacy and the nurture of the rejected or unattached child: it is also an imaginative and sensitive human enterprise where biology jostles passion, and where irresponsibility, inadequacy or wickedness is met by pity, concern and love. To presume to intervene by laws in this subtle and complex process is to invite condemnation as an intruder: reason and insight embedded within such laws, however mildly coercive, can be speedily resented.

Yet the need for sweeping changes is overwhelming. Scores of voluntary adoption societies exist, unevenly distributed throughout the country, some purporting to serve a locality and others claiming to operate nationally. Some of them have standards of service which are abysmal: these lack any professional skills or staff, dealing only on the basis of bizarre criteria with the selection of adoptive homes and the placement of children with parents who are often considered suitable primarily on the basis of their declared religious belief. The dilettante characteristics of too many of the adoption societies is encouraged by the perfunctory surveillance to which, by law, their standards are subject: indeed, approval of their registration has become reduced to a little more than a formality and it is done by local authorities more than half of whom have shirked exercising their existing powers to make their own social work department act as an adoption agency. Because we lack a comprehensive adoption service giving support and guidance to the unmarried mother as well as would-be adopters, available to all those needing it throughout the country, the choosing by society of parents for thousands of children each year is little more than a sinister game of roulette.

Outside the purview of these adoption societies of such varying quality come those adoptions arranged privately by matrons, gynaecologists, solicitors, busybodies or someone the hardpressed unmarried mother meets in the local launderette. Choosing parents for someone else's child is certainly too awful a responsibility to be left to any one person: but the muddlers and meddlers, who for morbid or mercenary motives intervene to play God, are given a dangerously free hand under our laws. Sometimes in my endeavours to arouse interest in adoption issues, I was able to bring some particular unhappy instances of these curious interveners to the attention of the House of Commons. One woman ingratiated herself with her society friends by having close links with a subsidized private maternity home in the East End. There, unmarried mothers who would give up their children to this lady bountiful were given beds free or at nominal cost. From an unregistered charity centre in the West End, this benefactor then distributed them to the wealthy sterile. How widespread her activities were became clear to me when I found myself, on raising the issues in the Commons, being subjected to considerable private opportuning on her behalf by some well heeled Tory M.P.s whose families had evidently found her centre a very useful baby supermarket.

Sometimes hardly less hazardous for the child are the direct adoptions arranged by a mother with colluding grandparents, aunts or elder sister, who wish to create legal relationships which differ from, and distort, the natural relationship not only of the adopters to the child but also of the child to his own mother. Too often in these adoptions the real circumstances are hidden from the child and his later discovery that his 'parents' are really his grandparents and that his 'older sister' is really his mother is the final damaging blow to a child who has already been brought up in an inevitably guilty and anxiety-ridden home.

Yet despite the damage that can be caused to the child's life when his future is settled by concealment strategies in the family, or when the child is handed over to a stranger by some untutored third party, the public reaction to such practices can be mild. If woman is no longer regarded as the property of her husband, a child is still widely held to be the property of his parents.

My breakthrough ultimately, however, came when I sensed the interest that could be stimulated when the 'property' was in issue, when a conflict arose between the desire of a foster parent to adopt a child whom she had tended for years and the natural mother who belatedly wished to reclaim her child. Then I observed all public indifference towards the adoption problem vanished. Because of such conflict situations, by the posing of provocative questions in the frame of a maientic dialogue, it was possible to act the pedagogue to a now attentive and disturbed public who could be taught that the complex decisions such disputes provoked were paradigms of the judgements that belonged to every adoption situation. The indignation felt when the battles over the future of a child were brought to public attention could be fanned into a blaze of protest as women empathized with the foster mother, the natural mother or indeed the child. I consciously, by speeches, questions in the House, and through the media, publicized the dilemmas and put into circulation phrases designed to catch the headlines: my description of tug-of-war children or tug-of-love children soon became the currency of sub-editors looking for an arresting paragraph.

Apart from the involvement of mothers at surface level in a dispute over parental and proprietal rights, there could be aroused at a more profound level the deep-seated emotions that have kept pristine for thousands of years the legend of the most famous adjudication in history, Solomon's renowned judgment. By tapping the self same springs which have perennially sustained the vigour of that biblical tale, I was to release forces which were to compel a government enquiry into the whole of our adoption law and practices.

The ancient Hebrew story of contending mothers, which in my battle for reform was to play such a significant part, is usually romantically recalled as the triumph, because of Solomon's insight, of the selfless mother over a cruel woman who was ready to have the babe killed. The adult memory tends to suppress the recorded facts of the story which is founded on harlotry and infanticide. Both the women concerned were prostitutes living alone in a brothel. Each had a child in the same house at about the same time with, strangely, no-one else present. The one mother smothered her own babe by 'accident', and then at night put her dead child by the side of the good sleeping mother, taking from her unsuspecting sleeping colleague the live child. On the morrow the good mother awoke to find only a dead child to suckle: immediately asserting the dead child was not hers she appealed to the king. The killing mother, who so desperately wanted to replace her lost child, then improbably agreed to Solomon's suggestion that the live child be hacked to pieces. This is indeed a strange story replete with odd embroidery and most unlikely responses. Yet its fascination remains in our secular world.

Is not the clue to its continued acceptance that secretly we know that this is not the story of two mothers and two children but of one mother and one babe? It bears psychological witness to the ambivalence of every woman to her own child, of her love for him and of her hate, of her feelings of fulfilment and of her feelings of destructiveness. The schizoid splitting in the tale, of the one woman into two, into good and bad, is imperfectly completed: the good mother still has her badness symbolized by her prostitute's status, so that subliminally we may learn without fear that evil and antagonism must live in every mother side by side with tenderness and maternalism. In the first part of the story the mother kills the child, but in the second part hate is defeated by love and the babe lives again in unison with the true mother. Solomon, the wisest of kings, confirms that although woman must have conflict between her role as individual and her role as mother, a healthy society enables the woman to resolve the struggle and attain happiness and self-esteem in a symbiotic relationship with her wondrous creation.

In every tug-of-war situation there is enacted before every woman the selfsame drama of the loving mother and the rejecting mother: and since both such mothers are encapsulated within every woman, it is not surprising that such incidents arouse a tumult of emotions. Most of the battles between foster parents who have children in long term care and the natural parents arise, in fact, out of poor case work by overburdened social workers who fail to maintain an adequate contact between foster parent and natural mother; but although laws in themselves cannot remedy the failures which precipitate such conflicts, their very existence enabled me to use them for fuller discussion of all adoption malpractices. Members of Parliament who had such instances occurring in their constituencies came to discuss them with me, and with such Members I was now able to form an all-Party group committed to pressurizing the Home Office to review our adoption and fostering laws. The Home Office still stalled: the children's department was already overstretched with preparations for other legislation and did not wish to take on further burdens. As our pressures mounted, they pleaded, predictably, more research was needed before any moves could be made. But the ill wind, which, following devaluation, blew Jim Callaghan out of the Treasury into the Home Office, brought me good fortune in my quest, for Jim Callaghan had a special reason to be concerned with the fate of children unendowed with two certain parents.

Callaghan, when a young boy, lost his father and the widow was left to fight a bitter struggle to maintain the family. The impress of these early years is irrevocably stamped upon the adult man. There are few men in the House whom I have known longer, since the chance that he represents a Cardiff seat means that I worked with him, long before I came into the House, as chairman of the Cardiff Labour Party, and I have, therefore, seen him play many roles.

The early loss of a father can leave a boy without an adequate model with whom to identify: it so often leaves a lad uncertain of whom he is and fantasy then intermittently takes over from reality. The boy is unable to visualize his future in terms of growing up like his father, and a faulty identity formation follows. Jim Callaghan is certainly not exempt from the syndrome associated with the fatherless child, and the multiplicity of political roles and stances he has assumed has led him to be frequently accused of lacking a fixed philosophy, of being too fluid an opportunist, and of being too professional a politician with an excess of facility. Such criticisms are not wide of the mark but they can lead to a serious under-assessment of the man.

Sometimes his role playing can be creative and socially most useful. Lacking the boundaries imposed upon a boy who has to model himself on a real living blemished father, the fatherless child can unrestrainedly picture himself even in adulthood as the limitless hero, like his fantasized father, and sometimes Jim Callaghan can play the conquering but restrained hero with great elan, as when, as Home Secretary, he supervised the Grosvenor Square demonstrations or walked, as a conciliator, through troubled Northern Ireland. Giving himself the part of the all wise, benevolent, but firm, father, he can play the role with a confidence that those of us whose fathers lived long enough to yield to us their frailties would be unlikely to attain. This capacity for what the existentialist psychologists may call self-actualization is one of his strengths. Indeed Jim Callaghan's role as a paternalistic conciliator in the Labour Party is not to be underestimated, and on more than one occasion he has helped to keep the Trade Union movement and the Labour Party together. The very fact that he is not cast in a fixed mould enables him to have the facility to empathize successively with each party to a dispute and make him a reconciler: his enemies, sensing the shallowness of his identifications, dismiss him as a humbug, but Oscar Wilde's apposite defence of hypocrisy as merely being a method of multiplying personalities should prompt one to temper such unsympathetic criticisms.

It is easy to mock at his evident uncertain self-image as he calls himself variously Leonard, James or Jim, and it is easy to be impatient as he determinedly dons his synthetic coat, following upon his leasing a small acreage, of Farmer Callaghan. But no-one can patronize him in the Chamber when he performs as a Party leader. Like actor friends of mine who can be so curiously uncertain of themselves in private, and so brilliant in the theatre, there is no one today who can so evenly and nonchalantly take the floor and command the ear of the House. It is his evident mastery of the House and his capacity to establish friendly acquaintanceships in the Commons – for deep friendships are of course unwanted encumbrances at Westminster – that has caused him almost invariably to be elected into the Shadow Cabinet over so many years at the top of the poll. Yet although by temperament an obvious choice as a reconciling leader in a Party always in danger of being rent with schisms, he has always drawn back even in the most favourable circumstances from making a sustained attempt to depose the existing leadership and take command.

The death of a father leaves a boy guilty. All secret death wishes of every boy against every father mean that when death does come, the boy irrationally feels responsible and guilty. But convicted murderers rarely commit a further murder, either in prison or when released. It is difficult to resist the view that Callaghan's early fatherlessness is an inhibitory factor restraining him from slaying the top authority figure in the Party. Making a virtue out of a compulsive inner necessity, he therefore places great stress on the value of loyalty. Although cynics may suspect such an observation in so labile a politician, his habit of growing into the ideal image he sets himself would cause one to prefer to go tiger hunting with him than with many of the politicians who so ostentatiously insist upon their fixed political principles.

In my desire to change our adoption laws, I certainly could not have had a more willing accomplice than the newly appointed Home Secretary. He had come to his new office shell-shocked. Devaluation and his subsequent resignation from the Chancellorship had left him stunned and depleted. He was too poor in his boyhood and it led him to be over-fascinated by money. Mixing with bankers and economists had shored him up, leaving him with a profound sense of security that he rarely had been able to enjoy. The total collapse of his assumptions and of the pound was felt as more than a policy failure: he was a shaken man, and he was consequently slow in playing himself into the Home Secretaryship. But his response to my importuning was generous and I was fortunate, too, in having a good ally in his wife Audrey who had for many years brought an informed interest, in her local authority work, to the fate of deprived children. She is an eminently sensible woman, and when I visited her when she lived at 11 Downing Street, or dined with the family in the top flat there, insulated from the flunkeys and officials below, I was gratified by her warm realism and her lack of pretensions: she stood out from some of the other Ministers' wives who lost their silly heads as they found themselves temporarily with more money and status than usual.

Jim Callaghan soon pressured his officials and before long my request for the appointment of an advisory committee charged with the task of reviewing the laws and practices of adoption in Britain, was granted. When the civil servants limited the terms of reference of the committee I was able with Callaghan's collusion to have them widened so that the review could be a genuinely comprehensive one. It had been arranged between the Home Secretary and myself that I should go on the committee, and this meant too, for political appearances, I should be joined by a Conservative M.P., Dame Joan Vickers, a dedicated woman whose private good works certainly do not lag behind her public activities. Almost all the others on the committee, as directors of social service departments or adoption societies, as paediatricians, child psychiatrists or jurists, had considerable field work experience in adoption: the exception was the chairman who was appointed after the original first choice declined the onerous task. The appointed chairman, Sir William Houghton, London's Director of Education, had personal roots which could make him sensitive to the disasters that could fall upon children; but his didactic headmasterly approach was soon causing tensions in the committee that had representatives of so many worthy but vested interests: after one tension-ridden day-long committee he went home to die that same night of a seizure. Judge Stockdale, one of our Members, took over the chair and together we were able to harness and harmonize the considerable clinical knowledge of our colleagues so that after almost three years of taking of evidence and tough decision making we were able to publish our unanimous report, a report which, in all probability will, in whole or part, be embedded in legislation in the 1974 session of Parliament.

To mark the conclusion of our work the committee held a dinner in July 1972 at the House of Commons to which Jim Callaghan, as the past Home Secretary, and Reg Maudling, as the current Home Secretary, were invited. Both accepted the invitations but only Jim Callaghan attended. Reg Maudling had been compelled to resign only a few days before. The day following the dinner Callaghan sent me a letter. He over-generously wrote: 'This is another reform that your own activity and zeal has been largely responsible for. You will have a wonderful collection of worthwhile scalps under your belt before you finish.

'And you do much more good in terms of human happiness than 90% of the work done in Parliament on what is called "political issues".'

Ironically, Maudling had written to me too but a little while before, after I had commented on certain Home Office policy suggestions he had made. He concluded his note: 'I hope in turn you will acquit me of sycophancy if I say there is no-one whose views on the subjects I was dealing with I would value higher than yours.' If it has to be a Conservative government which is to put through the adoption proposals with which I am associated, I cannot but regret that the Home Secretary who will supervise the operation will not now be poor Reggie Maudling.

Postscript

XV

Gradually some acceptance is being made of the fact that the fate of armies, political parties and nations may be determined by the physical pathology of their leaders. Bevin's heart block, Cripps's spinal infection, Churchill's strokes, Macmillan's prostate may all, it is reluctantly conceded, have influenced their decision-making. Now few doubt that Eden's inflamed bile duct and Nasser's diabetes made a grim contribution to the Suez debacle. Yet still there remains a stubborn refusal to face the fact that no less fateful consequences flow from the psychopathology of our leaders. Their actions are fundamentally influenced by the quality of their reality testing. If their feelings, affects and emotions so distort external events, then their relations to them may, with lamentable consequences for us all, be singularly inappropriate. We cannot therefore extend to the public man the same rights of privacy to which the private citizen is entitled.

The conventional politician, always seeking to elevate his personal prejudices into principles, hates what he describes as the personalization of politics. And much of the public colludes with him: as old faiths and certitudes collapse and the Church itself vacillates in its authority, the need for magical political leadership becomes dangerously strong. Too many in the community, although ambivalent to politicians, look to them to play the role once shared between God, the boss, the vicar, the father and the family doctor: and the politician, welcoming this overvaluation, is consequently provoked into megalomania rather than emotional growth.

The politician protects himself against anatomization by evoking every man's fear that his private fortunes may be pried into. Canons of taste and etiquette are erected, and those who will not accept the boundaries, beyond which enquiry into motivation must cease, are, for a little while, still treated with hostility and derision. But the tired formal pavane, still so primly danced between politician, some commentators and some sections of the public, cannot continue for much longer. We cannot afford such respectability.

Those who probe must bear the charge of scandalous scavenging. Yet to scrutinize even the sexual problems of political leaders is not simply to engage in a prurient exercise. My generation has lived through the terrible period in which Hitler's sexual problems became catastrophically en-meshed in the public domain through a symbolic resonance. His prob-lems were acted out at a time of socially resonating conditions. Despite his masculine show of uniforms, big boots and spurs, he certainly did no more than fumble in private with the pathetic Geli, his half-sister's daughter, who shot herself; and Eva Braun, though she tried to shoot herself for love of Hitler, never found before or after the episode, a fully potent lover. But consolation for private impotence may be found in the sense of multi-potence and even omnipotence to be derived from the highly charged, introactive group situation of the huge public meeting, where the orality of the orator can bring temporary balm to his deeply wounded self-esteem, and win him the full response which he has sought in vain from women. Sometimes, it is true, such aggressive, masterful and compelling displays of eloquence can, as with Nye Bevan, be accompanied by imaginative and healing reparations. But, nevertheless, despite the in-built checks within our political system, the informed community must, in such hazardous days, submit its leaders to insightful scrutiny. If, out of delicacy, it refrains, then the extent to which we can all become victims of the insatiable psychological needs of some of our political leaders, has never, in the history of man, been more awful.

We live in a milder political climate than that of the Weimar republic, the safeguards of our political community are stronger and none of the personalities dominating our political parties are as aberrant as Hitler and his gangsters. But we can afford no complacency: the lawlessness within our society grows, our political institutions are fragile and depend on consent, and the political maturity of which we rightly boast is inadequate to meet the new strains. Depth psychology provides us with a new armoury to assist man in conquering himself. If the Member of Parliament is to instruct the nation then he must be ready to submit himself to the careful surveillance of the findings of the new science, imperfect though they may still be. And those who have the greatest political influence in our society, the Prime Minister and the Leader of the Opposition, must expect, in the latter part of the twentieth century to be subjected to novel evaluations not available to the electorate of past days.

No decision taken in Parliament, since I have had the privilege to be a Member, has been more important than the vote to take our country into the European community: and I have felt the agony of that decision more than most of my colleagues since my vote to enter Europe, for the first time in my parliamentary life, for a while, painfully estranged me from my comrades in my constituency Party. Their disapproval was harder to bear because of my private judgement that Edward Heath's unrestrained enthusiasm to enter Europe was based, primarily, not upon an objective assessment, but came from weaknesses in his own temperament. Politicians can use public events as a screen upon which to project private travail: and, despite the constraints within our political system, Heath's determination to take us into Europe confirms that it is still possible for one man's irrational anxiety to become a nation's major political choice.

Once upon a time, for all of us, when first we were born, we had the bliss of what some of the psychoanalysts describe as primary love. Primary love is the relationship in which only one partner, the babe, may have demands and claims: the other partners, the mother and, through her, the whole environment, must have no interests, no wishes, no demands of their own. There is a complete identity of wishes and satisfactions: the environment must be in complete harmony with the demands and enjoyments of the babe. Such a paradisical condition does not last for long: only too soon the discovery that firm and independent objects exist destroys the babe's illusory world. From then on, the existence of external objects, resistant, aggressive and with ambivalent qualities, must be painfully accepted. No longer can the babe have the primitive relationship with the world which he had experienced as structureless friendly expanses. Now he has to acknowledge that vitally important parts of his world are both independent and inscrutable, creating a structure: from now on the world will consist of firm resistant objects and of spaces separating them.

Michael Balint who, before his recent death, was the distinguished president of the British Psychoanalytic Society has claimed that, although there are many gradations and shades, there are two basic ways in which people respond to this traumatic discovery. One is to create a world based on the fantasy that firm objects are reliable and kind, that they will always be there when one needs them, and that they never will mind, and never resent, being used for support. Those who so clingingly respond he described as ocnophilic types. But there is, too, another possible basic reaction to the discovery that the world does not belong to me. It is to attempt to recreate the lost world which goes back to life prior to the traumatic experience when objects emerge and destroy the primal harmony of the limitless contourless expanses. For these people, described by Balint as philobats, objects are felt as dangerous and unpredictable hazards. The philobatic world consists of friendly expanses dotted with these menacing objects. Safety lies among the expanses: and objects, above all people, are hazardous, to be vigilantly observed and decidedly kept at a distance.

The attitude of our politicians, and in particular of Edward Heath to the Common Market, adds a surfeit of suggestive clinical material to Balint's shrewd and important contribution to the typology of character. The two extreme types, ocnophil and philobat, I have seen locked at Westminster in an unselfconscious struggle as they plead for or against entry into Europe. The first group, replete with ocnophil bias, the virulent anti-common marketeers, clings to objects and cannot feel safe except when at home or in familiar surroundings; the second group resents ties and is thrilled and excited while journeying from place to place, and finds pleasure and pride in the skills which enables it to do so. Despite all the white papers and purportedly balanced views, the prolonged debate has been conducted in a miasma of personal prejudice, the arguments so often reflections of the distortions of the inner life of the participant. Even before M.P.s from all parties, over the years, have individually declared themselves, I have almost always found it possible to predict whether a man would speak for or against entry. Arguments and facts are selected by the contributor according to temperament and, released, as Members were for a long time, from the constraints of party whips and diktats, the individual predelictions were given freedom; and those who wanted to stay timidly at home and those who wanted recklessly to step out to the spaces abroad, all uninhibitedly indulged themselves. Enormous strains were inevitably felt in both parties as ultimately Party whips sought to drive members into lobbies quite alien to their fundamental temperament. Few issues in my lifetime have provoked more regressive adjustments to reality than the call to leave our motherland and take the journey into Europe.

For, of course, the original object to which both ocnophil and philobat are relating is the mother, or part of her. The ocnophil clings; the philobat distances: each in his way attempting to deal with the loved and hated mother, adjusting himself to his first anguishing discovery that she and her attributes are separate, independent of him. Those who may be sceptical of the existence of these early infantile adjustments to reality, and their ultimate invasion into adult political thinking, should glance at the games their children play. Rounders, musical chairs, hide and seek, oranges and lemons, all show the same design reminiscent of our earliest strivings to cope with the discovery of the external world, all revealing our earlier hesitant advances and retreats, in and out of the primary safe but illusory bliss. In the playground the child creates a zone of security, the 'home', the 'house'; outside the home is a catcher, a chaser, a seeker. The other players, leaving the security zone, the 'home', expose themselves in the hope that somehow or other they will reach security. And when seemingly we are grown up it is not only vicariously, watching cricket at Lords, when runs can usually only be scored by leaving the safe zone within the significantly named crease, do we re-enact our earlier fumbling to master our environment.

Some adults show their philobatic dispositions more obviously than may be revealed by a politician with the same bias. There are those like the pilots who feel safer in the skies than clinging to home, those who ski with zest on the slopes or drive fast with great stimulation on the road. For these men danger and fear are felt only if any object has to be negotiated: the pilot has to take off or land, the skier to negotiate trees and crevasses, the driver to mind other cars. Their philobatic world is indeed one of search for the friendly expanses, and wariness towards all firm objects. It is, in fact, the world of the acrobat: his thrills and his feeling of security come when he is not bound to land, not tied to mother earth. Up he goes, mastering the fixed and flying trapeze, the unsupported ladder. And all of us, calling up our thrills from our earliest beginnings, become yet more excited as we observe the distance from the ground increasing, and as the precariousness of his attachment to some firm structure – which in the last analysis means the earth – becomes even greater.

But it is to be noted that there is a marked ambivalence to mother earth. Always, extravagantly, the acrobat must assert his independence, always display flagrantly the symbol of a never-flagging, erect, potent penis. Narcissistically holding on to his pole, magically reinforcing his own potency and confidence, the acrobat tight-rope walker performs his feats, defying desperately the attraction, the gravity pull of the earth. The skier leaps from the slopes, holding quite close his phallic stick. The pilot rides high up with his joy stick. The earth will, they hope, be forgiving and receive them back in the end, but she is dangerous and destructive and an irresistible attraction which, if yielded to, will mean, to them, destruction.

Extreme philobats, no doubt, can in sports, climbing mountains or in speed boats, harmlessly indulge themselves, and milder ones can make good pilots although here there are hazards for clearly passengers cannot afford to have a pilot wrestling with too compulsive an attraction to the ground. The philobats may behave like those daredevil motorists, happy and accident-free on the highway, who repeatedly scrape their cars as they enter their own garages. But in politics such men need to be checked: those who have not in adulthood worked through sufficiently their earlier problems of adjustment to the external world, and oft times show it by their incapacity to relate appropriately to their mothers and thus to all womankind, may be unable to conduct their reality testing with the needed objectivity to which a trusting electorate is entitled.

Heath is the most enthusiastic, if not the most rationalist, propagandist to quit home waters and sail into the unknown. He has a complete assurance that we shall all arrive safely. Indeed it is his certainty on the complex Common Market issue that is most disturbing, even to those of us who have favoured entry. If, as I believe, there is merit in Balint's findings, then uneasily it has to be acknowledged Heath shows a rare catalogue of the traits this psychoanalyst attributes to the extreme philobat.

He keeps his distance from women and, indeed, from men. He escapes from land to sea and sails his well publicized yacht, demonstrating his masculine prowess; he conducts his choir or orchestra wielding the phallic baton, and, of course, all alone he plays his piano or organ. And he enjoys and shows great skill in negotiation with foreign bodies, a particular capacity that appears to give yet greater correspondence between his personality and the dispositions of the philobat delineated by Balint. Such a display of skills is to be expected; for those who, as babies, react in an extreme philobatic manner to the discovery that the harmonious mix-up of the primitive attitude to the world has ended, do so, as Balint describes, 'by developing exaggerated egocathexes leading to an undue preoccupation with the functions of their ego, the personal skills and neglecting the development of proper, intimate and lasting object relationships'. That his relationships lack intimacy is not only testified by his evident celibacy but in the complaints of more than one socially fluent Tory Minister who have told me how, outside the political matter in hand, they are reduced to silence in their attempts to bridge a lengthy conversation with him. Heath evidently distances himself from others in order to avoid the specific danger of exposing himself to narcissistic injury.

The real political dangers of the extreme philobat are not, however, to be found in the quirks or idiosyncrasies of his remote social life or personal leisure hobbies and interests. They lie in his supreme and unjustifiable confidence which stems from his determination to believe in his 'friendly expanses'. He can regress in his thinking to the primitive state where the world lacked unpredictable outside objects and consisted only of kindly substances which constituted these friendly expanses: and in his fantasy life he believes those friendly expanses will encompass his safety as a yacht in a kind sea, as a mother holds her babe, as perhaps our ancestors in phylogenesis were safely held by the ocean, or, as we ourselves were held by the amniotic fluid in our mothers' wombs. Thus he is always in danger of not making objective assessments on the basis of the realities of a situation, but on a denial of the evidence of any untrustworthy, unreliable and treacherous objects. The philobat can lapse into the firm but often unjustifiable belief that his skills will be sufficient to cope with all dangers, that it is up to him to conquer the world and, indeed, that the world will not mind being conquered. The philobatic world is not the world of the potent: it is the world of the omnipotent.

It must be acknowledged that the philobat can develop considerable skills: he needs them to get away from his undesirable objects. He can sometimes gain a consummate skill in his attempts to recreate something of the harmony that existed before the discovery of separate objects: but along with these often impressive skills, shown in his sustained efforts and his painstaking attention to details, there is the self-abandonment to an unrealistic fantasy, presuming friendliness where none exists and imposing optimistic views where none are justified. He expects the world to 'click in' with him: he does not make the needed realistic adjustment to the world. Inevitably, in politics, he is an excessively rigid personality.

Heath came to power proclaiming he was to create one nation: but that was to be his nation. His philobatic skills have certainly taken us into Europe: but his total denial of the inevitable consequences of the domestic policies he optimistically asserted would be acceptable has meant that he takes with him a deeply divided nation. His bland assumptions that his industrial relations policies would not be resisted by the Unions, despite the warnings of those who knew better, has led to disastrous strikes; and his magical belief that the market forces, when released, would solve all, has dissolved in the real world. The 'lame duck' philosophy, the scrapping of traditional regional aids, the notion that nationalized industries could be dismembered, all these illusory policies have, as the realities asserted themselves, been abandoned. His affirmed domestic policies, half-way through his term of office, are in a total shambles. In the House his attitudes have been interpreted as rigid and arrogant; but these are but the symptoms of his philobatic bias leading him to believe in his omnipotent capacity to command the world to come to heel: but since it is not so pliant, it is the whole nation, not merely Heath, who now suffer the consequences.

Often in the House of Commons we are able to contain each other's extravagances: and, indeed, over the European issue, the anxious, ocno-philic, extreme anti-common marketeers were able to deploy their neurotic agoraphobia to such effect that they almost thwarted Heath. But the auguries that, under this government, further philobatic mis-judgements of Heath can, within the Conservative Party, be checked are gloomy: for good reasons, most of Heath's ministerial colleagues are unlikely to act as correctives enabling more realistic appraisals to be made, and the opposition of Enoch Powell, bringing his own distorted sick vision, can only add to the confusions. The unlikelihood of the nation gaining relief from Heath's errors by differing perspectives coming from his Ministers is because most of them in fact are part of Heath's personal equipment. Clearly no one could so describe Quintin Hogg, but he was an object that was speedily safely banished to the Lords, despite his wish to remain in the Commons as Home Secretary, as he has told me. Nor could one so describe Maudling, but he unfortunately has banished himself, and Alec Douglas-Home is ageing. Apart, however, from Keith Joseph, most of the rest fulfil the inevitable constant philobatic need to avoid genuinely independent objects: extreme philobats cherish only those over whom they feel they have complete and absolute control, who they feel are really part of themselves, part in short of what, as Balint has pointed out, a sportsman will call his gear or equipment.

In my estimation the role some of Heath's Ministers perform for him is the same role as the pole does for the acrobat, as the phallic stick for the skier, or the bat for the cricketer. His whiz kids are a needed masculine corroboration. One of the exigencies of the biological differences between the sexes is that the man is for ever obliged to go on proving his manhood to the woman: for her there is no such analogous necessity. She performs her part by being, he by doing. The more uneasy a man is about his masculinity, the more exaggerated can his doing of something efficiently become. As Karen Horney has written 'The ideal of "efficiency" is a typical masculine ideal.' This was the ideal to which Heath and his corroborators were dedicated when they came to office, despising the indolent, the incompetent and the handicapped, determined to kill off all lame ducks. Their search for the Holy Grail was a flight from their deep-seated anxieties, for man, too, must feel as well as do. And denied emotions will, like murder, out. The debacle of their 'efficient' domestic policy-making is the price they and the nation pay for their attempt to repress their feelings.

The failure of the Labour governments of 1964–70 to fulfil the initial high hopes has been painfully felt by a now bewildered and depressed British Labour movement. A duty falls upon those of us who helped to raise those hopes to strive to diagnose the causes of our failure lest otherwise there spread an even more dangerous disenchantment with social democracy. Monism of interpretation of our failure has its hazards. No single method can ever be called upon to cope with, or to explain, the problems and stresses, the successes and failures of our present-day society; that must be attempted by the collaboration of all the scientific disciplines. Yet the contribution psychoanalysis can make towards illuminating and resolving some of the travail in the community has, in Britain, been largely ignored. Since it cannot be disputed that the Labour government's lack of success was to some measure due to the failure of the leadership, then some of the insights of depth psychology may help us to uncover, within the personalities of our leaders, the sources of our public political errors. We may thus even avoid repeating them.

At Westminster almost all the members are ambitious men: but none has been more ambitious than Harold Wilson. In all the biographies in which he himself has collaborated, the well-known story of Wilson senior taking a photograph of his young son on the steps of 10 Downing Street is consistently peddled in order to hint at the origin of Wilson's particular ambition. This well-publicized revelation is suspect, as indeed is the emphasis laid upon the influence of the father: for the primal source of the ambition, we need to look behind the screen and explore the significant devaluation of the influence said to have been exerted by Wilson's mother. But the early photograph of the boy nevertheless corroborates how inordinate was the ambition, how early it was formed, and the particular form it took. Most of the Labour M.P.s of Wilson's generation had been born into committed socialist families or had come into the Labour movement as their resentments against the savage capitalism of the 'twenties and 'thirties, which was causing them personal deprivation, found a resonance with their own adolescent strivings. But Wilson was not of this genre. He is a year older than I am but I had already been in the movement a decade before he had enrolled: indeed I had been arrested for my politics before he had joined the party. And most Labour M.P.s of my vintage could make a similar comment. Wilson was not swept into the Labour movement within which he found his ambition. He belongs, rather, to the small group of Labour M.P.s or ex-M.P.s, of whom the ebullient Woodrow Wyatt was one of the most talented, who, after Oxford, where Wilson was a liberal, and after the war, chose to become, in 1945, Labour candidates in order to enter the House. Wilson's ambition long preceded the ideational content. In the full sense he began as a career politician complete with his premiership fantasies and evidently with a strong parental expectation which he was to fulfil.

Ambition is always defended at Westminster as a virtue: and most M.P.s are defensive if it suggested that it can be a vice. Be that as it may, Wilson's ambitious strivings, even by the yardsticks of Westminster, have constantly remained limitless. It is not, however, the only characteristic which he shares with his colleagues but in which he excels them.

In the great talking shop of Westminster, both publicly and privately, he is the most incessant talker of us all. Tory M.P.s may complain of the awkward longueurs that sometimes discomfort them with Heath: but no Labour M.P. would make a similar complaint against Wilson.

In private as in public he has no reputation for brevity: many of his speeches are ruined by their longevity and his book, rendering his account of his governments, stands witness to his disregard for economical presentation. His role as Leader of the Party means he commands a deference which enables him often to talk without interruption and he takes full advantage of his position. When he speaks at you it is not a rapport that is being established: rather you feel he is relating to you by the only way open to him, by way of oral discharge. And not content to leave his words to be spoken once, a disproportionate amount of his conversation will be spent telling you of what he has recently said to the women of Bootle or the trades' council at Llanelli, and how large were his audiences and how well they responded. And he will recall meetings of long ago with an astonishing wealth of detail, savouring them yet again as would an ageing man recalling the affairs of his youth. His fluency, as his personal ambition, provided much of the dynamic which propelled Labour into power in 1964 and 1966: yet these traits also contributed to the fall of the Labour government.

There is, however, one other element within Wilson's disposition which distinguishes him from so many of his colleagues, and which made an important contribution both to Labour's climb to power in the 'sixties and to the subsequent collapse: it is Wilson's extraordinary optimism. The optimism of a leader can be of enormous importance to his followers, often so raising their morale that difficulties and obstacles, apparently insurmountable or overwhelming, are defied and overcome, and both in Cabinet and at a Labour Party conference Wilson's optimism has roused the flagging and reassured the fearful. Yet often such sustained sanguinity, in the face of reality, can lead to Wilson adopting positions which caused him to be labelled by so much of the press, in the latter stages of his government, as a Walter Mitty. Some of the gaffes obtained a humiliating notoriety, such as his declared belief that sanctions would bring the white Rhodesians to heel in a matter of weeks; and he went to his downfall in the election of 1970 in the euphoric belief that his personal appearances all over the country would lead to a further Labour government.

If, then, we are to begin to understand both the strength and weaknesses of Harold Wilson as a leader, we must turn to the sources from which the character traits of exceptional talkativeness, unfounded optimism and limitless ambition may spring. If we are to accept that he is the best leader Labour has, then discovery of even some hints of the aetiology of these traits may help us a little in ensuring that the Labour movement gains the advantages Wilson's dynamic provides, without becoming its victim. For the Labour movement to use Harold Wilson rather than to be used by him would undoubtedly be a feat: but the exercise is not impossible, and events appear to make the attempt inevitable.

The classical psychoanalytical view is that those elements of infantile sexuality which are excluded from participation in the sexual life of the adult individual undergo in part a transformation into certain character traits. In infancy all of us have an intense pleasure in the act of sucking, but psychoanalysts insist that this pleasure is not to be ascribed entirely to the process of taking food, but that it is conditioned in a high degree by the significance of the mouth as an erotogenic zone: some of that early enjoyed erotic activity finds a place in the kissing of adult lovers, but such is our oral erotic endowment that this outlet is insufficient to deplete its supply. The primitive form of obtaining pleasure through sucking has to persist under all sorts of disguises during the whole of our lives. Karl Abraham, the German Jew whose clinical work and writings have influenced so considerably the English schools of psychoanalysis, taught that certain traits of character can be traced back to a singular displacement in the oral sphere. Writing of people with such character traits he declared:

> Their longing to seek gratification by way of sucking has changed to a need to *give* by way of the mouth, so that we find in them, besides a permanent longing to obtain everything, a constant need to communicate themselves orally to other people. This results in an obstinate urge to talk, connected in most cases with a feeling of overflowing. Persons of this kind have the impression that their fund of thought is inexhaustible, and they ascribe a special power of some unusual value to what they say.

I have certainly sat too long as a Member of Parliament not to be aware of the clinical material which daily illustrates Abraham's theory inside the great talking shop of Westminster.

It is commonplace to describe the garrulous as suffering from verbal diarrhoea and M.P.s as gas bags. But the obvious temptation to ascribe such logorrhoea as an anal symptom is to be resisted: we have, as Abraham pointed out, to probe more deeply, and then find that some of the apparently pure anal traits are in fact an admixture, and that their ultimate source lies in oral eroticism. Here, too, Abraham teaches us, is the source of optimism: those who have found their sucking so highly pleasurable will bring with them into their adult lives an extraordinary confidence that they will continue to receive all they desire from life. But there are, too, those who, perhaps because of the tactless and brusque handling they receive before and at weaning, will never reconcile themselves to the reality that they have lost their pleasure sucking for ever: they deny the fact and fantasize that their mother's breast will flow for them for eternity. Such imperturbable optimism often gives them confidence, and their sanguine approach, when allied with energetic conduct, helps to bring about, at least for a while, the achievement of their aims: but such boundless ambition often prevents them facing the hostility of forces in real life none of us can wholly escape: they will deny at all costs that the breast environment has ever failed them.

When events go awry, the fault must always be elsewhere and responsibility must always be placed on some other interfering agency. Never, never, can such an adult admit that he is ever wrong in his optimistic assessment of the objective environment: he cannot admit that it is not ceaselessly benevolent for, if he did, he would be puncturing his whole enveloping fantasy. As a method of avoiding at all costs the knowledge that he is facing an antagonism he will deploy all his intellectual powers to prove that even the most mutually exclusive objects are not incompatible, and will indeed often attempt to pursue all of them: and as a consequence will usually not properly achieve any of them. Meantime such a personality wants around him no one who will disturb his worry-free dream: no critic, no voice in his circle, must be heard to say the emperor has no clothes.

And just as such irrational optimism can have its origins in the relationship between babe and breast, so can ambition. It was Melanie Klein, Karl Abraham's greatest pupil, who so arrestingly illuminated the source of ambition. She was one of the most beautiful old women I have met, and I found it easy to understand how she had managed to inaugurate such a distinct school of psychoanalysis in Britain. She claimed the spur of the grown man's overweening ambition is the baby boy's envy of his mother's breast. The enjoyment of the baby at the breast is often marred and overshadowed by feelings of envy, which may give rise to terrifying destructive wishes, and Melanie Klein's clinical material led her to the belief that the baby may react by imagining that he himself had given birth to the mother and was the original possessor of the envied breast. So it is not the baby who wishes to rob the mother, but the mother who has already robbed the babe. To the baby's insistence that it was he, not the mother, who came first, Melanie Klein traces the adult man's determination to have priority and primacy of place.

From such a disturbed and fantasized relationship there arise, according to Melanie Klein, other threats to the personality. Freud has told us that oral gratification which is rooted in a satisfactory relationship with the mother is the pre-requisite for experiencing full genital orgasm. Klein believes that if the babe's excessive envy of the breast impairs this oral gratification, the resultant hatred and anxiety is transferred to the vagina, so that a deep disturbance in the oral relationship paves the way for severe difficulties in the genital attitude towards women. The consequences are manifold. On the one hand it may lead to an impairment of genital potency, and on the other to a degree of promiscuity which betokens a compulsive need for genital gratification. Lloyd George and John Kennedy are obvious victims of this second alternative: but my view, necessarily impressionistic although reinforced by the many years which I have spent in talking incessantly to politicians, is that the most ambitious of them have little interest in genital sex. Parliamentary talk in smoke room, bars and tea rooms is surprisingly sexless. Some ambitious M.P.s are certainly more interested in having their egos massaged rather than their penises.

As children fantasize about their parents' sex life so does the electorate about the sex lives of their political leaders, but their speculations are usually wide of the mark. Wilson, like most Prime Ministers, has had to endure his share of such scandalous musings. There was a period when Members of Parliament were deluged with defamatory material making totally false accusations about his personal conduct. In the end, he was compelled to issue writs. Irritation was felt by many members of the Parliamentary Party because he did not rearrange his immediate entourage so as to demonstrate the falsity of these lying rumours and some felt that political prudence should in this situation take precedence over personal loyalty.

But Wilson, as so many political commentators have pointed out, does not easily discard the people whom he has appointed to work for him. He retains even those who have clearly failed, and he has a relationship of clinging dependence with his Ministers even when they have demonstrated their complete lack of ability. Certainly the public can calm its inflamed imagination: Harold Wilson is no Don Juan, as Heath is no Casanova. Both of them eschew any involvement in controversies concerned with sexual conduct. They will both vote in debates on capital punishment, and Wilson will express his opinion on Private Members' Bills relating to blood sports, but neither of them has ever voted on Bills which deal with family planning, divorce or abortion.

Far more relevantly, politically, if the Kleinian hypothesis is valid and if it is correct that oral sources of character formation influence Harold Wilson's behaviour more than most people's, are the feelings of persecution and omnipotence and the projective and other techniques which become necessary when an envious disturbed relationship exists with the breast. Chaucer has, with insight, warned us against envy: 'It is certain that envy is the worst sin that is: for all other sins are sins only against one virtue, whereas envy is against all virtue and against all goodness.' None of us is free from envy, but, when in some present adult situation an event prompts envy, the degree and intensity of feeling varies with the individual. The feeling of envy from its earliest souces can be re-activated, and if the individual has not established a secure relationship with the first object, with the breast, then when he feels he is losing, in adult life, the substitute for the first primal object – and the substitute can be a supporting political party upon whom he is dependent – his anxiety can mount disproportionately. Then all the persecutory anxieties that the babe felt towards the breast can flood his adult life, and all the feelings of omnipotent destruction that Klein had delineated as the possession of the babe can envelop the adult man.

Those who would dismiss as too extravagant such theorizing, even if it is drawn by the psychoanalysts from clinical material, will need to cast around for far more improbable explanations for some of the bizarre addresses to which on occasions Wilson has subjected the Parliamentary Labour Party members at their private meetings. One such address occurred during the series of debates that were arranged within the Parliamentary Labour Party between prominent supporters and opponents of our entering Europe, so that the Parliamentary Party could seek to reach a decision on the issue. The debate between Roy Jenkins and Barbara Castle inflicted a humiliating defeat upon a woman with whom Wilson has always had an especial relationship; Jenkins gave one of the finest speeches he has ever delivered and obtained a rare and deserved ovation in which quite clearly many of the hitherto floating voters in the Party joined. Wilson evidently felt severely threatened, although no one else seriously interpreted Jenkins' contribution as a personal threat to the Leader of the Opposition.

Before the next debate, between a different set of protagonists, commenced, Wilson peremptorily announced he was going to make a statement and to an amazed and stunned Parliamentary Party he unleashed a tirade which General Amin himself could not have excelled. The omnipotent delusions uncovered in this storm were even more magnified than on another famous occasion, when feeling threatened, Labour M.P.s were devalued by him as being dogs holding their licences, he implied, from him. The paranoid imprint upon this outburst, during the Common Market controversy, was saddening and all his capacity to interpret policy discussions as personal plots against him was given full play. Not a few of even the most unselfconscious Labour M.P.s believed he was on the edge of a nervous breakdown, as indeed, in my judgment, he was. Infantile fears accompany all men during their life, but once Wilson feels under threat he appears to have a veritable arsenal of infantile anxiety to draw upon, which he deploys to project upon and to distort political and economic actuality.

There is, Melanie Klein has stressed, a direct link between the envy experienced towards the mother's breast and the development of jealousy. Jealousy is based on the suspicion of and rivalry with the father who is accused of taking away the mother's breast and the mother. As the babe understands more of the external world and realizes he cannot keep his mother to himself as his exclusive possession, he becomes stricken with grief. Whether he will be able to find help against that grief in relation to his father or other people in his surroundings, largely depends on the emotions and experiences towards his 'lost unique object'. If that relationship is well founded, the fear of losing the mother is less strong and the capacity to share her is greater. Then he has the chance of experiencing more love towards his rivals; but conversely if the envy of the infant towards the breast is excessive, then even those innocent of challenges will be cast into the role of dangerous rivals.

With Wilson as Prime Minister, Ministers with warmer dispositions resigned, complaining of the distancing and suspicion-ridden coolness Wilson practised, preventing them from sharing in decision-making; and Roy Jenkins when at Number 11 Downing Street, although a corridor runs between the Chancellor of the Exchequer's home and the Prime Minister's, was to find he and his family were never invited socially to Number 10. It would be naïve to suggest that Wilson is not surrounded by ambitious politicians and that there are not others yearning for the prize he possesses: but Wilson notoriously sees jealous threats where none exist, and he and the Parliamentary Party then become victims of his basic mistrust.

There is in man, according to Erikson, a nuclear conflict of basic trust and mistrust which meets its crucial test during the rages of the teething stage, when the teeth cause pain from within and when one of the few ways the babe has of obtaining relief is by biting of nipple and breast which, however, are withdrawn from him. Teething seems to have a prototypal significance: if comfort and security are not felt by the child, if social trust is not established in the baby in the ease of his feeding, if the outer goodness of the succouring mother has not become an inner certainty, then the pain of teething, the inner harm, is intensely experienced as an external one and is projected upon those nearest to him, a mechanism which in adulthood in acute crises of confidence can characterize irrational attitudes of mistrust towards friends and adversaries alike. We are indeed formed in our mother's arms as well as in her womb. And if the babe has inadequately felt trust through care, if suddenness and adult ineptitude has made the unavoidable imposition of outer controls upon a babe appear to him as intolerable prohibitions, then the basis may be laid down of a manipulatory adult personality: outer control fails to be experienced as self control, and resentment against the rough coercion and manipulation imposed upon him leads to the compulsive need for the vengeful manipulation of others. Our pipe-biting leader, of biting speech, is acknowledged by all as being the supreme manipulator, and indeed, this capacity has, in the autumn Common Market Conference of 1972 saved the Party from disaster, but a babe's intolerance of being manipulated can be so fierce that the adult can go on manipulating for its own sake, obtaining a morbid enjoyment in the success of the manipulation irrespective of the social value of the operation.

More, even the political skills which are the privileged possession of the manipulatory personality can sometimes show in-built weaknesses which arise from the aetiology of his facility. At the end of the day Wilson, thanks to Ted Short's private intervention at the 1972 conference, saved the Party from destruction at the very brink of the abyss. But few in the Parliamentary Party would not agree that if Wilson had stood up earlier to Wedgwood Benn, who had provoked the crisis, such a display of hazardous brinkmanship would not have been necessary. Klein, in spelling out the characterological changes which can arise when the adult as a babe has not securely established his relationship with his first object, the breast mother, has pointed out that if for external reasons the persecutory anxiety increases he can be overwhelmed by the need to pacify persecutors at any cost. Confronted with the fanatical political visionary, Benn, that was the type of appeasement Wilson bestowed upon him: yet criticism of Wilson for such miscalculation must in turn be tempered by an understanding of the single-minded passion which propelled Benn and almost overwhelmed Wilson.

Benn's notorious attraction to some of the principles of Maoism, his constant wordy battle against political elitism, and his long expositions on the need for participation by the workers, his demands for referenda, all reveal his hostility to paternalism. Few men in British public life have, with such clamour and elan, projected into a vulgar popularist philosophy such a marked antagonism to established authority: his extravagances, as when in the summer of 1972 he sought to justify lawless striking picketers, sent a frisson through the more temperate groups within the Labour Parliamentary Party. Wherever an institution, a law, or a political view show any hint of being a surrogate of an authoritarian father figure, Benn is on the attack. Indeed his refusal to assume his father's title, and to enter the House of Lords, led him to conduct a tireless campaign which produced the constitutional changes which now enable the son of a peer to renounce the title and be an M.P. One thing was certain, Wedgwood Benn had no intention of following in the footsteps of his father, and entering the chamber of the patricians. He had fought his father in life when Lord Stansgate had, against his son's wishes, accepted the title, and he fought him too in death: but many of us wish the parricidal struggle could now be restricted to the private domain. It is its destructive intrusion into the affairs of the Labour Party to which we object.

He was not of course intended to be his father's heir: for he was a second son, a place in the family constellation which, as Alfred Adler long since pointed out, is prone to be filled by rebels finding the double authority of both a father and elder brother too hard to tolerate. But his older brother, who at the school where both boys attended together was, unlike the fractious Tony, enormously popular, unfortunately lost his life during the war. The concatenation of events that has led Benn to work out his marked ambivalences to paternalism in society, by conducting a campaign for the ultimate leadership of the Labour Party through denying the necessity of leadership was bound to have disturbing consequences.

His enthusiasm for new forms of 'democracy', expressed in pamphlets and speeches, flared up during the period from the 1970 election on: he has three sons and at this time they had reached their adolescence. Becoming the father of adolescent children, an experience in which I am presently sharing, can have the effect on the adult of what the child psychiatrist James Anthony describes as 'decompensation in retrospect'. The adolescent child prompts the reactivations of the father's own adolescent struggles with auto-erotic, homosexual and Oedipal conflicts. Few fathers are likely, when faced with their adolescent sons, to be unmoved by some of the reverberations echoing their own struggles to cope with the threat once felt to their own authority as a clamorous sexuality assailed them. The classic defence used by the adolescent to cope with his newly aroused sexual impulses is to deploy the defence mechanism of projection, to work out the sexual revolution against his father and against all the institutions of his father's generation. Adolescence is the period of rebellion and it becomes them: but it does not become influential middle-aged men who are the fathers of adolescents. From a conversation I had with Benn, after he had written to me inviting me to comment on one of his recently published pamphlets, I have no doubt that he is not exempt from some of the responses that are teased out from fathers who, for a disturbing while, have to assume the role of head of an adolescent family. It is indeed not by chance that many of his parliamentary colleagues have dubbed much of Benn's political thinking as adolescent.

His year of office as Party chairman was disastrous. Far from taking on the role of conciliator, he imposed upon a reluctant Parliamentary Party his absurd notion of a vague referendum on the Common Market, driving out Jenkins and Lever from the Shadow Cabinet and leaving our front bench bereft of Treasury spokesmen of calibre. During the referendum debate an incisive intervention in the House by Lever provoked him to a public comment which in my judgement could only be interpreted as meaning that Jews, because they were a minority, would be predisposed to be against referenda. I resented the comment and sent him a sharp note. He immediately sought me out, seeking to explain his comment was directed against the Common Market minority in the Labour Party, and not against Jews. I did not believe Hansard supported his interpretation and, rejecting his apologia, bluntly told him that because his father had been such a well-known and loyal supporter of Jewish causes there was no need for him to feel compelled to make such a comment. He sent me, after our altercation, a lengthy three-page letter, defending his interpretation of his comment, which inevitably ended telling me of all the support he had given Jewry. I was complaining, however, against him importing his Oedipal problems into the political scene: I was not alleging anti-semitism. Indeed it was clear from his letter to me that, undoubtedly, some of his best friends are Jews.

It was because Wilson felt, as a result of Benn's activities in 1972, a feeling of persecution that he behaved so weakly, vainly believing he could appease his tormentor: the fears of conspiracies that sometimes distort Wilson's judgements become inflamed when external conditions exist which he interprets as undermining his personal position. He is only at his best when he feels secure, reassured by his environment, and the most important environmental influence is now the Parliamentary Party and the Shadow Cabinet. Indeed if the Party is to obtain power, the Parliamentary Party must now give him genuine allegiance. The dynamic behind his limitless ambitions can help to carry the Party into government; his loquacity can be used to persuade the nation that benefits can still come from having a Labour government; his envy, sufficiently mortified and properly canalized, can be an instrument to be used in the fight for social justice against privilege – but the Parliamentary Party must exact returns for such fealty. There must be no yielding to Wilson's delusions of omnipotence which have already led to such disastrous escapades as the personality cult election of 1970: a practical programme of reform must be put to the nation with a clear intention of implementing it. He must be ready to accept, knowing it is not a personal threat, constant critical advice from strong colleagues with whom he must consult, and he must not be dependent upon any seedy group of sycophants or upon an incompetent personal secretariat: and if power comes to the Party, in order to make it more likely that the promises will be implemented, government posts must be distributed according to talent and not obsessively manipulated in an attempt to stifle any effective criticism of the leadership from any quarter. The absurdity of a government staffed by too many of the second rate while the talents of men like Michael Foot or Harold Lever are unused, or only deployed in times of crises for a short period in minor roles, must not again take place.

If it is contended, as it well may be, that such a prescription is psychologically improbable, the riposte must be that it depends as much upon the Parliamentary Labour Party as upon Wilson. My colleagues include sophisticated men, sufficiently self-conscious not to yearn for or to expect magical leadership. If they act, free from the tainting influences of possible patronage, power can be regained by the Party and, more important, used healthily. None of us is without blemish: we all of us, the Leader included, have talents and flaws. With greater self awareness and moral commitment we can, for the sake of our nation, and ourselves, use our constructive capacities and overcome our worst frailties.

The disenchantments that followed Wilson's government, and the policy inconsistencies of Heath, have left our national leadership confronted with the public opinions it crystallized at earlier points of time. Once the politicians have established a context, once they have created a *gestalt*, subsequent affronting inconsistencies then activate psychological processes which must include feelings of betrayal.

The betrayal is interpreted, as all betrayals, as a sign that no love or concern is genuinely felt, and the electorate, particularly the young, then use apathy as a defence against the anxiety felt by such a withdrawal of love. Apathy, not hate, is the opposite of love: and it is this apathy, against which the resentful politicians rail, which is a menace to our democracy.

The apathetic hear the words of the politician as double talk: and rather than respond to such duplicity the young, although desperately screaming that they want to 'communicate', become mute, except for some echoes of a tribal idiom without individuation. Sullenly, despairing of the betraying parent politicians, the mistrusting young turn away from the traditional political parties, scorn the very language of the elder statesmen, and, from their underground, use words coined in their special deviant cultures which depart weirdly from an understood term of reference and are as ambiguous as they are familiar. They deploy only a vocabulary of monorimes, expressive of force, lust and despair: and, in an attempt to drown this onslaught, too many of the still fantasizing politicians release a torrent of rhetoric that leaches away still further the power of words to evoke images, emotions or concepts that are related to reality and the common experience. The young are sulkily dumb, and deaf to the political leader: and the conventional contemporary political leader, besotted with his own speeches, bewitched by his own incantations, is in danger of losing the art of communicating to the new electorate.

Living out his own romance, the conventional politician does not wish to acknowledge the widening gulf between himself and his constituents. For it must not be overlooked that the politician casts himself as his own hero: too often he has not stepped out of the romantic role that, as a child, he wove to restore for him the bliss he enjoyed before a critical estimate of his parents' actual place in the larger social world brought the realization that he did not have, in reality, the advantages of parents with uncontested power. For all of us, as for him, once upon a time our parents were Olympians and we shared their special privileges and unconditional love without special efforts being made; but, later, when our gods prove hollow, most of us learn to acknowledge reality, but there are others, even in adult life, who secretly pretend their blemished parents are not the real parents, and in fantasy they hold themselves to be the foundling children of the gods or the kings. And, as in the fairy stories, as in *Cinderella* or in Wilde's *Importance of Being Earnest*, there comes the restoration and, instead of being the unacknowledged aristocrat living with foster parents, the yearned for recognition is attained and he lives happily ever after. The politician, like the impostor, wants to maintain that early fiction: for both of them an audience is absolutely essential, and for both of them it is from the confirming reaction of his audience that they can maintain their fable, and, as prince-heroes, live out their lives happily as the fairy stories tell us is to be their destiny. And sometimes the politician, feeling ashamed of his living lie, seeks to conceal his impostrous performance with the aid of old tricks, by ensuring that the listening audience is kept in the dark. And, indeed, to make certain that the audience is so blinkered, the politician can, on occasions, revert to the most child-like game of denial: I have shared platforms with nationally known political figures who, as they waxed most eloquent, determinedly shut their eyes! It is not so much admiration that this impostor type of politician needs: rather he requires constant confirmation of his 'reality'. Fortunately, such phonies are increasingly discerned, particularly by the apathetic young who turn determinedly away from them.

Yet there is another type of spurious leadership, largely engaged in extra-Parliamentary activities, to whom the estranged factory floor workers, as the apathetic young, are today dangerously susceptible. Apathy or a-pathos is a withdrawal of feeling: but there is a dialectical relationship between apathy and violence. Violence is the ultimate destructive substitute which surges in to fill the vacuum when there is no relatedness. The anonymous cannot endure their apathy interminably: they wish to force us to acknowledge that they do exist, and a leadership that proffers them violent words and destructive behaviour gives them the hope that they will shock both the community and themselves into feeling again. The very reaction they provoke gives them a renewed confidence to declare: 'We also are here'. In dockland, in the Trade Union branches, in adhoc tenants' associations, more conventional leadership finds itself displaced or challenged by disturbed men whose need to be in chronic opposition gives them the advantage that they have a rapport with those followers who only come alive through a defiance of authority.

This type of disturbed leadership, now only too prevalent, shows the consequences that arise in adult behaviour when the man, as a babe, lacks the good care which allows a fusion of his aggression and his eroticism. The paediatrician Winnicott has elegantly taught us that the motility that exists in the inter-uterine life, as the babe kicks in the womb, and that exists when a babe of a few weeks thrashes away with his arms, is the precursor to the aggression that has to be purposively organized by the child if he is to become a person. But, for some, the environmental chance, which enables the babe to ensure an integration of a personality, is denied. They become not the healthy adults whose behaviour is purposive and whose aggression is meant: they are the sick whose aggression is not meant, who are like the babe who kicks in the womb or thrashes away with his arms, and upon whom we project the notion that they mean to kick out or mean to hit when, in fact, we have no right to make such an assumption. They are, in short, the men who have not lived their earliest time constantly discovering and re-discovering the environment by using their motility as they snuggle and struggle within their mother's arms: they have not enjoyed that primal erotic experience within which they can fuse their aggression and love. For them contact with the environment has not been an experience of the individual: lacking loving care, they lacked a series of individual experiences, helping them on their way to integration, and suffered only an environment which was felt as an impingement.

The tragedy of men who have suffered such an early fate is that as adults they must constantly expose themselves to opposition that is vigorous, if not dangerous, because only in aggressive reaction to impingement can they feel real. Such persons may have erotic experiences but only if seduced, and since they do not enjoy in the act a fusion of their aggression and their eroticism, the erotic experience itself does not feel real: for they are doomed to have a personality which has developed falsely as a series of reactions to impingement, and their only hope of possessing a total sense of feeling real is when they can provoke situations which arouse resistance and opposition. They are the type of men who in politics delight in being in permanent opposition, and are afraid they will dissolve if they were to accept the responsibility of government: a handful of such men is an incubus upon the Parliamentary Labour Party since such character types persistently concoct extravagant policies which are guaranteed to estrange large sections of the community and keep Labour out of office for ever. But it is outside Parliament, in universities and on factory floors and in the underground, that such personalities are currently more usually finding their fulfilment, for their incitements to violence unfortunately are thought of as life belts by those who are drowning in apathetic despair.

There are, however, variants of this early determining pattern, marked by an emphatic disharmony between a babe's aggression and love, that provide the dynamic to a type of leadership which, within its limits, can fundamentally be remarkably successful. The style of Trade Union and political leadership provided by the coruscating Clive Jenkins often understandably prompts comment. He has an acid fluency, wit but little humour, and seems determined always, as presumably is his need, to be unloved. In this respect he is indeed the mirror image of most politicians, whose yearning to be loved so often blurs their capacity to make the right decisions. But whether a politician defiantly provokes the re-enactment of some early deprivation or, as is more usual, strives desperately to win the affection which he never had when his need was most urgent, the sensitive recoil. Neither love nor hate can be successfully commanded. To command them is to evoke at best pity, and at worst irritation. Some such explanation is necessary to explain how Clive Jenkins, so obviously more brilliant than most Trade Union leaders and M.P.s, found that he could not succeed in fulfilling his early wish to be chosen by a selection committee as a Labour candidate for a seat in the House of Commons.

Indeed I know of no politician in Britain who can court unpopularity so happily as Clive Jenkins. His speeches at Party and Trade Union conferences, even when logic-right and intellectually persuasive, are often, in tone, repellent. There seems a compulsive need to place a distance between himself and his audience as if, like dictators and troubadours, he is making certain that, if he is to be approved, liked or loved, he can only permit it from afar off. He mobilizes with extraordinary elan his hate, and directs a most destructive aggression against all the many objects of his dislike. Yet, even although he is so obviously seeking the applause and votes of his listeners, the very methods he deploys often seem a guarantee he will estrange those whom on a conscious level he is seeking to win over. Is this a case of a man who, with extraordinary dynamism, in his Trade Union and political activities is working out a compulsion to hate and be hated while all the time longing to love and be loved?

All political and Trade Union leaders are great talkers and none is more fluent than Clive Jenkins whose orations have a special rasping vibrance. The 'mouth ego' possessed by every infant exercises a profound influence on everyone, but his influence, transparently, is particularly marked on those of us who live our lives incessantly talking. For the infant the mouth is the organ of desire, the main instrument of activity, the predominate medium of satisfaction and frustration, the channel of love and hate: but the suckling situation, in which the mother's breast is the focal point, is also the first social relationship established by the infant, and that first relationship, chasteningly, can shape all our adult social relationships. The psychoanalyst Douglas Fairbairn has spelt out the possible characterological consequences when some excessive fixation takes place at our early oral phase and when an attitude appropriate to that stage persists in exaggerated forms into adult life.

One of the results that can emerge from some circumstances in our early oral life is the feeling that love is destructive and bad, that each man kills the thing he loves. When the child empties the breast, he can feel he has emptied his mother, and may be possessed with anxiety fearing he has destroyed his coveted object: and the fact that the mother customarily leaves him after suckling has the effect of contributing to that impression. He fears he cannot have his cake and eat it. If that babe later comes to feel that he is not really loved and valued as a person by his mother, the original traumatic situation can become emotionally re-activated and reinstated: he feels that the reason for his mother's apparent lack of love towards him is that he has destroyed her affection and made it disappear, and at the same time he feels that the reason for her apparent refusal to accept his love is that his own love is destructive and dangerous. Such a child can become a man who fears to love or be loved: he can indeed in order to protect himself substitute hate for love, and by rude-ness and quarrels be sufficiently objectionable to induce others to hate instead of love him. In any appraisal of Clive Jenkins's public responses and contributions the positive achievements he has made in organizing the white-collar workers of Britain must be weighed against the negative traits which have led him to be as disliked as he is admired in the Trade Union movement. A scrutiny of those traits, I believe, reveals residual traces of the symptomology which in its rare, pure and tragic form has been delineated by Fairbairn.

Such scrutinies of political leadership, are not, in my judgment, a misuse of psychoanalytical theory; although it certainly would become an abuse if political leaders were disparaged by interpreting their behaviour in terms of infantile motives without reference to the modifications of them produced by sublimation and sophistication. And those who out of malice, envy or hatred would pervert contemporary depth psychology and use it as a weapon of character assassination deserve condemnation: but the public interest now urgently requires that the insights, hard-won from the therapy of individuals, should be applied to political problems, for if political man now fails to make efforts to understand himself none of us will survive. Certainly the application of these theories to political prob-lems must in part be an advantage of surmise but much light, nevertheless, can already be shed, more than fitfully, on our selection of leaders and on the leaders themselves. We are today still dangerously yielding to un-conscious forces connected with leadership and the selection of leaders which relate more to neurotic gratification than to the testing of reality and the goals of democracy. The introduction into politics of these complexities may be unwelcome, but they aid in defining the problem of achieving and maintaining the goals of our democratic society: and a definition of a problem is often a necessary preliminary step to its solu-tion.

I have lived my life since I was a lad within the Labour movement: that movement has, during my life span, been the greatest single one in making our society more civilized. It is my hope, but not my certainty, that in the decade ahead it will become sufficiently self-aware to provide a political leadership, free from ruthlessness, that will help to make the nation healthier, more integrated, happier and more compassionate.

Select bibliography

ABRAHAM, KARL. Letters of Freud and Abraham (Hogarth Press).

ABRAHAM, KARL. Selected Papers on Psychoanalysis (Hogarth Press).

ABSE, D. WILFRED. Hysteria and related Mental Disorders (John Wright).

ABSE, D. WILFRED, NASH & JESSNER. Marriage Counselling in Medical Practice (University of North Carolina Press).

ABSE, D. WILFRED. Speech and Reason (John Wright).

ABSE, D. WILFRED and JESSNER, LUCIE. The Psychodynamics of Leadership: Excellence of Leadership in a Democracy, edited by Graubard, Steven and Holton, Gerlad (Columbia University Press).

ALVAREZ, A. The Savage God: A Study of Suicide (Weidenfeld & Nicolson).

ANTHONY, E. JAMES and BENEDEK, THERESA. Parenthood (Little, Brown & Co.).

BALINT, MICHAEL. Thrills and Regressions (Hogarth Press).

BELL, NORMAN W. and VOGEL, EZRA F. A Modern Introduction to the Family (Collier Macmillan).

BIRNBACK, MARTIN. Neo-Freudian Social Philosophy (Stanford University Press).

BRIERLEY, MARJORIE. Trends in Psychoanalysis (Hogarth Press).

BROFENBRENNER, URIE. Two Worlds of Childhood (Allen & Unwin).

BROWN, J. A. C. Freud and the Post Freudians (Cassell).

BROWN, NORMAN O. Life against Death (Routledge & Kegan Paul).

BURN, MICHAEL. The Debatable Land (Hamish Hamilton).

CAMERON, NORMAN. Personality Development and Psychopathology (Houghton Mifflin).

CROSSMAN, R. H. S. My Father (*Sunday Telegraph*, 16 December 1962).

DEVEREAUX, BROFENBRENNER and RODGERS. Child Rearing in England and the United States (*Journal of Marriage and the Family*, May 1969).

DICKS, HENRY V. Licensed Mass Murder (Chatto Heinemann).

EHRENZWEIG, ANTON. The Hidden Order of Art (Weidenfeld & Nicolson).

EHRENZWEIG, ANTON. The Psychoanalysis of Artistic Vision and Hearing (Routledge & Kegan Paul).

EISLER, K. R. Editor. Searchlight on Delinquency: New Psychoanalytical Studies (International Universities Press).

ERIKSON, ERIK H. Identity – Youth and Crisis (Faber and Faber).

ERIKSON, ERIK H. Childhood and Society (Pelican).

ETZIONI, AMITAI. The Kennedy Experiment – The Dynamics of Aggression. Edited by Megargee & Hokanson (Harper & Row).

FAIRBAIRN, W. R. Psychoanalytical Studies of the Personality (Routledge & Kegan Paul).

FENICHEL, OTTO. The Psychoanalytical Theory of Neurosis (Routledge & Kegan Paul).

FLETCHER, RONALD. The Making of the Modern Family. The Family and its Future, edited by Elliott, Katherine (J. & A. Churchman).

FLETCHER, RONALD. The Family and Marriage (Penguin).

FISHER, WM. F. Theories of Anxieties (Harper & Row).

FLUGEL, J. C. Studies in Feeling and Desire (Duckworth).

FLUGEL, J. C. Psychoanalytical Study of the Family (Hogarth Press).

FLUGEL, J. C. Population, Psychology and Peace (Watts & Co.).

FLUGEL, J. C. Men and their Motives (Kegan Paul).

FLUGEL, J. C. Man, Morals and Society (Penguin).

FLUGEL, J. C. The Psychology of Clothes (Hogarth Press).

FRANK, JEROME D. Sanity and Survival (Cresset Press).

FRANKL, VIKTOR E. The Doctor and the Soul (Souvenir Press).

FRANKL, VIKTOR E. Psychotherapy and Existentialism (Souvenir Press).

FREUD, ANNA. Normality and Pathology in Childhood (Hogarth Press).

FREUD, ANNA. Comments on Aggression (*International Journal of Psychoanalysis*, Volume 53, Part 2).

FREUD, ANNA. The Ego and the Mechanisms of Defence (Hogarth Press).

FREUD, SIGMUND. Collected Works (Hogarth Press).

FROMM, ERICK. The Fear of Freedom (Routledge & Kegan Paul).

GLOVER, EDWARD. The Roots of Crime (Imago).

GORER, GEOFFREY. Exploring English Character (Cresset Press).

GRAZIA, SEBASTIAN DE'. The Political Community: A Study of Anomie (University of Chicago).

GREENACRE, PHYLLIS. The Relation of the Imposter to the Artist (*Psychoanalytical Study of the Child*, Volume XIII, 1958).

GREENSON, RALPH. Screen Defences, Hunger and Screen Identity (*Journal of American Psychoanalytical Association*, Volume 6, 1958).

GRODDECK, GEORG. The Unknown Self (Vision Press).

GRODDECK, GEORG. The Book of the IT (Vision Press).

GUNTRIP, HARRY. Schizoid Phenomena, Object-Relations and the Self (Hogarth Press).

HA-AM, AHAD. Philosophia Judaica (East and West Library).

HART, BERNARD. The Pyschology of Insanity (Cambridge University Press).

HINDELL and SIMMS. Abortion Law Reform (Peter Owen).

HOLBROOK, DAVID. Sex and Dehumanisation (Pitman).
HORNEY, KAREN. Feminine Psychology (Routledge & Kegan Paul).

IREMONGER, LUCILLE. The Fiery Chariot (Secker & Warburg).

JAQUES, ELLIOTT. Measurement of Responsibility (Tavistock Publications).
JONES, ERNEST. Sigmund Freud: Life and Work (Hogarth Press).
JUNG, C. G. Psychological Types (Kegan Paul).
KAHN-FREUND, Professor OTTO. Matrimonial Property: Where do we go from here? (Joseph Unger Memorial Lecture).

KLEIN, MELANIE. Envy and Gratitude (Tavistock Publications).
KOHUT, HEINZ. The Analysis of the Self (Hogarth Press).

LANGER, WALTER. The Mind of Adolf Hitler (Secker & Warburg).
LASSWELL, HAROLD D. Politics: who gets what, when, how (Meridian).
LASSWELL, HAROLD D. The Analysis of Political Behaviour (Routledge & Kegan Paul).
LASSWELL, HAROLD D. Psychopathology & Politics (Viking Press).
L'ETANG, HUGH. The Pathology of Leadership. (Wm. Heinemann Medical Books Ltd.).
LOMAS, PETER. Editor. The Predicament of the Family (Hogarth Press).

MADDOX, JOHN. The Doomsday Syndrome (Macmillan).
MALTHUS, THOMAS R. Essay on the Principle of Population (Everyman's Library).
MAY, ROLLO. Love and Will (Souvenir Press).
McGREGOR, DOUGLAS. The Human Side of Enterprise (McGraw-Hill).
MITSCHENICH, ALEXANDER. Psychoanalysis and the Aggression of Large Groups (*International Journal of Psychoanalysis*, Volume 52, Part 2).

NAGERA, HUMBERTO. Editor. Basic Psychoanalytical Concepts and the Theory of Instincts (Allen and Unwin).
NAMIER, L. R. Personality and Powers (Hamish Hamilton).

PARSONS, TALCOTT. Social Structure and Personality (Collier Macmillan).
PETERS, H. F. My sister, my spouse (Gollancz).
POPPER, K. R. The Open Society and its Enemies (Routledge & Kegan Paul).

RADZINOWICZ, LEON. Ideology and Crime (Heinemann).

RANGELL, LEO. Aggression, Oedipus and Historical Perspective (*International Journal of Psychoanalysis*, Volume 53, Part 1).

RANK, OTTO. The Trauma of Birth (Kegan Paul).

REAY, LORD and VISSERS, H. J. An Analysis of the Personality of Harold Wilson (magazine feature).

REICH, W. Character Analysis (Vision Press).

REICHE, REIMUT. Sexuality and the Class Struggle (N.L.B.).

REIK, THEODOR. Ritual – Four Psychoanalytical Studies (Grove Press).

RIGNANO, EUGENIO. The Nature of Life (Kegan Paul).

ROAZEN, PAUL. Freud: Political and Social Thought (Hogarth Press).

RYCROFT, CHARLES. A Critical Dictionary of Psychoanalysis (Nelson).

RYCROFT, CHARLES. Reich (Fontana-Collins).

SCHUR, MAX. Freud: Living and Dying (Hogarth Press).

SEGAL, HANNA. Aggression (*International Journal of Psychoanalysis*, Volume 53, Part 1).

SEGAL, HANNA. Introduction to the Work of Melanie Klein (Hogarth Press).

SLOVENKO, RALPH. Editor. Sexual Behaviour and the Law (Charles C. Thomas).

STOKES, ADRIAN. The Invitation in Art (Tavistock).

STOLLER, ROBERT J. Sex and Gender (Hogarth Press).

STORR, ANTHONY. Human Aggression (Allen Lane).

STRACHEY, ALIX. The Unconscious Motives of War (Allen & Unwin).

TAYAR, GRAHAM. Personality and Power (B.B.C.).

TILLEARD-COLE, RICHARD and MARKS, JOHN. Scientific Aspects of Psychological Medicine (Roche).

WAELDER, ROBERT. Progress and Revolution (International Universities Press, New York).

WEIZMANN, CHAIM. Trial and Error (Hamish Hamilton).

WINNICOTT, D. W. Pain and Reality (Tavistock).

WINNICOTT, D. W. The Maturational Processes and the Facilitating Environment (Hogarth Press).

WINNICOTT, D. W. Through Paediatrics to Psychoanalysis. Collected Papers (Tavistock).

WINNICOTT, D. W. The Family and Individual Development (Tavistock).

WOLHEIM, RICHARD. Freud (Fontana).

WOOLF, MYRA. Family Intentions (HMSO).

ZILBOORG, GREGORY. The Psychology of the Criminal Act and Punishment (Hogarth Press).

Index